Neurodevelopment in the Post-Pandemic World

ADVANCE PRAISE FOR *NEURODEVELOPMENT IN THE POST-PANDEMIC WORLD*

"Drs. Colvin, Reesman, and Glen provide important insights and perspective on the long-term impact of Covid disruption on student learning and achievement. As a special education attorney, it is critical to understand how to analyze the psychological impact of disrupted learning and how that can affect special education eligibility and services."

—**Kimberly Glassman**, Esq, Law Office of Brian K. Bruber

"This very important and timely book presents all the relevant information about how the COVID-19 pandemic-induced school closures affected our children. It takes a holistic approach to the crisis and reviews the data behind children's education, mental health, and neurodevelopment experience during the pandemic. It is a fact-based, science-based approach that brings together all the horrible costs of the school closures that continue to affect our children. A must read."

—**Harry Anthony Patrinos**, World Bank

"In *Neurodevelopment in the Post-Pandemic World*, the authors provide a thorough examination of unprecedented learning losses, the raging mental health crisis, and the widening achievement gap. Strategies aimed at mitigating these harms are also explored. This comprehensive analysis is an indispensable resource for anyone concerned with correcting the damage that was done to America's children."

—**Margery Smelkinson**, Together Again
Montgomery County Public Schools

"Drs. Colvin, Reesman, and Glen show us history truly does repeat itself. *Neurodevelopment in the Post-Pandemic World* begins by discussing what we already knew: historically, prolonged school closures have a disproportionate impact on groups who are already disadvantaged. The impacts are not confined to academic concerns, however. Mental health, physical health, neurodevelopment, social development, and other areas critical for a successful transition to adulthood are all affected. Relying on prior research, Drs. Colvin, Reesman, and Glen make suggestions that we, as a society, can implement to ensure pandemic-era youth have the resources they need to mitigate the damage done by the pandemic and the restrictions associated with it. This book sounds the alarm of the damage that was done to our youth and is a must read for anyone working with children."

—**Jessica Hasson**, Quince Orchard Mental Health Group

"In *Neurodevelopment in the Post-Pandemic World*, Drs. Colvin, Reesman, and Glen masterfully dissect the profound effects of the COVID-19 pandemic on children's education, mental health, and neurodevelopment. Their insightful analysis offers an urgent, empathetic, and scholarly perspective that connects deeply with anyone vested in the well-being and future of our children. This book is an indispensable guide through the challenges of a post-pandemic world. These challenges will remain with us for the foreseeable future. This book provides hope and clear strategies for a resilient educational system."

—**Jaime A.B. Wilson**, Prescribing Medical Psychologist and Board-Certified Neuropsychologist

"Drs. Colvin, Reesman, and Glen have created a must-read resource for every level of psychological practitioner by weaving together the threads for understanding the far-reaching impact of the pandemic on children's education, mental health, and neurodevelopment. This in-depth discussion takes into consideration the differential impact on marginalized students, students of color, and those with disabilities across age ranges. They offer numerous recommendations for policy change, advocacy, and assessment and intervention considerations. Although the discussion is aimed towards Neuropsychologists, the information has direct relevance for School Psychologists, Rehabilitation Psychologists, and Forensic Psychologists."

—**Kathleen T. Bechtold**, Johns Hopkins University School of Medicine

"While there has been much debate re-litigating decisions made during the Covid-19 pandemic, this important book looks to the future. After expertly taking stock of what we know and summarizing the state of the research on how school closures and other disruptions affected multiple dimensions of childhood development, the authors lay out the ongoing implication of these impacts for tracking academic recovery, diagnosing developmental delays, and determining eligibility for various support services. This book will be an invaluable resource for practitioners and policymakers alike."

—**Vladimir Kogan**, Ohio State University, Professor, Department of Political Science

"*Neurodevelopment in the Post-Pandemic World* is an extremely timely, much needed, well researched and highly readable account of the impact of the Covid pandemic on the educational experience of students across the globe. The authors explore the long-term consequences, many of which are not yet known. Of great importance, the authors emphasize that children of color, children of lower SES, and children with disabilities have been impacted with significantly greater severity. This book is a must-read for educators, for educational administrators, for mental health professionals, and neuropsychologists as we all work to better understand and support the children who lived through this unprecedented global experience."

—**Kathleen Nadeau,** Psychologist and Founder of the Chesapeake Center for ADHD, Learning & Behavioral Health

"This text is a 'must have' for clinicians, all of whom will be in the challenging position of making complex diagnostic decisions in the post-COVID era. I extend my sincerest gratitude to Drs. Colvin, Reesman, and Glen for their comprehensive treatment of this important and timely topic!"

—**Joette James,** Licensed Psychologist, Board Certified in Clinical Neuropsychology

"This book is a remarkable analysis of evidence on the effects that the global experiment of prolonged school closures during the COVID-19 pandemic had on youth, and on the subsequent remediation efforts to prevent more learning loss. Bridging the worlds of education and mental health, the authors provide a sound guide not only for those health professionals working with pediatric populations, but also for parents, teachers, and other school professionals, as well as education researchers and policymakers, ready to support the 'COVID generation' moving forward."

—**Carol Vidal,** Child and Adolescent Psychiatrist

"This book is a must read for every educator, policymaker, and leader charged with our children's education. This book tackles the impacts of the COVID-19 prolonged school closure from every angle. The impacts on learning loss, mental health, and neurodevelopment are vividly illustrated and lessons for the future must be heeded. This is a must read for anyone in a leadership role in the world."

—**Babur Lateef,** Chairman At-Large, Prince William County Public Schools, Virginia

"This trio of neuropsychologists provide a stellar review of the emerging literature pertaining to COVID-19 impact on neurocognitive and mental health. They offer essential guidance for clinical practice and research that will likely only grow in relevance in the years to come."

—**Tricia S. Williams,** Associate Scientist, Clinical Neuropsychologist, Hospital for Sick Children

"What could be the lingering impacts of school closures on learning and behavior? How do we act in the best interests of youth? How do we make meaningful changes to policy and pedagogy to avoid later school closures whenever possible? This book provides a clear-eyed and timely review of these considerations with recommendations for practitioners, policymakers, and community partners going forward."

—**Jordan A. Booker,** University of Missouri

"*Neurodevelopment in the Post-Pandemic World* is a welcome, fact-based, deep dive into the widespread and ongoing effects of the rapid and drastic measures that were employed in response to the COVID-19 pandemic. More importantly, the authors present the information in a factual, non-political fashion, relying on specific irrefutable outcomes data to expose the multifaceted consequences, while raising points of dialogue and inquiry. While directed toward psychologists and neuropsychologists, *Neurodevelopment in the Post-Pandemic World* highlights the responsibility of all educational and health care professionals to not only take steps in the long process of correcting the failures of the pandemic response, but also make sure that such actions are not taken again in the future."

—**Mark T. Barisa,** Clinical Neuropsychologist

"The Covid pandemic didn't just devastate Americans physically, but its toll negatively affected our children's emotional and cognitive health. Drs. Colvin, Reesman, and Glen have written a comprehensive, scholarly, and extraordinarily timely text on the impact of Covid both directly and indirectly on America's children. Examining the science in context to a critical neurodevelopmental lens, the authors lay out systematically the various components of the pandemic and its adverse influence on multiple aspects of our children's growth. From school closures to the upswing in behavioral problems, impacts on academics and achievement, college youth, and unintended racial consequences, the influence of the pandemic is both quantifiable and persistent. Colvin, Reesman, and Glen provide a readable and well referenced treatise to interpret and respond to the impact of this critical juncture in time."

—**Timothy E. Wilens,** MD, Professor of Psychiatry, Harvard Medical School

Neurodevelopment in the Post-Pandemic World

The Altered Trajectory of Children's Education, Mental Health, and Brain Development

MOLLY COLVIN
JENNIFER LINTON REESMAN
TANNAHILL GLEN

OXFORD
UNIVERSITY PRESS

OXFORD
UNIVERSITY PRESS

Oxford University Press is a department of the University of Oxford. It furthers the University's objective of excellence in research, scholarship, and education by publishing worldwide. Oxford is a registered trade mark of Oxford University Press in the UK and in certain other countries.

Published in the United States of America by Oxford University Press
198 Madison Avenue, New York, NY 10016, United States of America.

CIP data is on file at the Library of Congress

ISBN 9780197762639

DOI: 10.1093/9780197762660.001.0001

Printed by Integrated Books International, United States of America

MIX
Paper
FSC FSC® C183721

The manufacturer's authorised representative in the EU for product safety is Oxford University Press España S.A. of el Parque Empresarial San Fernando de Henares, Avenida de Castilla, 2 - 28830 Madrid (www.oup.es/en)

To James, Kate, and Jack, for their love, laughter, and unwavering encouragement to follow my compass. And to my parents, who dedicated their professional lives to the pursuit of equality and excellence in public education. With deep gratitude for the bravery, keen intellects, and great company of my colleagues, Dr. Reesman and Dr. Glen. (MC)

For Clara, may this experience have taught you to never stop questioning and seeking knowledge. With deep gratitude for colleagues that demonstrate the promise and all that is good in clinical neuropsychology. Drs. Colvin and Glen, you are unmatched. (JR)

For Simon, Daire, Hope, and Hector, who never forgot for a moment to reach out to those who had no voice. I am also deeply grateful to my colleagues Dr. Colvin and Dr. Reesman for their tireless study and boundless optimism. (TG)

Contents

Acknowledgments

There are many people that have supported, encouraged, and helped us to shape this work and bring it to fruition. Katy Pasquariello: your attention to detail has helped to bring these threads together in managing a massive number of references with care. Nadina Persaud: thank you for believing in the importance of this project. To the reviewers who have helped us to frame and think critically about this work, thank you. Pete Duquette and David Zweig: thank you for your patience while this project took focus.

Introduction

In Spring 2020, in response to the burgeoning COVID-19 pandemic, a remarkable transformation of the childhood educational and psychosocial experience began. In the United States, most schools closed, transitioning to virtual education for periods ranging from a few weeks to more than a year (Burbio's K-12 School Opening Tracker, 2021), with continued, shorter term classroom closures through the next full academic year. The Secretary-General of the United Nations, Antonio Guterres, referred to school disruptions as "an education catastrophe" (UNESCO, 2020).

Research since that time has consistently shown that pandemic-related educational disruption, consistent with pre-pandemic research, is associated with attenuated learning gains and widening achievement gaps for students of color, emerging English speakers, students with economic disadvantage, and students with disabilities (National Assessment of Educational Progress [NAEP], 2022). Global learning losses are estimated to be the equivalent of more than a year of education, with long-term implications for gross domestic product growth (Jakubowski et al., 2023).

The duration of virtual instruction has also been associated with greater attenuation of learning gains (Oxner, 2021). Compounding concerns, studies have shown schools with the highest percentage of vulnerable students experienced the longest closures (Goldhaber et al., 2022).

As the pandemic began to recede, and schools reopened, other impacts became visible: chronic absenteeism dramatically increased (Fortin, 2022), and student enrollment declined or was delayed (Vazquez Toness & Lurye, 2023). Evaluation, diagnosis, and intervention for children with disabilities was significantly disrupted, with unknown impact on longer term outcomes for those high-risk groups (Allison & Levac, 2022). At the same time, rates of psychiatric dysfunction in children and adolescents increased measurably (Wong et al., 2023), a finding more than one study has linked to the effects of school closures because of the resultant increased exposure to risk factors for psychosocial dysfunction (Vidal et al., 2023). Youth already impacted by pre-pandemic disparities were disproportionately affected by psychosocial change during the COVID-19 pandemic.

Neurodevelopment in the Post-Pandemic World. Molly Colvin, Jennifer Linton Reesman, and Tannahill Glen, Oxford University Press. © Oxford University Press 2024. DOI: 10.1093/9780197762660.001.0001

This book explores the impact of pandemic-related education disruption in the United States, but it is critical to note that closures occurred globally. Studies have shown similar patterns of learning losses and increased disparities as seen in the United States (Di Pietro et al., 2020; Engzell et al., 2021; Maldonado & De Witte, 2022; Rose et al., 2021), with data from other countries ranging from optimistic (Sweden; Hallin et al., 2022) to disturbing (Uganda; Blanshe & Dahir, 2022). Although ample research has examined pandemic-related learning challenges in college students (Shoair et al., 2023), this publication focuses on American primary and secondary school students.

Another major focus of this book is to highlight the increased likelihood for negative outcomes in youth of color, those with disabilities, emerging English speakers, and those from economically disadvantaged households, with an eye toward remediation of losses and future policy. Neuropsychologists, in particular, will need to consider the neurocognitive and psychological impacts of educational disruption during the COVID-19 pandemic into the foreseeable future, recognizing that those from racial/ethnic minority groups, lower socioeconomic status, and with disabilities have been most affected. That said, other fields will be directly impacted by effects of prolonged disruption as well: school psychologists, psychiatrists, pediatricians, legislators, public health personnel, and attorneys will encounter pandemic-related issues, and the topics covered in this book are of direct relevance to their work.

It is our opinion that there is substantial evidence to support the idea that neurodevelopmental trajectories have been altered for some youth, and the long-term effects of any alteration are simply unknowable for the immediate future. Evidence will continue to accumulate well beyond this publication, but this book's framework for understanding evidence is built on a solid empirical foundation that will underpin new data as they emerge. This book is not an exploration of whether American schools *should* have shut during the COVID-19 pandemic, but an effort to discuss the long-term implications of these extraordinary disruptions, and to understand how developmental trajectories may have been altered in ways that are relevant to clinicians, educators, and policymakers now and into the future.

Walsh (2023) described the impact of educational disruption as "the other Long Covid," writing, "And so the US began an emergency experiment, one with no precedent and no foreseeable end, in what would happen to

America's children if we took away the place where they spend, on average, over a thousand hours a year." With that in mind, let us review the evidence.

References

Allison, K. M., & Levac, D. E. (2022). Impact of the COVID-19 pandemic on therapy service delivery and functioning for school-aged children with disabilities in the United States. *Disability Health Journal, 15*(2), 101266. https://doi.org/10.1016/j.dhjo.2021.101266

Blanshe, M., & Dahir, A. (2022, January 10). Uganda reopens schools after world's longest Covid shutdown. *The New York Times*. https://www.nytimes.com/2022/01/10/world/africa/uganda-schools-reopen.html

Burbio's K-12 School Opening Tracker. (2021). *Burbio*. https://about.burbio.com/school-opening-tracker

Di Pietro, G., Biagi, F., Costa, P., Karpinski, Z., & Mazza, J. (2020). The likely impact of COVID-19 on education: Reflections based on the existing literature and recent international datasets. *Publications Office of the European Union*. https://doi.org/10.2760/126686

Engzell, P., Frey, A., & Verhagen, M. D. (2021). Learning loss due to school closures during the COVID-19 pandemic. *Proceedings of the National Academy of Sciences U S A, 118*(17). https://doi.org/10.1073/pnas.2022376118

Fortin, J. (2022). More pandemic fallout: The chronically absent student. *The New York Times*. https://www.nytimes.com/2022/04/20/us/school-absence-attendance-rate-covid.html

Goldhaber, D., Kane, T. J., McEachin, A., Morton, E., Patterson, T., & Staiger, D. O. (2022). The consequences of remote and hybrid instruction during the pandemic. Research Report. Cambridge, MA: Center for Education Policy Research, Harvard University.

Hallin, A. E., Danielsson, H., Nordström, T., & Fälth, L. (2022). No learning loss in Sweden during the pandemic evidence from primary school reading assessments. *International Journal of Education Research, 114*, 102011. https://doi.org/10.1016/j.ijer.2022.102011

Jakubowski, M., Gajderowicz, T., & Patrinos, H. A. (2023). Global learning loss in student achievement: First estimates using comparable reading scores. *Economics Letters, 232*, 111313. https://doi.org/https://doi.org/10.1016/j.econlet.2023.111313

Maldonado, J. E., & De Witte, K. (2022). The effect of school closures on standardised student test outcomes. *British Educational Research Journal, 48*(1), 49–94. https://doi.org/https://doi.org/10.1002/berj.3754

National Assessment of Educational Progress (NAEP). (2022). Reading and mathematics scores decline during COVID-19 pandemic. *National Center for Education Statistics, Institute of Education Sciences, US Department of Education*. https://www.nationsreportcard.gov/highlights/ltt/2022/

Oxner, R. (2021, June 28). Texas students' standardized test scores dropped dramatically during the pandemic, especially in math. *The Texas Tribune*. https://www.texastribune.org/2021/06/28/texas-staar-test-results/

Rose, S., Badr, K., Fletcher, L., Paxman, T., Lord, P., Rutt, S., . . . Twist, L. (2021). Impact of school closures and subsequent support strategies on attainment and socio-emotional wellbeing in key stage 1. Research Report. *Education Endowment Foundation*. https://files.eric.ed.gov/fulltext/ED620409.pdf

Shoair, O. A., Smith, W. J., Abdel Aziz, M. H., Veronin, M. A., Glavy, J. S., & Pirtle, S. J. (2023). Pharmacy students' perceptions and attitudes toward face-to-face vs. virtual team-based learning (TBL) in the didactic curriculum: A mixed-methods study. *Medical Education Online, 28*(1), 2226851. https://doi.org/10.1080/10872981.2023.2226851

UNESCO. (2020). UN Secretary-General warns of education catastrophe, pointing to UNESCO estimate of 24 million learners at risk of dropping out. *UNESCO*. https://www.

unesco.org/en/articles/un-secretary-general-warns-education-catastrophe-pointing-unesco-estimate-24-million-learners-risk-0

Vazquez Toness, B., & Lurye, S. (2023). Thousands of kids are missing from school. Where did they go? *T. A. Press.* https://projects.apnews.com/features/2023/missing-children/index.html

Vidal, C., Holland, E. T., & Duriseti, R. S. (2023). Rejoinder 3: School closures: The trigger point in the decline in pediatric mental health outcomes during the COVID-19 pandemic. *Journal of Canadian Academy of Child and Adolescent Psychiatry*, *32*(2), 88–92.

Walsh, B. (2023). The other long Covid. *Vox.* https://www.vox.com/the-highlight/23584869/covid-coronavirus-school-closures-remote-education-learning-loss-psychological-depression-teens

Wong, B., Cross, S., Zavaleta-Ramírez, P., Bauda, I., Hoffman, P., Ibeziako, P., . . . Ougrin, D. (2023). Self-harm in children and adolescents who presented at emergency units during the COVID-19 pandemic: An international retrospective cohort study. *Journal of the American Academy of Child and Adolescent Psychiatry*, *62*(9), 998–1009. https://doi.org/10.1016/j.jaac.2022.11.016

1

The Good, Bad, and Ugly of School Closures and Virtual Learning

How Long Were American Schools Closed?

Global educational disruption related to the coronavirus (COVID-19) pandemic was unparalleled in breadth and duration (Colvin et al., 2022). When hybrid and partial closures are considered, North America had some of the world's most prolonged closures (Recch et al., 2023). However, there was extreme variability among states and districts, ranging from only 4 weeks in South Dakota (Ballotpedia, 2023) to more than 1 year in other areas (Burbio's K-12 School Opening Tracker, 2021). Even within districts, private schools opened for in-person classes more rapidly than public schools (Miller, 2020). Geographical variability was profound: the National Assessment of Educational Progress (NAEP)/Institute for Educational Studies 2021 survey of schools found 93% of Nebraska students were attending school in person in May 2021, compared to only 5% of California students. The same survey documented other disparities among groups for in-person classes: while more than two thirds of White students were attending school full time in person, fewer than half of students of color were enrolled in in-person classes (National Assessment of Educational Progress [NAEP], 2021).

But simply documenting availability of instruction has limitations, as described by Kurmann and Lalé (2023), who pointed out that in many schools, in-person instruction was available but the uptake was significantly limited. For example, the District of Columbia school district was the only entity granted a waiver of federally mandated testing in Spring 2021 because 88% of its students were still engaged in virtual learning (Katanyoutanant et al., 2021). The authors measured effective in-person learning (EIPL), using cell phone safe tracking data to map school presence. They found that for the 2020–2021 academic year, consistent with other data, EIPL was lowest for public schools, schools with higher numbers of students of color, and schools with lower pre-pandemic achievement test scores. They also found, counterintuitively, lower in-person attendance for schools in areas

Neurodevelopment in the Post-Pandemic World. Molly Colvin, Jennifer Linton Reesman, and Tannahill Glen, Oxford University Press. © Oxford University Press 2024. DOI: 10.1093/9780197762660.003.0001

of high affluence and education level, and surmised this may have reflected the greater ease of work-from-home arrangements for those professionals, and perhaps differences in risk perception based on social or political beliefs. Other data indicate only half of fourth and eighth graders were attending in-person, full-time school in May 2021; about 20% of fourth and eighth graders were still fully remote during the same time period (U.S. Department of Education, 2021).

Further complicating measurement of school closures is the lack of an operationalized definition of "open," which during the pandemic was used to refer to full pre-pandemic operations, or alternately, one day of in-person instruction per week in at least one grade (County of Los Angeles Department of Public Health, 2021).

Also, in some areas of the United States where schools reopened, instructional disruption continued for some time. Rolling closures and temporary reversion to virtual education continued well into Spring 2022 due to various factors such as prolonged quarantine periods for students testing positive and rising COVID-19 cases (Silva, 2022). In mid-January 2022, 5,000–7,000 schools did not offer in-person classes one or more days due to pandemic-related disruptions (Burbio's K-12 School Opening Tracker, 2022). In some states, post-pandemic teacher shortages resulted in provision of virtual instruction, concerningly, in lower performing schools, through the use of synchronous video streaming (Files, 2022).

These short-term closures have increasingly been a concern because of the risk that short-term school interruptions will become more normalized, without any empirical support for their impact; this is discussed in more detail in Chapter 10. In fact, even very brief interruptions have been shown to impact learning progress, and there may even be a "snowballing" effect that opens the door to future interruptions (Kraft & Monti-Nussbaum, 2021). To wit, in Fall 2023, as schools returned to in-person classes after summer, several nonpandemic school closures were reported in the news: in Kentucky, schools were closed due to severe bus driver shortages (Diaz, 2023), and in multiple states, classes were canceled or shortened due to heat advisories (Roston, 2023).

Impacts of Past School Closures

Because of the extraordinary extent of educational disruption, it was apparent even in Spring 2020 that quantifying and remediating the effects of school closures would be critical. However, there were sparse data on which to base predictions of impact on learning gains or societal functioning. Kuhfeld et al. (2020) described how pre-pandemic research on school closures and absenteeism is not easily generalizable to the COVID-19-related closures. Prior to the COVID-19 pandemic, short-term, localized, "reactive" school closures occurred during outbreaks that were severe enough to cause staffing shortages and mass student absenteeism, with these closures typically being brief (4–6 days) (Germann et al., 2019).

Researchers modeled potential impacts of a different sort of school closure: the preemptive school closure to mitigate viral impact and reduce household transmission (World Health Organization [WHO] 2009). The tactic was used during the influenza A H1N1 virus outbreak in 2009 (Shi et al., 2014), when the Centers for Disease Control and Prevention (2009) recommended preemptive short-term (5–7 days) school dismissals in targeted areas. Modeling studies on the impact of such closures have produced variable results because there is no consensus as to extent of preemptive closure (e.g., gradual/abrupt, partial/total, local/national) (Luca et al., 2018). Theoretical school dismissal models ranged from very brief (5–7 days) to 16 weeks in the most catastrophic modeled scenarios; the longest term closure response was recommended to be combined with holidays and/or a delayed start to a semester (Shi et al., 2014). It is worth noting that such simulation studies examined the impact of preemptive closures on transmission patterns, number of cases averted, and reduction of peak burden on the health care system (Germann et al., 2019) as opposed to economic, psychosocial, and academic costs, which makes their conclusions less applicable to the COVID-19 pandemic.

Historical Evidence on Prolonged Educational Disruption

In the absence of solid data on the effects of prolonged school closures, it is possible to examine historical comparisons. For instance, the Spanish Flu of 1918 led to urban school closures of about 80 days in two major districts (Smith, 2021). Li and Malmendier (2022) documented significant negative effects on high school completion and absenteeism for the school-age Spanish Flu cohort. Ironically, given that the same districts remained virtual for longer than many other cities in the COVID-19 pandemic (Burbio's K-12 School Opening Tracker, 2023), New York City, Chicago, and New Haven

(Connecticut) schools remained open during the Spanish Flu, in part due to public health and education officials' desire to maintain health surveillance for students and their families (Stern et al., 2010).

After Hurricane Katrina struck Louisiana in 2005, the hardest hit schools were closed for more than 5 weeks, with 20% of area students out of school for 2 months. Some of the most badly damaged schools were shut for 1 year, and although students could receive instruction in other areas, many students moved or never returned to school (Hill, 2020; Pane et al., 2006). Puerto Rico, devastated by the 2017 hurricanes Irma and Maria, never reopened about a quarter of functioning schools prior to that hurricane season (Katz, 2019). Closures disproportionately impacted those living in high-poverty areas, and higher academic workloads were distributed over shorter school days (due to power and water shortages) (Moreno, 2018). Disruption related to a major Ebola virus outbreak in Sierra Leone (2014–2015) led to school instruction via radio programming, followed by two abbreviated academic years with accelerated curriculum (Powers & Azzi-Huck, 2016). Condensed and/or accelerated learning has been documented in post-conflict societies as well: Sierra Leone schools were also disrupted by war from 1991 to 2002, but primary school students received adjusted instruction to facilitate their starting secondary school on time (Barrios-Tao et al., 2017).

Finally, the country of Ukraine provides a more recent comparison, although long-term data are not yet available as events are still unfolding: Ukrainian schools were closed or significantly altered for more than 7 months during the COVID-19 pandemic, followed by an estimated 2 months' disruption due to the war, with thousands of Ukrainian students who escaped to other countries not enrolled in school at all (Patrinos, 2022).

This prolonged wartime educational turmoil is reminiscent of academic and psychosocial disruption in Europe during World War II, which resulted in reduced educational achievement for a school-age cohort in countries heavily involved in the war (Ichino & Winter-Ebmer, 2004). In the United Kingdom there was a unique period of disruption for students: in 1939 the British government evacuated 800,000 urban children—many from working-class households—to rural areas to escape anticipated aerial bombardment (Huxford, 2019). The evacuation program, backed by the Ministry of Health, was voluntary, but there was a concerted government messaging program strongly advising evacuation to what were initially planned as large school camps, but which, due to cost concerns, became simply foster family placement (Johnston, 2021). Johnston documented how the official messaging campaign emphasized parental moral obligations to send children away and the anticipated benefits of evacuation, and ultimately minimized negative effects of the scheme. Johnston's quote from historian Julie Summers is startlingly familiar: "What is striking about the stories told by evacuees is that in the immediate post-war era this topic was barely, if ever, discussed. It was simply taken for granted that children would adjust to life." Johnston continues: "The external crisis of impending war drove the government to create evacuation as a solution. Yet, this ultimately generated another type of individual trauma which, if not wholly unforeseen, was not regarded as a pressing issue."

The impact of traumatic separation on child adjustment and mental health was widely studied. The psychoanalyst Anna Freud authored a report on the topic and opened the Hampstead War Nurseries for the care and study of children impacted by war (Midgley, 2007). Interestingly, another concern at the time was that moving children from an urban center, with higher rates of infectious childhood illnesses, to rural areas, with lower levels of immunity, would result in increased disease activity, and in fact, a temporary alteration of disease activity was documented (Smallman-Raynor & Cliff, 2015).

Even brief periods of school closure have been linked to attenuation of expected gains (Wong et al., 2014) and lower educational attainment (Jaume & Willén, 2019), so it is unsurprising that prolonged educational disruptions, such as those due to natural disasters, have been associated with lower academic achievement, with disproportionate impact on marginalized groups (Hallgarten, 2020; Smith, 2021). Nor is the altered trajectory of achievement necessarily a transient state: studies of educational losses after the 2005 Pakistan earthquake revealed continued decline in learning gains even after children returned to school (Recch et al., 2023). Surveys following the Ebola virus outbreak in Africa from 2013 to 2016 showed a quarter of Liberian students did not return to education after schools reopened (The World Bank, 2016). Delayed routine health care, treatment disruption for those with disabilities, loss of school social services, and economic strain also contribute to long-term effects of prolonged educational disruption (Benner & Mistry, 2020).

Massive Resistance: A Chapter in American History

A particularly discomfiting period in the nation's history provides more insight into the effects of prolonged educational disruption. In 1954, the

U.S. Supreme Court published its opinion in *Brown v. Board of Education*, ordering the desegregation of public schools (Kronholz, 2004). In response, after appeals were exhausted, there were legislative efforts to prevent school desegregation, termed the "Massive Resistance" campaign, which culminated in a complete shutdown of public schools in Prince Edward County, Virginia, through refusal to fund public education (Hershman, 2020). Provisions were made for White students to attend private facilities using county-funded vouchers, but Black children had no such options. Between 1959 and 1963, an estimated 1,700 Black children in the county did not receive public education (Green et al., 1966). A similar scenario played out in another city: in Little Rock, Arkansas, public high schools were closed by the governor in 1958–1959. Of the estimated 750 Black students who were displaced, 50% received no school at all (Encyclopedia of Arkansas, 2023).

Some of the Black students who were forced out of education moved to nearby counties, entered college early, or attended private school, but few received the requisite 4 years of schooling. There were various efforts to provide some degree of education, but instruction was purposefully limited, for example, summer "crash" remediation programs, so as not to release the county from its requirement to provide public education (Heaton, 2008). The U.S. Department of Justice led the effort to establish "Free Schools," which provided education for some Black students (Green et al., 1966) before public schools finally reopened.

Sponsored by the U.S. Department of Health, Education, and Welfare, successive studies assessed unfinished learning in the affected populations (Green et al., 1966; Green & Hofmann, 1965). In the first study of Prince Edward County affected students, Green and Hofmann administered the Stanford Binet Test and the Stanford Achievement Test to students separated into "Education" and "No Education" groups, but even the "Education" group only had an average of 1.5 years of instruction during the school closures. Students were tested in 1963 and 1964, which was near the completion of the Free School education intervention. While students who received some education demonstrated slightly higher achievement test scores than those with no education at all (1–1.5 grade equivalent level), their scores remained lower than those of children in neighboring areas whose education was uninterrupted. Children ages 6–11 years demonstrated the most significant differences, specifically in the area of language skills. With the resumption of instruction, achievement test scores did improve but reading skills remained below expectations. Intelligence test scores were lower for children who never attended school: a difference of nearly 20 points was observed between young children (age 7–9 years) with no education and those with partial education.

Green's 1966 follow-up study revealed that 11-year-old Black students in Prince Edward County scored about two grade equivalent levels lower on the Stanford Achievement Test than did their peers in neighborhood counties. High-school-age students in Prince Edward County scored more than two grades lower on reading tests compared to those in neighboring counties. Other educationally relevant skills were impacted by education disruption: basic skills such as time-telling, pencil use, and test-taking procedures were underdeveloped in the most affected group (Heaton, 2008). In a second follow-up study to assess the effects of the year-long Free Schools, Green et al. (1966) found that despite substantial test score gains, achievement of affected students remained low relative to national norms.

Heaton (2008) documented negative impact on educational attainment for Prince Edward County minority citizens who were of school age during the Massive Resistance period. Heaton also noted that data from the Prince Edward County cohort enabled estimation of the costs of prolonged, widespread educational disruption. Findings did provide room for some optimism: Heaton found adults who experienced the school closures as children lost about 1 year of educational attainment, compared to the projected 4–5 years. Impacts were greatest for older students, who were more likely to obtain employment rather than return to school much later.

Interestingly, a similar finding was noted 60 years later: a recent World Bank global study of impacts of prolonged school closures observed that older students were the least likely to return to school after closures (Sanchez et al., 2023). Heaton opined that the relatively reduced impacts were possibly due to partial educational efforts during the school closures. Heaton did not find significant differences between Prince Edward student outcomes and those of neighborhood counties in income, medical, or legal (incarceration) spheres. However, Heaton's findings contradict other studies: the county's poverty rate remained higher than surrounding areas, and the high school graduation rate remained lower (Kronholz, 2004), and educational achievement and income were lower for the Massive Resistance cohort that remained in the county during the shutdown compared to students who left during that period (Hale-Smith, 1993). In fact, concerns of the Virginia business community about the negative impact of educational instability on industrial development and workforce preparation prompted the eventual founding of Virginia's technical and community college programs (Hodges, 2019).

Research on Virtual Learning

Prior to the COVID-19 pandemic, virtual education was a billion-dollar industry (Metaari Press Release, 2020). By 2022, the market for online educational services had grown exponentially, from about $19 billion to nearly $200 billion; market projections predict further record growth, to an estimated $600 billion by 2030 (Vantage Market Research, 2023).

In the earliest months of the COVID-19 pandemic, many school districts rapidly transitioned to remote instruction. The scale of such broad and sustained implementation of virtual instruction was unprecedented: an estimated 93% of U.S. households with school-age children engaged in online instruction (McElrath, 2020). There was not a particularly large body of research on virtual learning; existing studies did not evaluate wholesale replacement of traditional instruction, especially for preschool and elementary settings (Koc, 2005). Instead, studies focused on skill enhancement in higher education and training programs, such as those for continuing education or certification. Interestingly, those studies highlighted challenges for the technology, including disparities in access to technology and low student engagement, especially for those with disabilities and those with fewer economic resources (Fu, 2013; Kamenetz, 2020; Linne, 2014; Vekiri, 2010). The Government Accountability Office published an analysis showing that even before the pandemic, students in virtual charter schools participated in achievement testing at a lower rate, with an average math proficiency rate about 25 percentage points lower than the rate for in-person traditional schools (21% and 46%, respectively) (U.S. Government Accountability Office [GAO], 2022).

For an accurate assessment of the contributions and impacts of prolonged virtual instruction, it is necessary to operationally define the method. Perhaps surprisingly, there is no consensus definition of remote learning, so virtual instruction programs varied substantially among schools (Wang et al., 2021). Models included hybrid instruction, on/off days in school, remote instruction in the classroom setting, synchronous (real-time) instruction, and asynchronous (prerecorded) presentations (Brady & Pradhan, 2020). According to the National Academy of Education (2021), there was even variability of instruction models within schools.

There was also wide variability by region and state in the duration of online learning; some school districts returned to in-person full-time instruction for the entire 2020–2021 school year, while others remained online for the entire academic year (MCH Strategic Data, 2021). In some states, nearly all students were in person by the end of the 2020–2021 school year (e.g., Montana, Wyoming, Florida), while in others (e.g., California, Oregon, and the District of Columbia), fewer than a quarter of students were in person (Burbio's K-12 School Opening Tracker, 2022; George et al., 2021). Jack and colleagues (Jack et al., 2023) showed that among 5,000 sampled American school districts, 43% of the 2020–2021 school year was dedicated to in-person instruction, 38% of the year required hybrid instruction, and 19% was devoted to virtual instruction.

Socioeconomically disadvantaged students were less likely to have learning-enhancing environments (e.g., private study space and home computers) and less likely to have active learning support from schools (e.g., being given a "learning pack" instead of online video conferencing with live interaction) (Andrew et al., 2020). Children from high-income households used online resources at higher rates compared to children from low-income households; children in lower income households were more likely to be learning using paper materials sent home from school (McElrath, 2020) or using screen time as replacement for schoolwork, rather than for learning support (Dore et al., 2021). These findings are consistent with reports of a shortage in online learning technology for students from poorly funded school districts or socioeconomically disadvantaged households during the pandemic (Nierenberg & Pasick, 2020).

A major factor in the efficacy of virtual instruction is accessibility to quality Internet and learning environments. While more than 9 out of 10 American households have at least one computer and one Internet provider contract (Martin, 2021), technology maintenance theory posits that the digital divide is now characterized not by the absence of technology or Internet, but by lack of sustained service, quality hardware, and skills, resources, and experience in navigating service/device disruptions; persons of color and those with fewer economic resources are less likely to exhibit high technology maintenance (Gonzales, 2016). Reynolds et al. (2022) interviewed primary and secondary school teachers in May and June 2020, after the first round of virtual instruction. Teachers in schools with more economically disadvantaged students noted greater "intermittency" of technology and fewer students with prior technology proficiency (e.g., a student's lack of email experience), leading to inability to receive critical materials. Interviewees noted that parents were often recruited to help with technology glitches. Other work has shown that Black (19%) and Hispanic (14%) persons were less likely to work from home ("telework") than Asian (38%) and White (24%) persons in the early pandemic period (Asfaw, 2022), so Black and Hispanic students were less likely to have a parent (a) working from home and (b) with prior technology proficiency, a finding borne out in other research (Anakwe et al., 2021).

This disparity is perpetuated by other factors: schools with more students from higher income households are more likely to have better Internet integration, making the transition to virtual instruction less disruptive (Garcia & Weiss, 2020). Parents with higher education levels and in higher income positions were more likely to transition to work-from-home arrangements, making student supervision and assistance more available (Bansak & Starr, 2021). A survey from the National Center for Education Statistics (Berger et al., 2022) detailed how electronic devices were shared by multiple students in one family, Internet bandwidth was highly variable across areas, and synchronous (real-time) instruction occurred more frequently in districts with more middle- and high-income households. The same survey revealed that fewer than half of teachers in public schools offered live (real-time) instruction, which is correlated with parental involvement (Marschall & Shah, 2020), compared to more than half of charter school instructors and nearly two thirds of private school teachers who offered in-person (real-time) lessons. (Reynolds et al., 2022) demonstrated that "paper packet" educational tools were used as alternative instructional materials, for instance, during the delay between order and delivery of take-home devices, or as hybrid materials, and that such packets were often discordant with online instructional content, and inconsistently offered across districts.

There is also disparity in reliance on virtual learning. Parolin and Lee (2021) found that schools with pre-pandemic indicators of educational and economic disparities (e.g., lower third-grade math scores, higher percentages of minority students and students experiencing homelessness) were more likely to fully rely on remote learning (Parolin & Lee, 2021). Other studies have replicated the finding that students of color are more likely to have been enrolled in remote learning (Dorn et al., 2020), and students from urban areas were also more likely to be enrolled in remote learning than students from rural areas (Schwartz et al., 2021).

In short, disparities in educational technology were "staggering" (Singer, 2023), and as described by (West, 2023), "prolonged school closures and the application of technology-dependent solutions have precipitated outcomes that are of grave and urgent concern" (p. 421). Interested readers may see Reynolds et al. (2022) and Golden et al. (2023) for review.

References

Anakwe, A., Majee, W., Noel-London, K., Zachary, I., & BeLue, R. (2021). Sink or swim: Virtual life challenges among African American families during COVID-19 lockdown. *International Journal of Environmental Research and Public Health, 18*(4290). https://doi.org/10.3390/ijerph18084290

Andrew, A., Cattan, S., Costa Dias, M., Farquharson, C., Kraftman, L., Krutikova, S., . . . Sevilla, A. (2020). Inequalities in children's experiences of home learning during the COVID-19 lockdown in England. *Fiscal Studies, 41*(3), 653–683. https://doi.org/10.1111/1475-5890.12240

Asfaw, A. (2022). Racial and ethnic disparities in teleworking due to the COVID-19 pandemic in the United States: A mediation analysis. *International Journal of Environmental Research and Public Health, 19*(4680). https://doi.org/10.3390/ijerph19084680

Ballotpedia. (2023). School responses in South Dakota to the coronavirus (COVID-19) pandemic. https://ballotpedia.org/School_responses_in_South_Dakota_to_the_coronavirus_(COVID-19)_pandemic

Bansak, C., & Starr, M. (2021). Covid-19 shocks to education supply: How 200,000 U.S. households dealt with the sudden shift to distance learning. *Review of Economics of the Household, 19*(1), 63–90. https://doi.org/10.1007/s11150-020-09540-9

Barrios-Tao, H., Siciliani-Barraza, J., & Bonilla-Barrios, B. (2017). Education programs in post-conflict environments: A review from Liberia, Sierra Leone, and South Africa. *Revista Electrónica Educare, 21*(1), 1–22. https://doi.org/10.15359/ree.21-1.11

Benner, A. D., & Mistry, R. S. (2020). Child development during the COVID-19 pandemic through a life course theory lens. *Child Development Perspectives, 14*(4), 236–243. https://doi.org/https://doi.org/10.1111/cdep.12387

Berger, M., Kuang, M., Jerry, L., & Freund, D. (2022). Impact of the coronavirus (COVID-19) pandemic on public and private elementary and secondary education in the United States (preliminary data): Results from the 2020–21 National Teacher and Principal Survey (NTPS). First Look. NCES 2022-019. *National Center for Education Statistics.* https://nces.ed.gov/pubsearch/pubsinfo.asp?pubid=2022019

Brady, A. K., & Pradhan, D. (2020). Learning without borders: Asynchronous and distance learning in the age of COVID-19 and beyond. *ATS Scholar, 1*(3), 233–242. https://doi.org/10.34197/ats-scholar.2020-0046PS

Burbio's K-12 School Opening Tracker. (2021). *Burbio.* https://about.burbio.com/school-opening-tracker

Burbio's K-12 School Opening Tracker. (2022). *Burbio.* https://about.burbio.com/school-opening-tracker

Burbio's K-12 School Opening Tracker. (2023). *Burbio.* https://about.burbio.com/school-opening-tracker

Centers for Disease Control and Prevention. (2009). CDC health update: School (K–12) dismissal and childcare facilities: Interim CDC guidance in response to human infections with the Influenza A H1N1 Virus, 2009. https://www.cdc.gov/h1n1flu/HAN/050109.htm

Colvin, M. K. M., Reesman, J., & Glen, T. (2022). The impact of COVID-19 related educational disruption on children and adolescents: An interim data summary and commentary on ten considerations for neuropsychological practice. *Clinical Neuropsychology, 36*(1), 45–71. https://doi.org/10.1080/13854046.2021.1970230

County of Los Angeles Department of Public Health. (2021). Appendix T-1: COVID-19 protocol for TK-12 schools. http://publichealth.lacounty.gov/media/Coronavirus/docs/protocols/AppendixT1_K12Schools-Retired.pdf

Diaz, A. (2023). Bus driver shortage closes schools in Kentucky. *CBS News*. https://www.cbsnews.com/video/bus-driver-shortage-closes-schools-in-kentucky/

Dore, R. A., Purtell, K. M., & Justice, L. M. (2021). Media use among kindergarteners from low-income households during the COVID-19 shutdown. *Journal of Developmental and Behavioral Pediatrics, 42*(8), 672–676. https://doi.org/10.1097/dbp.0000000000000955

Dorn, E., Hancock, B., Sarakatsannis, J., & Viruleg, E. (2020). COVID-19 and student learning in the United States: The hurt could last a lifetime. *McKinsey & Company, 1*, 1–9.

Encyclopedia of Arkansas. (2023). Lost year. https://encyclopediaofarkansas.net/entries/lost-year-737/

Files, K. (2022, October 21). MPS pilots use of remote teachers for in-person classes amid staffing shortage. *WUWM Milwaukee*. https://www.wuwm.com/2022-10-21/mps-pilots-use-of-remote-teachers-for-in-person-classes-amid-staffing-shortage

Fu, J. S. (2013). ICT in education: A critical literature review and its implications. *International Journal of Education and Development Using Information and Communication Technology (IJEDICT), 9*, 112–125.

Garcia, E., & Weiss, E. (2020). COVID-19 and student performance, equity, and U.S. education policy. Economic Policy Institute https://www.epi.org/publication/the-consequences-of-the-covid-19-pandemic-for-education-performance-and-equity-in-the-united-states-what-can-we-learn-from-pre-pandemic-research-to-inform-relief-recovery-and-rebuilding/

George, G., Dilworth-Bart, J., & Herringa, R. (2021). Potential socioeconomic effects of the COVID-19 pandemic on neural development, mental health, and K-12 educational achievement. *Policy Insights from the Behavioral and Brain Sciences, 8*(2), 111–118. https://doi.org/10.1177/23727322211032248

Germann, T. C., Gao, H., Gambhir, M., Plummer, A., Biggerstaff, M., Reed, C., & Uzicanin, A. (2019). School dismissal as a pandemic influenza response: When, where and for how long? *Epidemics, 28*, 100348. https://doi.org/10.1016/j.epidem.2019.100348

Golden, A. R., Srisarajivakul, E. N., Hasselle, A. J., Pfund, R. A., & Knox, J. (2023). What was a gap is now a chasm: Remote schooling, the digital divide, and educational inequities resulting from the COVID-19 pandemic. *Current Opinion in Psychology, 52*, 101632. https://doi.org/10.1016/j.copsyc.2023.101632

Gonzales, A. (2016). The contemporary US digital divide: From initial access to technology maintenance. *Information, Communication & Society, 19*(2), 234–248. https://doi.org/10.1080/1369118X.2015.1050438

Green, R., Hofmann, L. J., Morse, R., & Morgan, R. (1966). The educational status of children during the first school year following four years of little or no schooling. Michigan State University https://files.eric.ed.gov/fulltext/ED010118.pdf

Green, R. L., & Hofmann, L. J. (1965). A case study of the effects of educational deprivation on southern rural Negro children. *Journal of Negro Education, 34*(3), 327–341. https://doi.org/10.2307/2294204

Hale-Smith, M. E. (1993). The effect of early educational disruption on the belief systems and educational practices of adults: Another look at the Prince Edward County school closings. *Journal of Negro Education, 62*(2), 171–189. https://doi.org/10.2307/2295192

Hallgarten, J. (2020). Evidence on efforts to mitigate the negative educational impact of past disease outbreaks (K4D Helpdesk Report 793). https://opendocs.ids.ac.uk/opendocs/handle/20.500.12413/15202

Heaton, P. (2008). Childhood educational disruption and later life outcomes: Evidence from Prince Edward County. *Journal of Human Capital, 2*, 154–187.

Hershman, J. (2020). Massive resistance. *Encyclopedia Virginia*. https://encyclopediavirginia.org/entries/massive-resistance

Hill, P. (2020). What Post-Katrina New Orleans can teach schools about addressing COVID learning losses. *Center on Reinventing Public Education*. https://crpe.org/what-post-katrina-new-orleans-can-teach-schools-about-addressing-covid-learning-losses/

Hodges, R. A. (2019). Massive resistance and the origins of the Virginia Technical College system. *Inquiry, 22*(2), n2.

Huxford, G. (2019). *Child evacuees in the Second World War: Operation Pied Piper at 80*. https://history.blog.gov.uk/2019/08/30/child-evacuees-in-the-second-world-war-operation-pied-piper-at-80/

Ichino, A., & Winter-Ebmer, R. (2004). The long-run educational cost of World War II. *Journal of Labor Economics, 22*(1), 57–87. https://doi.org/10.1086/380403

Jack, R., Halloran, C., Okun, J., & Oster, E. (2023). Pandemic schooling mode and student test scores: Evidence from US school districts. *American Economic Review: Insights, 5*(2), 173–190. https://doi.org/10.1257/aeri.20210748

Jaume, D., & Willén, A. (2019). The long-run effects of teacher strikes: Evidence from Argentina. *Journal of Labor Economics, 37*(4), 1097–1139.

Johnston, M. (2021). Operation Pied Piper: Britain's forgotten war children. https://booksandideas.net/Operation-Pied-Piper-Britain-s-Forgotten-War-Children#:~:text=On%20the%20eve%20of%20the,marred%20by%20accusations%20of%20abuse.

Kamenetz, A. (2020). What do students need to recover when school closes for months? *National Public Radio*. https://www.npr.org/2020/04/01/825056995/what-do-students-need-to-recover-when-school-closes-for-months

Katanyoutanant, T., Kwon, S., McNeilly, M., Hemberg, B., Thurlow, M. L., Lazarus, S. S., . . . Liu, K. K. (2021). The 95 percent state assessment participation requirement: Current landscape, state challenges, and recommended strategies. NCEO Report 429. *National Center on Educational Outcomes*. https://nceo.umn.edu/docs/OnlinePubs/NCEOReport429.pdf

Katz, J. (2019, September 12). The disappearing schools of Puerto Rico. *The New York Times*. https://www.nytimes.com/interactive/2019/09/12/magazine/puerto-rico-schools-hurricane-maria.html

Koc, M. (2005). Implications of learning theories for effective technology integration and pre-service teacher training: A critical literature review. *Journal of Turkish Science Education, 2*(1), 2–18.

Kraft, M. A., & Monti-Nussbaum, M. (2021). The big problem with little interruptions to classroom learning. *AERA Open, 7*, 23328584211028856. https://doi.org/10.1177/23328584211028856

Kronholz, J. (2004, May 17). After 45 years, a school lockout still reverberates. *The Wall Street Journal*. https://www.wsj.com/articles/SB108474643453412817

Kuhfeld, M., Tarasawa, B., Johnson, A., Ruzek, E., & Lewis, K. (2020). Learning during COVID-19: Initial findings on students' reading and math achievement and growth. Northwest Evaluation Association. https://www.nwea.org/uploads/2020/11/Collaborative-brief-Learning-during-COVID-19.NOV2020.pdf

Kurmann, A., & Lalé, E. (2023). School closures and effective in-person learning during COVID-19. *Economics of Education Review, 95*, 102422. https://doi.org/10.1016/j.econedurev.2023.102422

Li, K., & Malmendier, U. (2022). School closures, inequality, and politics—Evidence from the 1918 Spanish Flu. https://eml.berkeley.edu/~ulrike/Papers/Pandemic_Draftv2_June2022.pdf

Linne, J. (2014). Adolescents from low-income sectors: The challenge of studying in a time of digital environments. *International Journal of Adolescence and Youth, 19*(4), 434–443. https://doi.org/10.1080/02673843.2014.942792

Luca, G., Kerckhove, K. V., Coletti, P., Poletto, C., Bossuyt, N., Hens, N., & Colizza, V. (2018). The impact of regular school closure on seasonal influenza epidemics: A data-driven spatial transmission model for Belgium. *BMC Infectious Disease, 18*(1), 29. https://doi.org/10.1186/s12879-017-2934-3

Marschall, M. J., & Shah, P. R. (2020). Linking the process and outcomes of parent involvement policy to the parent involvement gap. *Urban Education, 55*(5), 699–729.

Martin, M. (2021). Computer and internet use in the United States: 2018. *American Community Survey Reports.* https://www.census.gov/library/publications/2021/acs/acs-49.html

McElrath, K. (2020). Nearly 93% of households with school-age children report some form of distance learning during COVID-19. *United States Census Bureau, 2*(3), 4.

MCH Strategic Data. (2021). COVID-19 IMPACT: School district operational status updates for Fall 2022. https://www.mchdata.com/covid19/schoolclosings

Metaari Press Release. (2020). 2019 global edtech investments reach a staggering $18.66 billion. *Markets Insider.* https://markets.businessinsider.com/news/stocks/2019-global-edtech-investments-reach-a-staggering-18-66-billion-1028800669#

Midgley, N. (2007). Anna Freud: The Hampstead war nurseries and the role of the direct observation of children for psychoanalysis. *International Journal of Psychoanalysis, 88*(Pt 4), 939–959. https://doi.org/10.1516/v28r-j334-6182-524h

Miller, C. (2020, July 16). In the same towns, private schools are reopening while public schools are not. *The New York Times.* https://www.nytimes.com/2020/07/16/upshot/coronavirus-school-reopening-private-public-gap.html

Moreno, C. (2018). A year after Hurricane Maria, school closures make trauma worse for Puerto Rico's children. *Huffington Post.* https://www.huffpost.com/entry/hurricane-maria-school-closures-children-puerto-rico_n_5ba05da1e4b013b0977e2f59

National Academy of Education. (2021). Educational assessments in the COVID-19 era and beyond. https://naeducation.org/wp-content/uploads/2021/02/Educational-Assessments-in-the-COVID-19-Era-and-Beyond.pdf

National Assessment of Educational Progress (NAEP). (2021). NAEP 2021 School Survey. National Center for Education Statistics, Institute of Education Sciences, U.S. Department of Education. https://nces.ed.gov/nationsreportcard/subject/about/pdf/2021_may_school_survey_dashboard.pdf

Nierenberg, A., & Pasick, A. (2020, October 14). Why students can't get laptops. *The New York Times.* https://www.nytimes.com/2020/10/14/us/students-laptops-digitial-divide.html

Pane, J. F., McCaffrey, D. F., Tharp-Gilliam, S., Asmus, G. J., & Stokes, B. R. (2006). *Student displacement in Louisiana after the Hurricanes of 2005: Experiences of public schools and their students.* Santa Monica, CA: RAND Corporation. https://www.rand.org/content/dam/rand/pubs/technical_reports/2006/RAND_TR430.pdf

Parolin, Z., & Lee, E. K. (2021). Large socio-economic, geographic and demographic disparities exist in exposure to school closures. *Nature Human Behaviour, 5*(4), 522–528. https://doi.org/10.1038/s41562-021-01087-8

Patrinos, H. A. (2022). Learning Losses in Ukraine can amount to over one year. *Education, Economics and Public Policy.* https://hpatrinos.com/2022/05/02/learning-losses-in-ukraine-can-amount-to-over-one-year/

Powers, S., & Azzi-Huck, K. (2016). The impact of Ebola on education in Sierra Leone. https://blogs.worldbank.org/education/impact-ebola-education-sierra-leone

Recch, F., Petherick, A., Hinton, R., Nagesh, R., Furst, R., & Goldszmidt, R. (2023). Education data needs and challenges for building back from COVID-19. *Epidemics, 43*, 100673. https://doi.org/10.1016/j.epidem.2023.100673

Reynolds, R., Aromi, J., McGowan, C., & Paris, B. (2022). Digital divide, critical-, and crisis-informatics perspectives on K-12 emergency remote teaching during the pandemic. *Journal of the Association for Information Science and Technology, 73*(12), 1665–1680. https://doi.org/https://doi.org/10.1002/asi.24654

Roston, E. (2023). As school started in the U.S., so did the school closures for heat. *TIME.* https://time.com/6312416/as-school-started-in-the-u-s-so-did-the-school-closures-for-heat/

Sanchez, A., Gregory, L., Crawford, M., Oviedo, B., M.E., Herman, R. S., & Ahlgren, E. (2023). *Learning recovery to acceleration: A global update on country efforts to improve learning and reduce inequalities*. Washington, DC: World Bank Group.

Schwartz, H. L., Diliberti, M. K., Berdie, L., Grant, D., Hunter, G. P., & Setodji, C. M. (2021). *Urban and rural districts showed a strong divide during the COVID-19 pandemic: Results from the Second American School District Panel Survey*. Santa Monica, CA: RAND Corporation. https://doi.org/10.7249/RRA956-2

Shi, J., Njai, R., Wells, E., Collins, J., Wilkins, M., Dooyema, C., . . . Rainey, J. J. (2014). Knowledge, attitudes, and practices of nonpharmaceutical interventions following school dismissals during the 2009 Influenza A H1N1 pandemic in Michigan, United States. *PLoS One*, *9*(4), e94290. https://doi.org/10.1371/journal.pone.0094290

Silva, D. (2022). In states where Covid cases are again on the rise, schools weigh safety measures, closures. *NBC News*. https://www.nbcnews.com/news/us-news/states-covid-cases-are-rise-schools-weigh-safety-measures-closures-rcna27709

Singer, N. (2023, September 6). Dependence on tech caused "staggering" education inequality, U.N. agency says. *The New York Times*. https://www.nytimes.com/2023/09/06/technology/unesco-report-remote-learning-inequity.html

Smallman-Raynor, M. R., & Cliff, A. D. (2015). Operation Pied Piper: A geographical reappraisal of the impact of wartime evacuation on scarlet fever and diphtheria rates in England and Wales, 1939–1945. *Epidemiology and Infection*, *143*(14), 2923–2938. https://doi.org/10.1017/s0950268815000175

Smith, W. C. (2021). Consequences of school closure on access to education: Lessons from the 2013–2016 Ebola pandemic. *International Review of Education*, *67*(1–2), 53–78. https://doi.org/10.1007/s11159-021-09900-2

Stern, A. M., Reilly, M. B., Cetron, M. S., & Markel, H. (2010). "Better off in school": School medical inspection as a public health strategy during the 1918-1919 influenza pandemic in the United States. *Public Health Report*, *125* (Suppl 3), 63–70. https://doi.org/10.1177/00333549101250s309

U.S. Department of Education. (2021). Monthly school survey. https://ies.ed.gov/schoolsurvey/mss-dashboard/

U.S. Government Accountability Office (GAO). (2022). K-12 education: Department of Education should help states address student testing issues and financial risks associated with virtual schools, particularly virtual charter schools. Report to Congressional Requesters. GAO-22-104444. https://www.gao.gov/products/gao-22-104444

Vantage Market Research. (2023). Online education/e-learning market—Global industry assessment & forecast. https://www.vantagemarketresearch.com/industry-report/online-education-e-learning-market-2028#:~:text = Snapshot&text = Global%20Online%20Education%2FE%2DLearning,17.2%25%20over%20the%20forecast%20period

Vekiri, I. (2010). Socioeconomic differences in elementary students' ICT beliefs and out-of-school experiences. *Computers & Education*, *54*, 941–950. https://doi.org/10.1016/j.compedu.2009.09.029

Wang, T., Towey, D., Ng, R. Y., & Gill, A. S. (2021). Towards post-pandemic transformative teaching and learning: Case studies of microlearning implementations in two post-secondary educational institutions. *SN Computer Science*, *2*(4), 271. https://doi.org/10.1007/s42979-021-00663-z

Wong, K. K., Shi, J., Gao, H., Zheteyeva, Y. A., Lane, K., Copeland, D., Hendricks, J., McMurray, L., Sliger, K., Rainey, J. J., & Uzicanin, A. (2014). Why is school closed today? Unplanned K-12 school closures in the United States, 2011-2013. *PloS one*, *9*(12), e113755. https://doi.org/10.1371/journal.pone.0113755

West, M. (2023). An ed-tech tragedy? Educational technologies and school closures in the time of COVID-19. https://unesdoc.unesco.org/ark:/48223/pf0000386701&sa = D&source = docs&ust = 1694462757220029&usg = AOvVaw33bgPnSXpahzBUCqLdbcAE

The World Bank. (2016). The socio-economic impacts of Ebola in Liberia. https://www.worldbank.org/en/topic/poverty/publication/socio-economic-impacts-ebola-liberia
World Health Organization (WHO). (2009). Reducing transmission of pandemic (H1N1) 2009 in school settings: A framework for national and local planning and response. Geneva, Switzerland: WHO Press. https://www.who.int/publications/i/item/reducing-transmission-of-pandemic-(h1n1)-2009-in-school-settings

2

Absenteeism and Delayed Enrollment

Increase in Chronic Absenteeism: Students Lost in the System

Chronic absenteeism, defined as missing more than 10% of classes (Attendance Works, 2023a), was associated with lower graduation rates (Liu et al., 2021), poorer academic achievement, and lower executive function scores (Ansari & Gottfried, 2021) even prior to the COVID-19 pandemic. Chronic absenteeism is also correlated with poorer vocational, health, and psychological outcomes (Robert Wood Johnson Foundation, 2016), and has a negative impact on the development of cognitive and social skills (Dick & Riddell, 2010). The impact of chronic absenteeism may be magnified for specific groups, including students from households with fewer socioeconomic resources Balfanz and Byrnes (2012).

Chronic absenteeism increased during the COVID-19 pandemic and school closures. For the 2015–2016 school year, the U.S. Department of Education (DOE) (2021) estimated a chronic absenteeism rate of 16% nationwide, which increased by 25% for the 2020–2021 school year. The DOE numbers may underestimate student losses in some states because of differences in when and how attendance was calculated and reported during the pandemic. For instance, New York City public schools did not report absenteeism data for two years during the pandemic, and in some places students were marked as present simply if contact was made with a parent (Edelman, 2022). In New Jersey, surprisingly high attendance rates of nearly 100% were inconsistent with the state's previous rates, other states' data, and teacher reports (Wall, 2020).

Surveys indicated virtual classes were plagued by attendance rates of 25% or less in some areas (Zota & Granovskiy, 2021). Some school districts stopped taking attendance during the pandemic for virtual classes (Jacobson, 2020), or they eliminated failing grades, which may have decreased incentives for attendance (Tadayon, 2020). In many states, students with positive COVID-19 tests or symptoms, and sometimes even students with potentially infectious classmates or family members, had to quarantine for a designated period, leading to higher absenteeism rates (Jones, 2021). Attendance

Neurodevelopment in the Post-Pandemic World. Molly Colvin, Jennifer Linton Reesman, and Tannahill Glen, Oxford University Press. © Oxford University Press 2024. DOI: 10.1093/9780197762660.003.0002

Works, a nonprofit initiative to reduce chronic absenteeism, surveyed state attendance policies and found that state definitions of a "day of attendance" differed widely. Further, data on truancy and differentiation of excused versus unexcused absences are limited (Attendance Works, 2023b).

In five states—California, Connecticut, Michigan, Ohio, and Virginia—rates of chronic absenteeism doubled during the pandemic (Chang et al., 2022). In Tennessee, chronic absenteeism rates almost doubled (Patrick et al., 2021), and was 40% in the Los Angeles Unified School District for middle and high school students in 2020 (Ponce, 2021) ultimately peaking at more than 45% (Tadayon, 2023). Brown et al. (2023) analyzed data from Philadelphia schools, documenting an overall chronic absenteeism rate of 46% during the 2021–2022 school year. In areas where pre-pandemic high school chronic absenteeism was a major challenge, rates dramatically increased for elementary and middle schools, to as high as 73% for one elementary school. Dee (2023) found that every state experienced an increase, ranging from 4% to 22%, in chronic absenteeism, corresponding to a nationwide rate nearly double the pre-pandemic rate.

Concerningly, there is strong evidence of racial and economic disparities in absenteeism: rates increased more for African American and Hispanic students and emerging English learners than for White students and more notably for students from socioeconomically disadvantaged families (Young, 2021). Hill and Prunty (2023) reported that rates of chronic absenteeism tripled in California in 2021–2022, with rates exceeding 40% for Black, Pacific Islander, and Native American students, and a near-tripling of the chronic absenteeism rate for Latino students from 13% to 35%.

Chronic absenteeism also negatively impacts children with disabilities at higher rates than their nondisabled peers. Kouroupa et al. (2023) found higher rates of absence and chronic absenteeism in a group of students with neurodevelopmental disorders (autism or intellectual disability) engaged in virtual instruction compared to students learning in person. Nationwide reports from 2013 to 2014 indicated that elementary school students with disabilities and served under the Individuals with Disabilities Education Act (IDEA) were 1.5 times more likely to be chronically absent as their peers without disabilities (Cortiella & Boundy, 2018).

According to previous studies, transportation access is associated with reduced absenteeism for vulnerable students (Edwards, 2022), which is a concern because of an unprecedented school bus driver shortage during the pandemic, delaying the start of classes and resulting in discontinued bus routes in some areas (Axios, 2022; Wingate, 2021). The rates of other major predictors of chronic absenteeism (discussed in more detail in later chapters) increased during the pandemic, including acute health conditions, injury/illness, disengagement, and poverty (Balfanz & Byrnes, 2012; D'Souza et al., 2023; Gottfried et al., 2022; Jones, 2021; Kaiser et al., 2021).

Chronic absenteeism also increased among school personnel. Teacher absenteeism is associated with measurable negative effects on learning achievement (Clotfelter et al., 2009), and increased during the pandemic. This may reflect greater mental health symptoms reported by teachers compared to other professions, with more symptoms reported by teachers in remote instruction compared to in-person classes (Kush et al., 2022). Instructor chronic absenteeism was reported to have increased in 70% of schools (Institute of Educational Sciences, 2023), with teacher absenteeism particularly pronounced (missing more than 10% of school days) in schools with higher numbers of students of color (Sparks, 2022) and students from marginalized backgrounds (Greene & Butcher, 2023).

In a rather unexpected and dramatic development, the staggering increase in chronic absenteeism has not been a transient phenomenon. In 2022, schools continued to report high rates of chronic absenteeism, even in states that resumed in-person learning relatively quickly (Belsha, 2023). In the District of Columbia, chronic absenteeism was still 48% in 2022 (Coffin & Rubin, 2023). In Connecticut, the absenteeism rate remained stubbornly high through November 2022, at about 25%, similar to the 2021 rate and more than double the pre-pandemic absenteeism rate (Calvert, 2022). In Los Angeles County Unified School District (LAUSD), the chronic absenteeism rate rose to nearly 50% (Esquivel & Gomez, 2022), and was still reported to be 35% in 2023 (Tadayon, 2023). In some states (e.g., Massachusetts and Connecticut), chronic absenteeism was twice pre-pandemic rates in 2022-2023 (Dee, 2023). Stevenson (2023) found that schools with the longest closures (e.g., California, District of Columbia, Maryland, etc.) demonstrated the largest increases in chronic absenteeism.

More persistent absenteeism rates have been blamed on seasonal flu and respiratory syncytial virus (RSV) outbreaks. However, data suggest the increased rates are not simply due to COVID-19 illness-related absences or the recent viral outbreaks: Esquivel and Gomez (2022) reported LAUSD data showing 30% of absences were unrelated to pandemic quarantines. Similarly, in North Dakota, parents shared that absences reported to be COVID-related were due to other causes, such as social anxiety or stress over falling behind in class (Belsha, 2022). This is an important point: an educator quoted in Belsha's article noted the possibility that being out for an extended time for COVID-19 quarantine could cause stress over falling behind in class, potentially leading to failure to return to class. Harris (2023) speculated that for younger children, school may be viewed as more like daycare, and missing class therefore as less harmful. For older students, absenteeism may reflect the fact that current coursework is dependent on prior curriculum content, which may have been truncated or missed entirely during school closures.

Mehta (2023) interviewed school administrators to query perceived reasons for persistent chronic absenteeism. Factors ranged from school bus driver understaffing, increased mental health concerns, to anxiety about the safety of large gatherings of people. Interestingly, though, in a Scottish longitudinal study, all forms of absenteeism, whether due to illness, truancy, or family holidays, were inversely related to achievement (Klein et al., 2022).

In a deeply moving article on local efforts to reduce chronic absenteeism, MacGillis (2024) described interviews with parents, school administrators, and those tasked with locating missing students and encouraging return. Families described in the article suffered from challenges ranging from difficulty returning to old routines to lack of school clothing or frequent moves. MacGillis questioned whether school had become "optional" for families who became disengaged during school closures. Remarkably, MacGillis noted:

> Absenteeism underlies much of what has beset young people in recent years, including falling school achievement, deteriorating mental health—exacerbated by social isolation—and elevated youth violence and car thefts, some occurring during school hours. But schools are using relatively little of the billions of dollars that they received in federal pandemic-recovery funds to address absenteeism. The issue has also attracted surprisingly little attention from leaders, elected or otherwise, and education coverage in the national media has focused heavily on culture-war fights. (MacGillis, 2024)

Decreased Enrollment, Delayed Entry to the School System, and Students Lost to the System

In addition to the persistent increases in chronic absenteeism for enrolled students, there has been a decrease in student enrollment since the COVID-19 pandemic across the nation's schools. In some cases, the decline reflects exacerbation of a pre-pandemic trend. For instance, the San Francisco Unified School District has lost 9,000 students since 2014 (Tucker, 2022), a dramatic enrollment decline that has worsened budget shortfalls because education funds are tied to enrollment and attendance. Indeed, Montgomery County, Maryland, schools were criticized for misreporting missing students, despite accepting funding tied to their enrollment (Pagnucco, 2023).

An extraordinary report by the Associated Press and Stanford University (Vazquez Toness & Lurye, 2023) examined 21 states where data were available, and documented that enrollment in public education fell by 700,000 students since the onset of the pandemic. The authors determined that about 100,000 of those students likely moved to private education. Approximately 180,000 students registered for home schooling. The student population in the 21 states fell by another 180,000 due to factors such as moving out of state and declining birth rates. The authors surmised that the remaining 230,000 students were simply unaccounted for across the 21 states with data.

Accompanying the worrisome decrease in enrollment has been a perhaps unforeseen development: delayed entry of students into the educational system. Kindergarten enrollment had the steepest decline. Delayed kindergarten entry has been most pronounced for families with limited financial resources and in school districts that only offered remote learning. In New York City, a staggering 33% fewer children enrolled in kindergarten in 2022 compared to pre-pandemic years (Bardolf & Edelman, 2023). According to the U.S. Census Bureau (2023), the percentage of 3-to-6-year-olds enrolled in preschool dropped by 9 percentage points from 2019 to 2021, from 51.1% to 41.8%, and the number of preschool enrollees in 2021 was the smallest since data collection began in 2005. Enrollment declined for both public and private schools.

As a result, tens of thousands of children may enter formal education at an older age (Goldstein & Parlapiano, 2021), without the foundational skills typically acquired in kindergarten. Ferenchik (2023) quoted the superintendent of the Columbus, Ohio, school district as stating that kindergarten students are entering school without foundational skills, resulting in only 15% of new students demonstrating expected progress by midyear. Results from the 2022 administration of the Program for International Student Assessment (PISA), which reports findings specific to the United States and other countries, indicated students who attended kindergarten and preschool for 1 or more years scored higher in math testing at age 15 than those without kindergarten, even after socioeconomic level—a major predictor of math scores—was taken into account (OECD, 2023). Furthermore, chronic absenteeism may begin in kindergarten, but there appears to be a period of adjustment in grades K–2 when attendance rates increase (Balfanz & Byrnes, 2012). Thus, if potential kindergarten students are not enrolled at all during what appears to be a critical period for adjustment, the trajectory of attendance may be altered.

In addition to the negative impact of chronic absenteeism and delayed enrollment on multiple outcomes, they have a major impact on school budgets, as budgets are based in part on attendance and enrollment (Villanueva, 2022). For example, schools must spend allocated dollars as if they will have 100% attendance; if attendance is 60%, funding reflects that number instead (Arundel, 2022). Prior to the pandemic, Fay (2018) reported that a California school district with a 98% attendance rate lost more than $1 million annually due to absenteeism. The decline in student enrollment may compound an impending fiscal cliff (Krausen et al., 2023): federal Elementary and Secondary School Emergency Relief (ESSER) funding, scheduled to end in 2024, will prompt districts that invested ESSER funds into recurring costs to face challenging decisions of how to meet budget shortfalls due to declining enrollment while experiencing increased need. In a related vein, there is a more recent concern about the "school closure cliff" (Redelmeier, 2023). Redelmeier analyzed district enrollment data in Louisiana and found White students comprised a quarter of all students yet made up only 12% of students who experienced permanent school closures. Numerous schools have shut since the pandemic began, due to declining enrollment, a trend that began with Hurricane Katrina.

School districts will naturally seek to decrease absenteeism and maintain enrollment. With various financial incentives tied to attendance, schools may become creative in preventing budget cuts. In fact, Washington state, which has the "Becca Law" requiring schools to provide remedial instructions or other interventions for students with unexcused absences (Mueller, 2022), recently announced HB 1834 (2022), creating a new category of excused absence: unlimited use of "mental health days" that require no documentation at all from medical or psychiatric providers (Lafferty, 2022). This policy would be quite effective in eliminating unexcused absences that count against district budgets. However well-intentioned, such efforts may compound negative pandemic-era impacts for youth.

References

Ansari, A., & Gottfried, M. A. (2021). The grade-level and cumulative outcomes of absenteeism. *Child Development*, *92*(4), e548–e564. https://doi.org/10.1111/cdev.13555

Arundel, K. (2022). States look to ease funding declines spurred by low student attendance. *K-12 Dive.* https://www.k12dive.com/news/states-look-to-ease-funding-declines-spurred-by-low-student-attendance/617228/

Attendance Works. (2023a). Chronic absence. *Attendance Works.* https://www.attendanceworks.org/chronic-absence/the-problem/

Attendance Works. (2023b). Monitoring data matters even more: A review of state attendance data policy and practice in school year 2022–23. *Attendance Works.* https://www.attendanceworks.org/monitoring-data-matters-even-more-a-review-of-state-attendance-data-policy-and-practice-in-school-year-2022-23/

Axios. (2022). Vanishing bus routes. *Axios.* https://www.axios.com/2022/08/29/vanishing-bus-routes

Balfanz, R., & Byrnes, V. (2012). Chronic absenteeism: Summarizing what we know from nationally available data. *Baltimore: Johns Hopkins University Center for Social Organization of Schools*, *1*(1), 1–46.

Bardolf, D., & Edelman, S. (2023, August 5). Kindergarten enrollment rates among highest declines as families flee NYC DOE. *The New York Post.* https://nypost.com/2023/08/05/families-fleeing-public-schools-starting-with-kindergarten/

Belsha, K. (2022). Why are students missing so much school? The answer may lie in the chronic absenteeism "black box." *Chalkbeat.* https://www.chalkbeat.org/2022/10/13/23403250/chronic-absenteeism-pandemic-attendance-quarantines

Belsha, K. (2023). Many schools went all in to fight chronic absenteeism. Why are kids still missing so much class? *Chalkbeat.* https://www.chalkbeat.org/2023/9/28/23893221/chronic-absenteeism-attendance-santa-fe-orlando-schools/

Brown, J., Purcell, D., & Graham, K. (2023, May 31). Unexcusable: Philly schools' chronic absence crisis. *Philadelphia Inquirer.* https://archive.is/Mbr6G#selection-191.0-203.17

Calvert, S. (2022, December 28). High rates of chronic absenteeism persist at U.S. schools. *The Wall Street Journal.* https://www.wsj.com/articles/high-rates-of-chronic-absenteeism-persist-at-u-s-schools-11672232415

Chang, H., Balfanz, R., & Byrnes, V. (2022, September 27). Pandemic causes alarming increase in chronic absence and reveals need for better data. *Attendance Works.* https://www.attendanceworks.org/pandemic-causes-alarming-increase-in-chronic-absence-and-reveals-need-for-better-data/

Clotfelter, C. T., Ladd, H. F., & Vigdor, J. L. (2009). Are teacher absences worth worrying about in the United States? *Education Finance and Policy*, *4*(2), 115–149.

Coffin, C., & Rubin, J. (2023). State of D.C. schools, 2021–22: In-person learning, measuring outcomes, and work on recovery. *D.C. Policy Center.* https://www.dcpolicycenter.org/publications/schools-21-22/

Cortiella, C., & Boundy, K. B. (2018). *Students with disabilities and chronic absenteeism (NCEO Brief #15).* University of Minnesota.

Dee, T. S. (2023). Higher chronic absenteeism threatens academic recovery from the COVID-19 pandemic. *OSF Preprints.* https://doi.org/10.31219/osf.io/bfg3p

Dick, B. D., & Riddell, R. P. (2010). Cognitive and school functioning in children and adolescents with chronic pain: A critical review. *Pain Research and Management*, *15*, 354812. https://doi.org/10.1155/2010/354812

D'Souza, D., Empringham, J., Pechlivanoglou, P., Uleryk, E. M., Cohen, E., & Shulman, R. (2023). Incidence of diabetes in children and adolescents during the COVID-19 pandemic: A systematic review and meta-analysis. *JAMA Network Open*, *6*(6), e2321281. https://doi.org/10.1001/jamanetworkopen.2023.21281

Edelman, S. (2022, April 2). Chronic absenteeism in NYC public schools hits alarming 40%. *The New York Post.* https://nypost.com/2022/04/02/chronic-absenteeism-in-nyc-public-schools-hits-alarming-40/

Edwards, D. S. (2022). How does school bus transportation affect student attendance and achievement? Policy Brief. *National Center for Research on Education Access and Choice.* https://files.eric.ed.gov/fulltext/ED622132.pdf

Esquivel, P., & Gomez, M. (2022, April 28). LAUSD failed students with disabilities during pandemic, federal investigation finds. *Los Angeles Times.* https://www.latimes.com/california/story/2022-04-28/lausd-failed-disabled-students-under-remote-learning-during-pandemic-investigation-finds

Fay, L. (2018, October 26). What's the cost of your child missing school? $47 a day in this California beach town. *Forbes.* https://www.forbes.com/sites/the74/2018/10/26/whats-the-cost-of-your-child-missing-school-47-a-day-in-this-california-beach-town/?sh = 36a5929467ca

Ferenchik, M. (2023, December 17). Will lowering reading standard goals hurt Columbus City Schools third graders? *The Columbus Dispatch.* https://www.dispatch.com/story/news/education/2023/12/17/will-lowering-reading-standard-goals-for-columbus-twill-lowering-reading-standard-goals-hurt-columbu/71878288007/

Goldstein, D., & Parlapiano, A. (2021, August 7). The kindergarten exodus. *The New York Times.* https://www.nytimes.com/2021/08/07/us/covid-kindergarten-enrollment.html

Gottfried, M., Page, L., & Edwards, D. (2022). District strategies to reduce student absenteeism. *EdResearch for Recovery.* https://files.eric.ed.gov/fulltext/ED626055.pdf

Greene, J. P., & Butcher, J. (2023). The alarming rise in teacher absenteeism. *The Heritage Foundation.* https://www.heritage.org/sites/default/files/2023-07/IB5322.pdf

Harris, A. (2023, November 8). Where are all the missing students? *The Atlantic.* https://archive.is/2023.11.08-123807/https://www.theatlantic.com/ideas/archive/2023/11/american-schools-absenteeism/675892/#selection-571.0-576.0

HB 1834. (2022). An act relating to student excused absences for mental health reasons. https://lawfilesext.leg.wa.gov/biennium/2021-22/Pdf/Bill%20Reports/House/1834%20HBR%20PL%2022.pdf

Hill, L., & Prunty, E. (2023). Exploring the spike in chronic absenteeism among K–12 students. *Public Policy Institute of California.* https://www.ppic.org/blog/exploring-the-spike-in-chronic-absenteeism-among-k-12-students/

Institute of Educational Sciences. (2023). School Pulse Panel. Institute of Educational Sciences. https://ies.ed.gov/schoolsurvey/spp/

Jacobson, L. (2020). Present and accounted for? Coronavirus-related school closures create attendance challenges. *K-12 Dive.* https://www.k12dive.com/news/present-and-accounted-for-closures-create-attendance-challenges/574412/

Jones, C. (2021). Absenteeism surging since schools reopened. *EdSource.* https://edsource.org/2021/absenteeism-surging-since-schools-reopened/661507

Kaiser, S. V., Watson, A., Dogan, B., Karmur, A., Warren, K., Wang, P., ... Bardach, N. S. (2021). Preventing COVID-19 transmission in education settings. *Pediatrics, 148*(3). https://doi.org/10.1542/peds.2021-051438

Klein, M., Sosu, E. M., & Dare, S. (2022). School absenteeism and academic achievement: Does the reason for absence matter? *AERA Open, 8.* https://doi.org/10.1177/23328584211071115

Kouroupa, A., Allard, A., Gray, K., Hastings, R. P., Heyne, D., Melvin, G. A., ... Totsika, V. (2023). The association between home learning during COVID-19 lockdowns and subsequent school attendance among children with neurodevelopmental conditions. *Child: Care, Health and Development, 49*(5), 846–851. https://doi.org/https://doi.org/10.1111/cch.13113

Krausen, K., Caparas, R., McClellan, P., Willis, J., & Perez, A. (2023). Is there a "fiscal cliff" on the horizon for California school districts? Planning for financial sustainability in an uncertain time. *WestEd.* https://www.wested.org/wp-content/uploads/2023/07/Is-There-a-Fiscal-Cliff-on-the-Horizon-for-California-School-Districts.pdf

Kush, J. M., Badillo-Goicoechea, E., Musci, R. J., & Stuart, E. A. (2022). Teachers' mental health during the COVID-19 pandemic. *Educational Researcher, 51*(9), 593–597.
Lafferty, K. (2022). Washington students to get "mental health day" excused absences. *King 5 News.* https://www.king5.com/article/news/education/washington-students-mental-health-excused-absences/281-55c4ce17-ea2d-48b5-bb5a-8c2d408d6939
Liu, J., Lee, M., & Gershenson, S. (2021). The short-and long-run impacts of secondary school absences. *Journal of Public Economics, 199*, 104441.
MacGillis, A. (2024, January 15). Has school become optional? *The New Yorker.* https://www.newyorker.com/magazine/2024/01/15/has-school-become-optional
Mehta, J. (2023). 3 years since the pandemic wrecked attendance, kids still aren't showing up to school. *NPR.* https://www.npr.org/2023/03/02/1160358099/school-attendance-chronic-absenteeism-covid#:~:text = Before%20the%20pandemic%2C%20about%208,doubled%20to%20around%2016%20million
Mueller, M. (2022). Mental health related absences: Guidance to support implementation of House Bill 1834. https://ospi.k12.wa.us/sites/default/files/public/attendance/pubdocs/Guidance_on_Mental_Health_Related_Absences_final.pdf
OECD. (2023). PISA 2022 results: Factsheets. *OECD.* https://www.oecd.org/publication/pisa-2022-results/country-notes/united-states-a78ba65a/#chapter-d1e11
Pagnucco, A. (2023). State Inspector General: MCPS reports incorrect enrollment. *Montgomery Perspective.* https://montgomeryperspective.com/2023/06/26/state-inspector-general-mcps-reports-incorrect-enrollment/
Patrick, S., Woods, S. C., Bala, N., & Santelli, F. (2021). Schooling during COVID-19: Fall semester trends from six Tennessee districts. *Tennessee Education Research Alliance.* https://peabody.vanderbilt.edu/tera/covid-19/covid19-fall-semester-trends/#h2
Ponce, A. (2021). Educational recovery now: LA's children and schools need a comprehensive plan. https://greatpublicschoolsnow.org/wp-content/uploads/2021/03/EdRecoveryNow_Final_3-29-21.pdf
Redelmeier, R. (2023). A school closure cliff is coming. Black and Hispanic students are likely to bear the brunt. *The Hechinger Report.* https://hechingerreport.org/a-school-closure-cliff-is-coming-black-and-hispanic-students-are-likely-to-bear-the-brunt/
Robert Wood Johnson Foundation. (2016). The relationship between school attendance and health. https://files.eric.ed.gov/fulltext/ED592870.pdf
Sparks, S. (2022). Teacher and student absenteeism is getting worse. *Education Week.* https://www.edweek.org/leadership/teacher-and-student-absenteeism-is-getting-worse/2022/07
Stevenson, J. (2023). Chronic absenteeism worse in states that closed schools longer. *Brownstone Institute.* https://brownstone.org/articles/chronic-absenteeism-worse-in-states-that-closed-schools-longer/
Tadayon, A. (2020). Letter grades? Pass/no pass? A's for all? Districts differ on grading online learning. *EdSource.* https://edsource.org/2020/letter-grades-pass-fail-as-for-all-districts-differ-on-grading-online-learning/629466
Tadayon, A. (2023). California districts see more chronic absenteeism than before pandemic. *EdSource.* https://edsource.org/2023/california-districts-still-see-more-chronic-absenteeism-than-before-pandemic/688787
Tucker, J. (2022). Applications to SFUSD schools stagnate, a worrying sign as district struggles with declining enrollment. *San Francisco Chronicle.* https://www.sfchronicle.com/sf/article/Applications-to-SFUSD-schools-stagnate-a-17012205.php
U.S. Census Bureau. (2023). Census Bureau releases school enrollment report press release number CB23-TPS.64. https://www.census.gov/newsroom/press-releases/2023/school-enrollment-report.html
U.S. Department of Education. (2021). Chronic absenteeism in the nation's schools. https://www2.ed.gov/datastory/chronicabsenteeism.html

Vazquez Toness, B., & Lurye, S. (2023). Thousands of kids are missing from school. Where did they go? *T. A. Press.* https://projects.apnews.com/features/2023/missing-children/index.html

Villanueva, C. (2022). Count every student: Attendance-based funding leaves too many students behind. *Every Texan.* https://everytexan.org/2022/09/21/count-every-student-attendance-based-funding-leaves-too-many-students-behind/

Wall, P. (2020). N.J. eased its attendance rules during the pandemic. Then Newark said 99.8% of students were present. *Chalkbeat.* https://newark.chalkbeat.org/2020/9/23/21452648/newark-remote-learning-attendance-spring

Wingate, K. (2021, August 22). COVID-19 pandemic amplifies school bus driver shortage concerns. *USA Today.* https://www.usatoday.com/story/money/2021/08/22/back-to-school-bus-driver-worker-shortage-covid-pandemic/7825434002/?gnt-cfr = 1

Young, D. (2021, May). SFUSD lost touch with 8,800 students during the pandemic. *The San Francisco Bay View National Black Newspaper.* https://sfbayview.com/2021/05/sfusd-lost-touch-with-8800-students-during-the-pandemic/

Zota, R. R., & Granovskiy, B. (2021). Remote learning for K-12 schools during the COVID-19 pandemic. CRS Report R46883, Version 3. *Congressional Research Service.*

3

Attenuated Learning Gains

Measurement and media coverage of unfinished learning have been criticized as unhelpful or even pejorative by some (Fishman, 2021), as such evidence may imply individual blame or actual loss of previously acquired skills. However, the issue is more complex, and effects of unfinished learning extend well beyond decline in achievement scores for a discrete period. Alban Conto et al. (2021) performed regression analysis for 13 lower income countries and found that, consistent with prior studies on the effects of educational disruption, missing up to a year of school was associated with reduced acquisition of foundational skills in reading and math. According to the World Bank guide for recovery of learning losses (World Bank et al., 2022), foundational learning is required to develop core abilities in reading and math skills, and in the modern era, digital competencies and social-emotional skills. Students most negatively affected by educational disruption will be unable to learn material requisite for future learning gains. Furthermore, students with reduced learning gains are more likely to experience mental health challenges—and the reverse is true: children with mental health challenges are more vulnerable to learning challenges. Thus, detailing the extent and content of unfinished learning is fundamental to designing remediation plans and identifying those in most need of assistance.

What Is "Learning Loss" and How Is It Measured?

Terminology is quite varied for alterations in learning progress. As Patrinos et al. (2022) noted, any search for relevant data may include the phrases "learning loss," "learning slide," "education gap," or "achievement gap." Angrist et al. (2021) considered learning loss to be a combination of both actual loss—forgetting of material over time, as may occur in the "summer slide"—and opportunity cost, or the absence of learning that would have occurred had schools not closed. Betthäuser, Bach-Mortensen and Engzell used the term "learning deficit" to refer to both slowed pace of

Neurodevelopment in the Post-Pandemic World. Molly Colvin, Jennifer Linton Reesman, and Tannahill Glen, Oxford University Press. © Oxford University Press 2024. DOI: 10.1093/9780197762660.003.0003

expected learning and loss of previously acquired skills and learning. Colvin et al. (2022) used the phrase "attenuation of learning gains"; the same authors use the following terms synonymously with learning loss: slower than typical progress, lower level performance compared to pre-pandemic or other cohorts, and having met fewer learning goals. Generally speaking, in the United States, learning progress is measured by standardized test score changes. However, Patrinos et al. (2022) opined that points and percentiles are not easily compared, and advocated the use of months of learning loss, converted to standard deviations, as measurement; for instance, 1 year of school learning equates to .33 standard deviation using their system. Thus, while loss of one quarter of one standard deviation of learning over 2 years may not sound like much, it equates to more than half a year of instruction.

The World Bank (2023) published an extensive document on learning recovery planning which is helpful for understanding the concept of learning losses as they relate to grade levels and content mastery. In their example, upon completion of third grade, students are expected to have learned the math operations of addition, subtraction, multiplication, and division. Being one grade level behind in terms of learning gains may mean students did not finish learning multiplication or division skills, which makes it more likely they will require learning support in future grades to maintain progress. The World Bank guide to learning described the importance of this "foundational learning," the skills that pave the way for future learning in ever-expanding areas, important enough to future learning to be prerequisites. The World Bank publication provides an excellent example of how disruption in foundational learning can impact skill development over time: although a ninth-grade literature course may not be totally dependent on an eighth-grade literature class, the same cannot be said for second-grade reading skills, which are heavily reliant on first-grade reading instruction.

In addition to standardized testing scores, most notably "the Nation's Report Card," the National Assessment of Educational Progress (NAEP), other measures of learning progress can be obtained from diverse sources. These data are surprisingly challenging to curate, as there is no single official repository for data, methodological differences preclude easy comparison, and sometimes, the information is simply difficult to access, as it is not made publicly available in the usual routes (Melzer, 2023). In short, in addition to national standardized testing, there are state tests, think tank reports, state Department of Education websites, not-for-profit organization papers, research studies, specialist group publications (such as the National Center for Learning Disabilities), school district reports, and news article/journalistic investigations. Colvin, Reesman, and Glen (2022) recommended that clinicians familiarize themselves with data specific to their districts, which can be facilitated by seeking out quantitative and qualitative information from these sources.

Modeling Studies on Learning Loss

Early in the pandemic, estimation of any impact of prolonged educational disruption relied on simulation models instead of actual test scores. Those models projected greater negative impacts for students from economically disadvantaged households, for younger children and those from households with lower educational levels (Fuchs-Schündeln et al., 2022), and significant learning losses in reading and math (Kuhfeld, Tarasawa, et al., 2020), as well as widening academic achievement gaps, particularly in math, among socioeconomic groups due to inequities in technology access and learning support (Center for Research on Education Outcomes, 2020; Kuhfeld, Soland, et al., 2020). Coe et al. (2020) predicted that the previous decade's narrowing of the achievement gap among groups could be reversed.

Evidence for Attenuation of Learning Gains

Perhaps most remarkable about the new research on learning progress after school closures is the consistency of findings. Achievement data and other indicators of learning progress have been highly consistent with projections (Bailey et al., 2021), and consistent across states and other countries (Di Pietro et al., 2020; Engzell et al., 2021; Maldonado & De Witte, 2021; Rose et al., 2021). Studies consistently reveal greater impact on students of color, students with disabilities, students from low-income households, and students with limited English proficiency.

Longer duration of virtual learning had a negative impact on students, a finding replicated internationally (Jakubowski et al., 2024). Districts with the fewest in-person classes exhibited the greatest decline in numbers of students meeting grade expectations (Oxner, 2021), and this most impacted students from marginalized groups (JerseyCan, 2021; Ponce, 2021; Young, 2021). Jack, Halloran, Okun, and Oster (2023) examined 2020–2021 test scores and found that districts with full-time face-to-face instruction exhibited lesser declines in math and English/language arts (ELA); districts with larger proportions of students of color showed the greatest benefit of in-person learning in terms of losses. Astounding differences were recorded between scores for Michigan students who were remote for the entirety of the 2020–2021 academic year versus those who were in person: proficiency rates on the Michigan Student Test of Educational Progress (M-STEP) were 20 to 30 percentage points lower for virtual students compared to their peers in live classrooms (Michigan Board of Education, 2023).

Analyses of school assessment data for math and reading suggest a more negative impact on math learning, with early studies showing more students falling in the lowest score quartiles (Kuhfeld, Tarasawa, et al., 2020) and fewer students reaching math learning goals (Dorn et al., 2020) compared to earlier years. Dorn et al. (2021) examined data for more than 1.5 million students in 40 states and found lower math and reading scores equivalent to delays of 5 months in math and 4 months in reading. The authors referred to this as "unfinished learning" due to abrupt school closures in 2020 and the resulting slower pace of learning through 2021.

While reading scores have been less dramatically impacted than math, analyses of assessment data have shown increases in numbers of "at-risk" reading scores for younger students. This is likely because younger students are developing readers and "reading to learn" at early grades, while for older students, reading is a more established skill. Still, there is evidence of disproportionate impact on Black and Hispanic students (Jacobson, 2021). The most marginalized students (students of color, those from impoverished homes, emerging English learners, and students with disabilities) are most likely to show lower-than-expected learning gains since the pandemic began (JerseyCan, 2021; Ponce, 2021; Young, 2021).

Learning progress is not only demonstrated by standardized test scores. It is also marked by maturation of skills such as recognizing and meeting task time limits, social reciprocity in the class setting, and dispute resolution. There are numerous qualitative indicators that students who missed a prolonged period of in-person school have suffered. Suspension rates have increased (California School Boards Association [CSBA], 2022), as have reports of disruptive behaviors (Einhorn, 2022). There are reports of youth being unable to perform tasks typically attained during a given period of in-person skill learning, tasks that are central to basic work productivity like working with others and making change.

Students lost an estimated 25% of instructional time in the 2019–2020 academic year due to pandemic-related educational disruption (National Association of School Psychologists, 2020). It is difficult to estimate lost instructional time for subsequent years, given state and district variation in instruction formats as well as the nature and quality of instruction. Regardless, fewer instructional hours for students resulted in reductions of curriculum content (Maryland State Department of Education, 2020). For example, 57% of math lessons were omitted at some grade levels in a large, suburban school district in Maryland, including topics such as telling time and understanding money (Khan, 2021). Even for more mature students who missed, for instance, a final year of high school or college, scores may be lower on professional skills exams, resulting in a "lower degree of competency" (Belkin et al., 2023).

There are ample studies on impacts in other countries (Jakubowski et al., 2023). Hallin et al. (2022) found that in Sweden, where elementary and middle schools did not close, there was no measurable attenuation oflearning gains in reading, nor any disproportionately greater loss for students from disadvantaged households. This finding strongly suggests learning losses are not due to general pandemic-related stress.

In contrast, Engzell et al. (2021) assessed learning progress in the Netherlands, which had relatively brief school closures (8 weeks) and, interestingly, has the world's highest broadband access rate, and still found learning loss equivalent to about one fifth of an academic year, larger for students from home with lower parental education. In Uganda, where schools were shut for nearly 2 years, longer than any other country, learning loss has not yet been measured, but it has been projected to be equivalent to a cumulative loss of 2.8 years of education (Angrist et al., 2021). This dire number does not even factor in Ugandan school closures again in November 2022 during an outbreak of Ebola virus (Datzberger & Brian, 2022). Gaps have increased between lower achieving or economically disadvantaged children and others, concentrating learning losses in the most vulnerable groups (Moscoviz & Evans, 2022).

Patrinos et al. (2022) analyzed studies on learning loss from 20 countries and found an average .17 standard deviation loss, equivalent to about a half year of school, across countries. They also found that students fell further behind where schools were closed for longer periods, and found that gains were closer to expectations once schools returned to in-person classes. It is worth noting that in addition to learning loss related to school closures in low-income countries, youth in those regions suffered from the compounding effects of suspended childhood vaccination programs and other medical supportive services, and severe economic strain (Buffie et al., 2023).

In the United States, studies have shown that higher education has also been impacted by school closures and the switch to virtual learning. College students report greater satisfaction with face-to-face learning compared to virtual instruction (Shoair et al., 2023). An influential study by Kofoed et al. (2021) compared students in virtual classes with those receiving in-person instruction at West Point Military Academy—a relatively homogeneous environment, with respect to financial support, nonacademic responsibilities, social setting, and coursework. Grades for those in virtual classes were nearly a quarter of a standard deviation lower than those receiving in-person instruction, and students with pre-pandemic academic challenges were more likely to demonstrate those differences. Another study found that undergraduate students with disabilities were unable to access previously granted accommodations after their universities switched to virtual instruction (Gin et al., 2021).

Enrollment in community colleges declined precipitously as schools initiated virtual learning, with students of color leaving schools in greater numbers. Fewer failing grades were observed, perhaps reflecting more leniency in grading (Bulman & Fairlie, 2022).

Scores on professional skills testing also have demonstrated declines. Belkin, Chapman, and Kesling (2023) reported that scores fell by 10% on a test of engineering fundamentals, and pass rates for other professional skill assessments fell during the same period. The percentage of students meeting all four benchmarks for college readiness on the ACT college admissions examination fell from 27% in 2018 to 25% in 2022; the percentage of students scoring below proficiency for understanding complex text rose from 53% to 57%, and the average test score fell to its lowest level in 30 years (ACT, 2022). The average ACT score fell again in 2023, by a further third of a point (ACT, 2023). The percentage of test takers in the graduating class of 2023—students who were in their first year of high school at the beginning of the pandemic—meeting none of the college readiness benchmarks rose to the highest level recorded: 43.3%. Verbal skills scores on the Criteria Basic Skills Test, a measure of basic employment readiness administered to millions of job applicants annually, declined 11 points for male test takers below age 25 during the pandemic (Belkin et al.,

2023). The pass rate for graduates of nonaccredited doctoral programs on the Examination for Professional Practice in Psychology (EPPP) fell from 55.03% in 2017–2019 to 46.70% for 2020–2022 (Association of State and Provincial Psychology Boards [ASPPB], 2023). Falling test scores have also been recorded in a military setting which may directly impact military readiness: average scores on the Armed Services Vocational Aptitude Battery are down nearly 10% since the pandemic began, a phenomenon military leaders blamed on remote schooling (Britzky, 2022). Over time, there will undoubtedly be more research on vocational achievement and wages for the COVID-19 pandemic college cohort, which has not been unscathed by school closures and pandemic disruption.

Colvin et al. (2022) summarized early evidence of attenuation of learning gains for U.S. children in primary and secondary school, and the remainder of this chapter will detail the most up-to-date data on learning progress.

NAEP: The Nation's Report Card

When contemplating changes in academic achievement progress, it is important to realize that even prior to the pandemic, there were indications of a plateau in gains for younger students. Academic gains for public and private school students are tracked nationally using the National Assessment of Educational Progress (NAEP) federally sponsored testing, administered every 2 years at grades four, eight, and twelve (National Assessment of Educational Progress [NAEP], 2019). Performance is described in scores as well as percentages of students reaching Basic, Proficient, and Advanced levels of achievement. As Fensterwald (2022a) observed, NAEP score changes of "small" magnitude (e.g., 3 points) are considered significant.

Since 2013, the trajectory of gains in achievement has been inconsistent, and in 2015, for the first time ever, scores actually declined (Jackson, 2018). In the years since, growth has remained relatively stable for most groups, but inconsistency remained: for example, for the lowest performing students, 2017 NAEP scores declined while growth was measured for higher performing students (National Assessment of Educational Progress [NAEP], 2017). The instability of growth in NAEP scores continued through 2019, when reading scores were lower for grades four and eight, and lower in math for grade eight (National Center for Education Statistics, 2019). The reason for this disruption of stable growth in achievement scores is unclear, but it has been speculated to reflect various factors such as curriculum changes and/or decreased education spending due to the 2008 recession (Jackson, 2018).

2019 was the last year the NAEP was administered prior to the pandemic. The scheduled 2021 NAEP assessment was delayed to 2022 (for fourth graders and eighth graders in reading and math). 2023 tests were completed in Spring 2023 and are due for release in 2024.

In 2022, NAEP math testing (delayed from 2019) scores declined in 51 states/jurisdictions. Math scores for fourth graders declined in all regions and in 43 states, on average showing a decline of 5 points when compared to 2019 scores (National Assessment of Educational Progress [NAEP], 2023b). The percentage of fourth graders scoring below the Basic level of mastery increased to 25%. Fourth-grade math scores were lower compared to 2019 in 23 of 26 participating urban school districts. Math scores declined even for higher performing students, by 8 points on average nationwide.

For eighth-grade students there was an increase in the number of public school students performing below the Basic level in math, with 38% of eighth graders performing below the Basic level nationally, compared to 2019. Math scores declined in most urban districts (22 of 26). Higher performing students exhibited less decline (–1 point) compared to low-performing students (–6 points).

Jordan (2023) reported an analysis of NAEP 2022 test scores. The number of fourth-grade students from low-income households with significant absenteeism (defined as missing more than 3 days in the month prior to testing) nearly doubled from 2015 to 2021, from 22% to 41% of test takers. Rates of significant absenteeism in more economically advantaged students doubled as well, from 15% to 29%. There was also a correlation between absenteeism and lower NAEP scores, most markedly for eighth-grade test takers from economically disadvantaged households, whose scores were on average 15 points lower than students with no absences in the previous month. This stark difference is concerning because an academic year of learning is thought to correspond to 10–12 points on the NAEP.

In 2022, 26 urban school districts participated in the Trial Urban District Assessment (National Assessment of Educational Progress [NAEP], 2023a), a specialized NAEP initiative funded by Congress in 2002 to compare urban schools with higher percentages of students of color, larger district size, and greater numbers of students eligible for free or reduced lunch programs (National Assessment of Educational Progress [NAEP], 2023d). The results of the 2022 assessment of fourth and eighth graders were compared with

2019 scores (National Assessment of Educational Progress [NAEP], 2023c). For fourth-grade students, math scores in 23 districts were lower in 2022 compared to 2019, by as much as 15 points in some areas. For eighth-grade students, scores were significantly lower in 22 districts in 2022.

Also in 2022, in contrast to the regular NAEP tests, were NAEP long-term trend (LTT) assessments, typically completed every 4 years (National Assessment of Educational Progress [NAEP], 2023e) to evaluate learning progress during the pandemic. The National Center for Education Statistics, the federal program that oversees NAEP assessment, conducted special testing in NAEP reading and math for students 9 years of age (National Assessment of Educational Progress [NAEP], 2022b), comparing scores from 2020 and 2022. The largest-ever drop in average reading scores (5 points) was measured, along with the first-ever decline in math scores (7 points). Again, greater decline in scores was observed in lower performing student groups, and the preexisting gap in math achievement between Black and White students widened by 8 points.

Regarding disparities in virtual learning, participants were queried for virtual learning experience: 70% of test takers reported having engaged in virtual learning in the 2020–2021 school year. Statistically significant differences were observed between high- (at or above 75th percentile) and low- (below 25th percentile) performing students: 83% of high-performing students reported having an electronic device for schoolwork all the time, compared to just over half (58%) of low-performing students. Nearly half of high-performing students reported access to high-speed Internet, a quiet place to work, and teacher availability, compared to only a quarter to a third of low-performing students.

More recently, there was release of LTT data collected from age 13 students from October 2022 through May 2023 (National Assessment of Educational Progress [NAEP], 2023a). Average reading scores for those students declined by 4 points nationwide, while math scores declined by 9 points. Declines were twice as large in math (–15 points) for the lowest performing student group compared to the highest performing students (–7 points). Average declines in math were greater for Black, Hispanic, and American Indian/ Alaska Native students compared to White students.

Results of the LTT analysis are viewed as evidence of the persistence of pandemic-related educational losses (St. George, 2023). Mahnken (2023) pointedly noted that the LTT math exam measures different skills than the regular NAEP "report card" tests, with more focus on basic skills rather than conceptual problem solving, so it may be that higher level math concept skills have demonstrated even more decline than the LTT data suggest.

NAEP assesses other subjects, including science, writing, civics, and history, with only civics and history test data being available at the time of this writing. Eighth-grade civics scores in 2022 declined for the first time since testing began, erasing two decades of increases (National Assessment of Educational Progress [NAEP], 2022a). History scores for the same group continued an 8-year trajectory of decline, with a statistically significant difference between 2018 and 2022 scores.

NWEA/MAP

The Northwest Evaluation Association (NWEA) is a not-for-profit research organization that performs academic testing, the Measures of Academic Progress (MAP) (NWEA, 2023). The MAP Growth Test measures individual progress, and test item difficulty is modified in response to test taker responses (rather than being a single test form for all examinees). It allows for comparison across multiple grades, which Goldhaber et al. (2022) believe is most appropriate for assessing progress during the COVID-19 pandemic, as many students are performing below grade level. Goldhaber and fellow authors published an influential analysis of MAP growth scores in reading and math for 2.1 million students (grades three through eight) from more than 9,000 schools across 49 states. The authors compared MAP growth data with pre-pandemic growth scores. Unique to the Goldhaber study, students were grouped by high (California, Virginia, DC) and low (e.g., South Dakota, Florida, Texas) duration of remote instruction and high, middle, or low school poverty level (based on rates of participation in the national Free and Reduced-Price Lunch Program).

One startling finding was that in "high virtual" states, high-poverty schools spent *2 months longer* in virtual instruction compared to low-poverty schools. Both math and reading growth scores declined, measured in standard deviations.

The authors compared Fall 2021 achievement scores to expected achievement according to pre-pandemic growth estimates (2017–2019). There was a negative impact of remote/hybrid instruction on achievement, most notably for high- and middle-poverty schools (although even low-poverty schools that remained remote showed decline): high-poverty *and* low-poverty schools that were in person lost only 15% of a year's learning. In contrast, low-poverty/remote schools lost 27% of an academic year's learning. Remarkably, *high-poverty/remote schools lost 40% of a year's learning.*

For schools open during the 2020–2021 academic year, the math achievement gap among low-, middle-, and high-poverty schools did not widen further. The school's poverty level was not a significant predictor of learning losses for schools with in-person instruction, but for schools remaining virtual, the learning loss in high-poverty schools was double that for low-poverty schools. In short, longer duration of remote instruction increased math disparities between low- and high-poverty schools.

Reading score growth reductions were of lesser magnitude but similar in pattern, demonstrating negative impacts of remote/hybrid education. However, in-person instruction was not as protective against losses, leading the authors to opine that reading scores may reflect broader home disruption with the pandemic, compared to math learning, which is typically done in the school setting.

Strunk et al. (2023) reported an analysis of Michigan's state test results (Michigan Student Test of Educational Progress [M-STEP]) and NWEA MAP growth scores, comparing a pre-pandemic cohort (students who advanced from grades three to four to grades six to seven in 2016–2019) with a pandemic cohort (students who advanced from grades three to four to grades six to seven in 2019–2022). They also assessed changes across the pandemic-era evaluations from 2020 through Spring 2022. Compared to relatively modest declines in ELA scores, math achievement growth declined precipitously during the pandemic compared to the pre-pandemic cohort, and disparities were most evident for students of color and those from households with economic disadvantage. Consistent with other studies, students receiving in-person instruction in 2020–2021 exhibited greater achievement growth than students who received remote instruction for part of that same year or for the entire year. Like many other states, Michigan student achievement scores did not meet expectations even prior to the pandemic, but in 2020–2021, achievement fell further behind. Also, as other studies suggest (Lewis & Kuhfeld, 2022), 2021–2022 scores indicate a modest rebound of growth, with ELA scores returning to expected levels. Math declines were persistent, and the authors observed rebounding growth was not sufficiently accelerated to allow growth "catch up," or return to the level of progress expected had educational disruption not occurred. They estimated a near doubling of math growth (140%–180% of typical growth) would be required for students to meet the 50th percentile of pre-COVID-19 achievement progress.

State Reporting

The 2015 Every Student Succeeds Act (ESSA) (U.S. Department of Education, 2023), which replaced the No Child Left Behind Act of 2002, requires states to assess ELA and math annually in grades three to eight and again during high school. Science is assessed three times between grades three and twelve (The Education Trust, 2016). Each state provides some level of academic proficiency testing. A comprehensive summary of all states' test scores is beyond the scope of this publication, but interested readers can search for the agency in their state (e.g., Illinois Assessment of Readiness; Illinois State Board of Education, 2023).

The COVID-19 School Data Hub (COVID-19 School Data Hub, 2023) is a repository for state "snapshots" of test scores in one database that has allowed researchers to assess effects of school closures on learning (Halloran et al., 2021). However, states vary considerably in the level of detail and timing of public releases. That said, two major points can be made with published state test data thus far. First, scores on achievement tests show significant loss in achievement gains following school closures in 2020; second, those losses appear to be persistent in many studies. A selection of published data is reported in this section; these are data made available to the public via state press releases, state Department of Education reports, news articles, investigative reports, and social media posts.

In the District of Columbia, a nonprofit organization (Empower K-12, 2022) first reported the area's test scores in December 2020. Results were dismaying. The group reported DC students lost 4 months of learning in math and 1 month of reading learning, with at-risk groups demonstrating greater decline. Evidence of further losses in math were noted through Fall 2020 (Empower K-12, 2020). The District of Columbia faced particular challenges, as more than half its pupils are students of color, who have been shown by multiple studies to be disproportionately affected by school closures, and nearly half (49%) are categorized as "at risk." The DC Department of Education report (Coffin & Rubin, 2023) for 2021–2022 showed the percentage of students meeting or exceeding learning expectations dropped from 37% to 31% in ELA, with a decline from 21% to 15%

for at-risk students. In math, the declines were greater: from 31% to 19% for students overall, and from 16% to 6% for at-risk students.

In 2021, Tennessee data showed declines in students meeting grade expectations during school closures, with those in remote learning the longest showing the greatest declines (Mangrum, 2021). The Tennessee state assessment results for 2022 and 2023 (Tennessee Department of Education, 2023) showed increases in statewide test scores, almost across the board, from 2021. Still, the number of students in the lowest performing quartiles remained at the highest levels since 2017 (Mangrum, 2022).

Reed, Ma, and Gerde (2023) analyzed scores from an urban Midwestern area and found that second-grade students' scores on a state reading/language arts writing prompt test were lower in Fall 2020 compared to second-grade students' scores in Fall 2019. They evaluated writing skills based on five factors (focus, organization, development, grammar, and mechanics) for first graders in 2019, prior to pandemic school closures, and first graders in 2020. The latter group demonstrated lower writing scores. The pandemic closures group also scored lower on writing tasks once they moved to second grade, compared to second-grade writing scores prior to the pandemic.

In New Jersey, the first results of state testing from 2020 to 2021 (and the first assessment results since the 2018–2019 school year) were not released until April 2023 (Strupp, 2023). Just over a third of students exhibited proficiency in math, a decline of 8 percentage points. Proficiency levels declined in ELA as well, from 58% to 49%. Statewide, fewer than half (42%) of third-grade students met proficiency standards in ELA, masking significant racial disparities: 52% of White students met proficiency standards, compared to 26% of Black students and 28% of Hispanic students, and 71% of Asian/Pacific Islander students. Only 17% of students with disabilities met the proficiency standards, and 24% of economically disadvantaged students. In math, results were similar: fewer than half of students statewide met proficiency standards (45%), with startling differences among groups (59% of White students compared with 23% of Black students, and about 25% of students with disabilities or economic disadvantage). Those trends were broadly similar across grades three to nine (New Jersey Department of Education, 2023).

Some indicators of math progress have been particularly dire. Montgomery County, Maryland, public schools released data in March of 2023 for the 2021–2022 academic year. Math proficiency fell by about half in 2022, from 42% to 23%. Math proficiency for students of color also declined precipitously (e.g., from 22% to 9% for Black middle-school students, and

18% to 7% for Hispanic and Latino students; Espey, 2023). Modest gains in both ELA and math were noted even among students with disabilities and at-risk students, but scores remained 3–9 points below those noted just prior to the pandemic.

Maryland assessment of ELA and math gains in Spring 2022 (Maryland State Board of Education, 2023) indicated that ELA scores returned to baseline or near-baseline levels after a decline in 2021 (assessment data were not available for 2020). However, math declines were substantial, 3 to 4 times larger than declines in reading, with fewer students meeting proficiency thresholds than pre-pandemic. Declines in percentage of students meeting proficiency ranged from 6 to 14 points below 2019 numbers, even in Spring 2022. The report, following three cohorts of students across grades three to eight, also shows a decrease in math gains: students exhibited a dramatic decline in percentage of students meeting proficiency in math, for instance, falling from 39% prior to the pandemic to 8.7% in 2021 and rising to 18.2% in 2022 in grade eight.

Kogan (2023) examined Spring 2023 achievement and progress scores in the state of Ohio. Gains were documented for both reading and math compared to 2021 scores. Remarkably, reading scores in the state recovered to levels comparable to pre-pandemic scores. However, math scores remained measurably behind expectations—the equivalent of 1–2 months' math instruction for elementary students. For middle school and high school students, however, math scores remained about a half year behind in terms of unfinished learning: recovery of achievement gains for those grade groups was slower compared to younger students. Kogan also measured an increase in the size of the pre-pandemic achievement gap for students of color, those with economic disadvantage, and those from urban settings and public schools. Because absenteeism rates were not available at the time of writing, the Ohio data do not compare gains for schools with higher rates of chronic absenteeism, although to some extent there is overlap, as Kogan did demonstrate slower and lower magnitude of gains for urban schools and students of color and those with economic disadvantage—groups at greater risk for higher chronic absenteeism rates.

Importantly, test scores also declined in Florida, where schools returned with a mandated in-person option in Fall 2020. About half of students grades three to eight achieved satisfactory or better scores on math testing in 2021, a decline of 10% from 2019 (WLRN, 2021). Scores on ELA testing declined less precipitously, by approximately 3%. Of interest, the state report indicated that schools with more in-person instruction exhibited less decline than those with more virtual attendance, but the percentage of virtual students participating in testing was extremely small (2%) compared to in-person or "innovative" programs, so broader conclusions must be limited. It is critical to note the report indicated that pre-pandemic achievement gaps between White students and students of color did not widen, as noted in other areas of the country, and instead either remained static or narrowed slightly (despite overall declines in scores).

Other state-level data indicate major changes related to educational disruption in the pandemic. State reporting, in addition to the analysis of scores by Strunk et al. (2023), revealed alarming changes for students in Michigan schools, some of which were shut an entire year and suffered brief closures for other reasons, including delays in air conditioning installation and teacher burnout (Hope, 2022). Graduation rates dropped from 64.8% to 46% in Flint (2021), with many more students on a delayed pace for graduation.

Fuller, Swiderski, Mikkelsen, and Bastian (2023) reported on the effect of the pandemic on North Carolina student grades, looking at absenteeism, grades, and student retention. The authors found the effects of educational disruption worsened every outcome evaluated, with major disparities in the effects across groups, marginalized groups being most negatively impacted. One interesting finding was that middle schoolers were less likely than high schoolers to have been retained a grade, despite lost instructional time and even failed classes. This suggests the middle-school cohort may advance to higher grades without completion of foundational learning expected in earlier grades.

In 2023, the Center for Education Policy Research at Harvard University (CEPR) and the Educational Opportunity Project (EOP) at Stanford University collaborated to produce a district-level interactive view of learning loss: the Education Recovery Scorecard (ERS) (Center for Education Policy Research [CEPR] at Harvard University & Educational Opportunity Project [EOP] at Stanford University, 2023). Because states set their own NAEP proficiency thresholds, comparison of 2019 and 2022 scores had, until then, not been possible. To create a new scale more comparable across grades and states, the ERS project combined information from the U.S. Department of Education EDFacts data (which includes achievement test scores), 2022 publicly released school data from state websites, and 2019/2022 NAEP scores for fourth- and eighth-grade students. The Educational Opportunity Project of Stanford University (Fahle et al., 2023) also developed a collection of national academic performance; their "Education Recovery Explorer" is an interactive database comparing 2019 and 2022 scores in reading and math for students in grades three to eight.

Fahle et al. (2023) analyzed data from the EOP's Stanford Education Data Archive (SEDA) to detail learning losses across 7,800 school districts in 41 states, comparing those data with achievement scores from 2009–2022 to estimate change, specifically focusing on change scores from 2016–2019 and 2019–2022. The authors, consistent with other studies, found the average learning loss in math from 2019 to 2022 (about half a grade level) was nearly double any isolated decline noted in previous years; reading gains were also attenuated disproportionately to losses noted in prior years. Consistent with other studies, the greatest declines in achievement scores were seen in districts with high numbers of students of color and in high-poverty areas, and in areas with greater duration of remote/hybrid instruction in 2020–2021. Attenuation of learning gains was greatest for districts in areas with more pandemic-related alteration of social life (e.g., more recent mask wearing, avoidance of gatherings), as well, which Fahle et al. (2023) opined may have reflected psychosocial disquiet or perceived safety risk, factors that can influence learning progress.

Fahle et al. (2023) also attempted to address the question of whether lower achievement gains were a transient phenomenon or would be a persistent one, noting that factors such as youth "resilience" or higher pandemic-related measurement error could feasibly lead to a quicker rebound of achievement progress. However, the authors found that through the entire measurement period, large declines in test scores, for whatever reason, resulted in scores persistently lower than average in subsequent years. Thus, the authors opined that pandemic-related losses would most likely be persistent as well, in the absence of significant mitigating efforts.

PISA Test Results

Most recently, results from the Programme for International Student Assessment (PISA), sponsored by the intergovernmental Organization for Economic Cooperation and Development (OECD), were reported. Although this book focuses on data on learning losses in the United States, PISA testing samples 15-year-old students across the globe, and specifically reports data for students from the United States, and 2022 test results were released in 2023 (OECD, 2023). Results can be compared to the previous assessment in 2018 (2021 testing was delayed due to the pandemic). Math scores were measured at historically low levels, with declines in scores for both high- and low-achieving students. Reading and science scores remained stable; for reading skills, this stability may reflect reading being a more consolidated skill at the age of 15. The proportion of students scoring below basic proficiency levels in math increased by 8 points, with 34% of U.S. test takers scoring below proficiency in math. The makeup of PISA test takers is important to consider in interpreting results: the largest group of U.S. test takers (39%) fell into the highest socioeconomic quintile, so results may be less representative of the nation's student body as a whole. Jakubowski et al. (2024) analyzed PISA data, estimating the impact of school closures by measuring deviation from recent trends in performance. The authors assessed losses in scores to be equivalent to about 7 to 12 months of learning, with schools shut for longer periods showing greater losses.

Do the Data Underestimate Learning Loss?

To consider this question, it is helpful to point out an unexpected finding in data published by the ERS that merits some discussion: California scores. A rather unexpected turn of events took place in October 2022 when NAEP scores were released, showing test score gains in only one district out of 26 included nationally: the Los Angeles Unified School District (LAUSD) (Reilly, 2022). LAUSD superintendent Alberto Carvalho said the gains were due to LAUSD policies, such as solid middle-school attendance, home computer distribution, high-intensity tutoring, and teacher training (Fensterwald, 2022a).

For those closely following state educational data reporting, this was a remarkable finding. After all, the California School Board Association had reported results of the 2022 performance assessment (the Smarter Balanced Summative Assessment, or the Alternate Assessment): student performance in ELA was 12 points below standard, and 52 points below standard in math. Chronic absenteeism in California more than doubled in 2021–2022, to 30% (California School Boards Association [CSBA], 2022). News reports warned of a "five alarm fire" for California student math scores (Fensterwald, 2022b). Referencing the superintendent of the LAUSD, Reilly (2022) wrote:

> While the NAEP results offered the most comprehensive national picture to date of how student learning was affected during the COVID-19 pandemic, California state test data painted a different picture for Los Angeles. The state's Smarter Balanced Assessment (2022b) revealed a drop in the percentage of Los Angeles students who met or exceeded standards in language arts and math in 2022. Based on those results, students in the district lost the equivalent of five to six years of learning on average, Carvalho said. "That's how deep, how cutting the regression was," he says. "And obviously, the loss was even more severe for the students who were in academic crisis prior to the pandemic. (Reilly, 2022)

Along those lines, California schools have relatively higher proportions of students who have been shown to suffer disproportionately negative impact of school closures, such as English learners and students of color (California Department of Education, 2019). Finally, California experienced some of the nation's longest school closures (Goldhaber et al., 2022). All of these factors have been consistently shown to correlate with lower achievement test scores (Colvin et al., 2022), so it is difficult to reconcile test score gains with these other factors.

This question is important because, across the nation, states are looking for empirically based interventions and evidence for which remediation efforts are most effective. Based on preliminary reporting, the California school data may spur some states to replicate their policies on remediation, assessment, and reporting, so understanding the strengths and vulnerable aspects of reported data is essential. The same caution stands for other states, of course, and the variables that follow should be assessed in analysis of any state's data. For example, Florida data initially appeared to show minimal learning loss, but closer analysis revealed significant disparities among districts, with some showing steep declines in test scores and others showing minimal change (WLRN, 2021). Thus, it would be unwise to view the state's educational experience during the pandemic as a homogenous entity—its data suggest complex interactions among disparities in remote education, socioeconomic factors, and other variables.

Fensterwald (2022a) offered analysis of the California learning gains data. He noted that in 2019, the LAUSD suffered a significant decline in scores compared to 2017. Students only took 20% of the test, in an effort to minimize testing time. Fensterwald pointed out that a federal agency that administers the National Center for Education Statistics (NAEP), in an unpublished opinion, stated it had analyzed the results and found no evidence enrollment declines colored the scores. That said, 2019 results did not include charter schools, while those schools were included in 2022; those charter schools are reportedly in more affluent areas and typically demonstrate higher achievement scores. Funds budgeted for intensive tutoring went unused in 2021–2022, so administrators' claims that tutoring was responsible for the results do not seem feasible. Fensterwald quoted one researcher who noted challenges in data comparison for states and districts with different sample sizes.

Critical review of state-level data is not always easy. For instance, in this case, based on Assembly Bill 130 (AB130, 2021), the California Department of Education can now only report data from the current year on the California School Dashboard (California School Boards Association [CSBA], 2022), whereas prior to that time, performance levels for two years of data were reported (including change from the prior year—either an increase or decline in performance measures). Likewise, the same document indicates increased graduation rates in California likely reflected "accommodations designed to give a boost to students most impacted by COVID-19." It is unclear exactly what the accommodations were, to whom they were granted, and whether they remain in place.

Other considerations may include the high, and increased, absenteeism rate in California, which doubled to 30% in 2022, higher in some areas, and its significant declines in school enrollment. Research has shown those missing students are typically the lower performing pupils, so it may be that the lowest performing students are simply not accounted for in the California data, at greater levels than noted in some other states.

Participation rate is a related variable to consider. In Spring 2021, fewer than 25% of California students participated in assessment (California Department of Education, 2022a). This phenomenon is not limited to California: DC schools recorded participation rates about 20 percentage points lower in Fall 2020 compared to 2019 testing. This lower participation rate was most pronounced for students from schools with higher percentages of at-risk students: schools with the lowest percentage of at-risk students enjoyed an 81% participation rate, while schools where more than 70% of students were classified as at risk, the participation rate in testing was only 66%, down 30 percentage points from 2019. The Maryland Public Schools Report (2023) indicated 20,000 fewer students were included in most assessment data, raising the question of whether results may underestimate disruption of learning gains. Standardized testing companies have also expressed concerns that scores may underestimate losses because the highest risk students are no longer participating in testing. Thus, districts with rebounding scores despite higher numbers of factors associated with declining scores may show recovery due to attrition. Previous publications have suggested data from 2020–2021 should not even be included in future assessments of learning loss (Shepard, 2020).

Casual analysis of scores across districts using the ERS interactive site reveals major disparities in learning losses across various groups, for instance, low-poverty districts versus high-poverty districts, which may appear as a mean performance level when viewed statewide.

Betthäuser et al. (2023) performed a systematic review of 42 studies from 15 countries, including the United States, on the pace of learning progress 2 years into the pandemic. Of interest for those following research on pandemic-era learning progress, the authors excluded studies at risk for bias, such as those with selection bias (under-representation of at-risk groups), missing data, or those that do not account for trends over time (e.g., comparing just two points in time rather than data points over time). These sources of biases may be a factor in other studies on learning loss.

There are a few more considerations regarding national and state test scores that may contribute to existing results being an underestimate of learning losses. Pandemic-related school closures resulted in significant disruption of the test-taking schedules for public and private schools across the nation. Waivers were granted for statewide assessment in 2020, so an entire year's data is simply missing on performance, support needs, or school accountability data, with no clear federal guidance on how to mitigate this loss of data. In 2021, the Department of Education allowed for "flexibility" in state assessment, for instance, offering abbreviated or remote testing or extending the deadline for required testing by 3–6 months.

The contribution of waivers for performance assessment is further complicated by variable application of waivers. In 2021, the U.S. Department of Education Office of Elementary and Secondary Education issued a letter announcing states would be given flexibility in testing and reporting, and this was following the year-long unprecedented waiver of state-level testing in 2020 (U.S. Department of Education, 2021). In California, virtual examination is still being offered for the English Proficiency test (California Department of Education, 2023). According to the National Academy of Education (2021), at the end of 2021, there were still significant alterations of test administration: testing windows were expanded, remote or in-person testing varied by district, either pencil-and-paper or computer-based testing was allowed in some cases, and some states allowed exams to be supervised remotely. Remote test taking could be impacted by environmental (home) distractions or Internet connectivity challenges. Also, although coursework was in many cases modified during school closures, test content was not. Finally, students in some cases entered the school building for the first time on the date of testing, and often plexiglass dividers and masks were required, which are not variables accounted for in previous assessment eras. The NAEP wrote that valid interpretation of 2020–2021 test data would be exceptionally difficult and would require contextual information.

The percentage of NAEP test takers identified as having disabilities was higher in 2022 than in 2019 (National Assessment of Educational Progress [NAEP], 2023b), which seems somewhat inconsistent with reports of lower rates of evaluation and diagnosis of educationally relevant disabilities during the pandemic (Barnett & Jung, 2021). Also, the percentage of public school students taking the test was lower in 2022 compared to 2019, due in part to the addition of charter schools to the database (Fensterwald, 2022b; National Center for Education Statistics, 2021). For eighth-grade testing groups, in 2022 there was a lower percentage of students from the Northeast United States, and a higher percentage from the South compared to 2019, which likely reflects more rapid school reopening in southern states. This is important because studies have shown longer duration of virtual school is correlated with lower test scores (Goldhaber et al., 2022).

Finally, a lower percentage of students eligible for free or reduced-cost lunch was observed in the NAEP 2022 sample, of interest because the national free lunch and breakfast programs were expanded significantly during the pandemic, a government benefit that ended in 2022 (Goldstein, 2023). Thus, seemingly a higher percentage of students receiving meals through the program would be expected. The lower percentage suggests those students may have been less represented in the NAEP test-taking groups, which would be consistent with reports of high-risk students lost to the system—in other words, vulnerable students lost to chronic absenteeism or dropout (Vazquez Toness, 2023) may simply not be reflected in the NAEP data.

It is important to note that the influential Goldhaber et al. study did not include data from schools if fewer than 60% of students completed the test. This highlights the potential for the remarkable evidence of learning loss to be an underestimate of changes; at least, analysis has shown a correlation between absenteeism and pandemic-era NAEP scores (Jordan, 2023), so it stands to reason those not represented in achievement test data are more likely to be lower performing. Also, the sample included a lower percentage of Hispanic students and lower percentage of high-poverty schools than are noted at the national level, and those factors have both been correlated with lower achievement scores (Carnoy & Garcia, 2017; National Assessment of Educational Progress [NAEP], 2022b).

Is There a Rebound Effect?

There is conflicting data on whether learning losses described earlier are temporary or persistent, or worse, will be compounded over time. Dorn et al. (2021)—who described their results as "an optimistic scenario"—predicted a "K-shaped recovery" in which some students recover previous learning rates but others fall further behind. In a meta-analysis of 39 studies on learning progress, Di Pietro (2023) found a decrease in achievement scores across 19 countries of about .19 standard deviations, comparable, according to the author, to the impacts of disruptions due to major disasters like Hurricane Katrina. Di Pietro found no evidence for significant recovery of losses after the first year of pandemic-related disruption. Importantly, the author emphasized that methodological factors—the use of methods that do not account for pre-pandemic trajectories—may result in underestimation of impacts on student performance.

Lewis and Kuhfeld (2022) analyzed achievement growth for about 7 million students across more than 20,000 schools, comparing scores from 2016 to 2019 to scores from 2020 to 2022. Although the pandemic cohort did exhibit lower achievement scores, pace of growth was faster in 2021–2022, and about 10%–20% of previous losses were eliminated by Fall 2022. However, it is important to note that it remains unclear whether the accelerated learning is a transient effect.

In a 2023 follow-up, Halloran et al. (2023) analyzed early evidence for test score recovery, comparing the extent of decline in test scores in 21 states from 2019 to 2021 with the percentage of recovered test scores through Spring 2022. They found that 20% of test score decline in ELA rebounded, while 37% of math test score declines were recovered. The authors evaluated the impact of factors such as duration of remote learning, district demographics, and pre-pandemic achievement scores, and perhaps surprisingly found little correlation with recovery rates. For example, similar rates of score recovery were observed in districts with the highest levels of students from groups who showed the greatest decline, and districts with lower rates of at-risk students.

ELA scores showed full recovery in some districts, while others showed continued decline from 2021 to 2022. Interestingly, math scores demonstrated at least some recovery in every state sampled. The variation in ELA score recovery by state does suggest that some recovery policies may be more effective than others, although the authors could not elucidate the particulars in their study.

State-level results in some areas indicate continued concerns. In New Jersey, standardized test scores from spring 2023 showed no increases in reading proficiency for third-grade students (Waters, 2023)—despite more than $2 billion in emergency funding for remediation. Overall, reading and math proficiency increased by about 2 percentage points, far below the increases required to erase attenuated gains. In Michigan, scores on the Michigan Student Test of Educational Progress (M-STEP) for grades three to seven were lower in 2023 compared to 2019; administration of the test was not required and was in some cases done remotely in 2020–2021. Third graders' reading proficiency scores declined significantly, and overall, reading and math scores declined by 4–6 percentage points compared to 2019, despite the influx of remediation funds (Macek, 2023).

Oster's 2023 finding that students with the most dramatic decline in learning progress exhibited the most recovery mirrors Green's 1966 results in the study of Black students who suffered prolonged educational disruption after desegregation orders. Green wrote that only the children with an absence of formal schooling during Massive Resistance made significant gains in intelligence testing, suggesting that reopening schools most dramatically benefitted those most harmed.

Overall, there is ample reason to suspect learning losses will not rebound as once hoped. Fahle et al. (2023) analyzed data from nearly 8,000 school districts and found that learning losses were larger in magnitude and more variable than any declines noted in previous years. They found that large declines were associated with persistent lower scores in successive grades, which would suggest persistence of the more significant learning losses. This is consistent with evidence showing the persistence of previous disruptions. The authors cautioned against the assumption that pandemic-era declines in achievement will disappear or regress to the mean. They also pointed out the logistical near-impossibility of the massive scale of accelerated learning required, involving coordination of thousands of instructors and curriculum schedules and the individual and varied needs of millions of students. Calculation of the potential scale of the problem showed that even if districts were able to provide a high-quality tutoring intervention to 10% of its students (a large number in terms of remediation), the effect would be an increase of 0.1 grade equivalent level, a number dwarfed by the scale of learning losses in some areas.

References

AB130. (2021). Education finance: Education omnibus budget trailer bill. https://leginfo.legislature.ca.gov/faces/billNavClient.xhtml?bill_id=202320240SB114

ACT. (2022). ACT profile report. https://www.act.org/content/dam/act/unsecured/documents/2022/2022-National-ACT-Profile-Report.pdf

ACT. (2023). Fewer high school seniors ready for college as ACT scores continue to decline. https://leadershipblog.act.org/2023/10/act-scores-decline.html

Alban Conto, C., Akseer, S., Dreesen, T., Kamei, A., Mizunoya, S., & Rigole, A. (2021). Potential effects of COVID-19 school closures on foundational skills and country responses for mitigating learning loss. *International Journal of Educational Development, 87*, 102434. https://doi.org/10.1016/j.ijedudev.2021.102434

Angrist, N., de Barros, A., Bhula, R., Chakera, S., Cummiskey, C., DeStefano, J., . . . Stern, J. (2021). Building back better to avert a learning catastrophe: Estimating learning loss from COVID-19 school shutdowns in Africa and facilitating short-term and long-term learning recovery. *International Journal of Educational Development, 84*, 102397. https://doi.org/https://doi.org/10.1016/j.ijedudev.2021.102397

Association of State and Provincial Psychology Boards (ASPPB). (2023). Psychology licensing exam scores by doctoral program. https://cdn.ymaws.com/www.asppb.net/resource/resmgr/eppp_/asppbdoctoralreport2023.pdf

Bailey, D. H., Duncan, G. J., Murnane, R. J., & Au Yeung, N. (2021). Achievement gaps in the wake of COVID-19. *Educational Researcher, 50*(5), 266–275. https://doi.org/10.3102/0013189x211011237

Barnett, W. S., & Jung, K. (2021). Seven impacts of the pandemic on young children and their parents: Initial findings from NIEER's December 2020 preschool learning activities survey. *National Institute for Early Education Research.* https://nieer.org/sites/default/files/2023-08/NIEER_Seven_Impacts_of_the_Pandemic_on_Young_Children_and_their_Parents.pdf

Belkin, D., Chapman, B., & Kesling, B. (2023, August 2). "How do I do that?" The new hires of 2023 are unprepared for work. *The Wall Street Journal.* https://archive.is/2023.08.02-094245/https://www.wsj.com/amp/articles/lost-learning-remote-pandemic-workplace-skills-new-employees-51351b33#selection-143.5-143.70

Betthäuser, B. A., Bach-Mortensen, A. M., & Engzell, P. (2023). A systematic review and meta-analysis of the evidence on learning during the COVID-19 pandemic. *Nature Human Behaviour, 7*(3), 375–385. https://doi.org/10.1038/s41562-022-01506-4

Blanshe, M., & Dahir, A. (2022, January 10). Uganda reopens schools after world's longest Covid shutdown. *The New York Times.* https://www.nytimes.com/2022/01/10/world/africa/uganda-schools-reopen.html

Britzky, H. (2022). COVID-19 had an "appalling" impact on American students' test scores. That's bad news for the military. *Task & Purpose*. https://taskandpurpose.com/news/military-recruitment-student-test-scores/

Buffie, E. F., Adam, C., Zanna, L. F., & Kpodar, K. (2023). Loss-of-learning and the post-Covid recovery in low-income countries. *Journal of Macroeconomics, 75*, 103492. https://doi.org/10.1016/j.jmacro.2022.103492

Bulman, G., & Fairlie, R. (2022). The impact of COVID-19 on community college enrollment and student success: Evidence from California administrative data. *Education Finance and Policy, 17*(4), 745–764.

California Department of Education. (2019). English learner, immigrant, and migratory students: 2017–18 demographic information report. https://www.cde.ca.gov/sp/el/er/documents/eldemographics1718.pdf

California Department of Education. (2022a). 2021–22 chronic absenteeism rate. https://dq.cde.ca.gov/dataquest/DQCensus/AttChrAbsRate.aspx?agglevel = State&cds = 00&year = 2021-22

California Department of Education. (2022b). 2021–22 assessment data show impact of COVID-19, demonstrate importance of state recovery efforts. https://www.cde.ca.gov/nr/ne/yr22/yr22rel50.asp

California Department of Education. (2023). COVID-19 accountability FAQs. https://www.cde.ca.gov/ta/ac/cm/covid19faq.asp

California School Boards Association (CSBA). (2022). California school dashboard release marks a new starting point for improvement. https://www.csba.org/en/Newsroom/PressReleases/2022/California-School-Dashboard-release#gsc.tab = 0

Carnoy, M., & Garcia, E. (2017). Five key trends in US student performance. *Economic Policy Institute*, 51–56. https://files.epi.org/pdf/113217.pdf

Center for Education Policy Research (CEPR) at Harvard University, & Educational Opportunity Project (EOP) at Stanford University. (2023). *The Education Recovery Scorecard*. https://www.google.com/url?q = https://educationrecoveryscorecard.org/about/&sa = D&source = docs&ust = 1691605260375231&usg = AOvVaw1oMJwa1q5fu7maYAAFnDI3

Center for Research on Education Outcomes. (2020). *Estimates of learning loss in the 2019–2020 school year*. Stanford, CA: Stanford University.

Coe, R., Weidmann, B., Coleman, R., & Kay, J. (2020). Impact of school closures on the attainment gap: Rapid evidence assessment. *Education Endowment Foundation*. https://dera.ioe.ac.uk/id/eprint/35707/1/EEF_(2020)_-_Impact_of_School_Closures_on_the_Attainment_Gap.pdf

Coffin, C., & Rubin, J. (2023). State of D.C. schools, 2021–22: In-person learning, measuring outcomes, and work on recovery. *D.C. Policy Center*. https://www.dcpolicycenter.org/publications/schools-21-22/

Colvin, M. K. M., Reesman, J., & Glen, T. (2022). The impact of COVID-19 related educational disruption on children and adolescents: An interim data summary and commentary on ten considerations for neuropsychological practice. *Clinical Neuropsychology, 36*(1), 45–71. https://doi.org/10.1080/13854046.2021.1970230

COVID-19 School Data Hub. (2023). The pandemic schooling mode and assessment outcomes data series. https://www.covidschooldatahub.com/research

Datzberger, S., & Brian, M. (2022). Ebola: Uganda's schools were closed for two years during COVID, now they face more closures—something must change. *The Conversation*. https://docs.google.com/document/d/1U2PiMF4x0y-t3paNQFMsa9lWWi9jWPYhrQQvM4QA3QI/edit

Di Pietro, G. (2023). The impact of Covid-19 on student achievement: Evidence from a recent meta-analysis. *Education Research Review, 39*, 100530. https://doi.org/10.1016/j.edurev.2023.100530

Di Pietro, G., Biagi, F., Costa, P., Karpinski, Z., & Mazza, J. (2020). The likely impact of COVID-19 on education: Reflections based on the existing literature and recent international datasets. *Publications Office of the European Union.* https://doi.org/10.2760/126686

Dorn, E., Hancock, B., Sarakatsannis, J., & Viruleg, E. (2020). COVID-19 and learning loss—disparities grow and students need help. McKinsey & Company. https://www.mckinsey.com/industries/public-and-social-sector/our-insights/covid-19-and-learning-loss-disparities-grow-and-students-need-help

Dorn, E., Hancock, B., Sarakatsannis, J., & Viruleg, E. (2021). COVID-19 and education: An emerging K-shaped recovery. *McKinsey & Company.* https://www.mckinsey.com/industries/education/our-insights/covid-19-and-education-an-emerging-k-shaped-recovery

The Education Trust. (2016). The Every Student Succeeds Act. Washington, DC.

Einhorn, E. (2022). Advocates fear suspensions could add to pandemic pain for vulnerable students. *NBC News.* https://www.nbcnews.com/news/education/school-suspension-covid-mental-health-rcna10329

Empower K-12. (2020). COVID 19 impact on student achievement and academic growth in DC. https://www.empowerk12.org/research-source/covid-impact-achievement-dc

Empower K-12. (2022). Positive indicators for academic recovery in DC. https://www.empowerk12.org/research-source/covid-impact-achievement-dc

Engzell, P., Frey, A., & Verhagen, M. D. (2021). Learning loss due to school closures during the COVID-19 pandemic. *Proceedings of the National Academy of Sciences USA, 118*(17), e2022376118. https://doi.org/10.1073/pnas.2022376118

Espey, E. (2023). Middle school math proficiency plummets over pandemic, state data shows. *MoCo360.* https://moco360.media/2023/03/10/middle-school-math-proficiency-plummets-over-pandemic-state-data-shows/

Fahle, E. M., Kane, N. T. J., Patterson, T., Reardon, S. F., Staiger, D. O., & Stuart, E. A. (2023). School district and community factors associated with learning loss during the COVID-19 pandemic. *Harvard Center for Education Policy Research, Cambridge, MA.* https://cepr.harvard.edu/sites/hwpi.harvard.edu/files/cepr/files/explaining_covid_losses_5.23.pdf

Fensterwald, J. (2022a). LAUSD's stunning reading score on NAEP: Illusion, real or something in between? *EdSource.* https://edso urce.org/2022/la-unifieds-stunning-reading-score-on-naep-illusion-real-or-something-in-between/681723

Fensterwald, J. (2022b). Student math scores touch off "five-alarm fire" in California. *EdSource.* https://edsource.org/2022/student-math-scores-a-five-alarm-fire-in-california/669797

Fishman, E. (2021). How the rhetoric of "learning loss" is harming schools. *The Progressive.* https://progressive.org/public-schools-advocate/learning-loss-harming-schools-fishman-210404/

Fuchs-Schündeln, N., Krueger, D., Ludwig, A., & Popova, I. (2022). The long-term distributional and welfare effects of Covid-19 school closures. *The Economic Journal, 132*(645), 1647–1683. https://doi.org/10.1093/ej/ueac028

Fuller, S., Swiderski, T., Mikkelsen, C., & Bastian, K. (2023). In school, engaged, on-track? The effect of the pandemic on student attendance, course grades, and grade retention in North Carolina (EdWorkingPaper: 23-747). Annenberg Institute at Brown University. https://doi.org/10.26300/58h9-3r54

Gin, L. E., Guerrero, F. A., Brownell, S. E., & Cooper, K. M. (2021). COVID-19 and undergraduates with disabilities: Challenges resulting from the rapid transition to online course delivery for students with disabilities in undergraduate STEM at large-enrollment institutions. *CBE Life Science Education, 20*(3), ar36. https://doi.org/10.1187/cbe.21-02-0028

Goldhaber, D., Kane, T. J., McEachin, A., Morton, E., Patterson, T., & Staiger, D. O. (2022). The consequences of remote and hybrid instruction during the pandemic. Cambridge, MA: Center for Education Policy Research, Harvard University.

Goldstein, A. (2023, April 22). A pandemic experiment in universal free school meals gains traction in the states. *Florida Phoenix.* https://floridaphoenix.com/2023/04/22/a-pandemic-experiment-in-universal-free-school-meals-gains-traction-in-the-states/

Hallin, A. E., Danielsson, H., Nordström, T., & Fälth, L. (2022). No learning loss in Sweden during the pandemic evidence from primary school reading assessments. *International Journal of Education Research, 114*, 102011. https://doi.org/10.1016/j.ijer.2022.102011

Halloran, C., Hug, C. E., Jack, R., & Oster, E. (2023, April). Post COVID-19 test score recovery: Initial evidence from state testing data. NBER Working Paper No. w31113. https://ssrn.com/abstract=4413850

Halloran, C., Jack, R., Okun, J. C., & Oster, E. (2021). Pandemic schooling mode and student test scores: Evidence from US states. *American Economic Review: Insights, 5* (2): 173–190.

Hope, J. (2022). Michigan school performance took a major hit from COVID lockdowns. *Michigan Capitol Confidential.* https://www.michigancapitolconfidential.com/news/michigan-school-performance-took-a-major-hit-from-covid-lockdowns

Illinois State Board of Education. (2023). Illinois assessment of readiness.

Jack, R., Halloran, C., Okun, J., & Oster, E. (2023). Pandemic schooling mode and student test scores: evidence from US school districts. *American Economic Review: Insights, 5*(2), 173–190.

Jackson, K. (2018). Could the disappointing 2017 NAEP scores be due to the great recession? *Education Next.* https://www.educationnext.org/could-disappointing-2017-naep-scores-due-to-great-recession/

Jacobson, L. (2021). One year into pandemic, far fewer young students are on target to learn how to read, tests show. *The 74 Million.* https://www.the74million.org/one-year-into-pandemic-far-fewer-young-students-are-on-target-to-learn-how-to-read-tests-show/

Jakubowski, M., Gajderowicz, T., & Patrinos, H. A. (2023). Global learning loss in student achievement: First estimates using comparable reading scores. *Economics Letters, 232*, 111313. https://doi.org/https://doi.org/10.1016/j.econlet.2023.111313

Jakubowski, M., Gajderowicz, T., & Patrinos, H. A. (2024). COVID-19, school closures, and student learning outcomes: New global evidence from PISA. http://documents.worldbank.org/curated/en/099932301112496929/IDU16cf7d0801f2091478b1934914b47c3ab4027

JerseyCan. (2021). A time to act: COVID-19 academic slide in New Jersey. https://jerseycan.org/wp-content/uploads/sites/7/2021/03/Presentation-A-Time-to-Act-COVID-19-Academic-Slide-in-NJ.pptx-1.pdf

Jordan, P. (2023). Have policymakers overlooked a major contributor to the dismal 2022 NAEP results? *FutureEd.* https://www.future-ed.org/have-policymakers-overlooked-a-major-contributor-to-the-dismal-2022-naep-results/

Khan, A. (2021). Montgomery County families question omitted content from virtual curriculum. *Fox 5.* https://www.fox5dc.com/news/montgomery-county-families-question-omitted-content-from-virtual-curriculum

Kofoed, M. S., Gebhart, L., Gilmore, D., & Moschitto, R. A. (2021). Zooming to class?: Experimental evidence on college students' online learning during Covid-19. *SSRN Electronic Journal.* https://docs.iza.org/dp14356.pdf

Kogan, V. (2023). Student achievement and learning acceleration on Spring 2023 Ohio state tests. John Glenn College of Public Affairs at The Ohio State University. https://glenn.osu.edu/sites/default/files/2023-08/Spring2023_OST_1.pdf

Kuhfeld, M., Soland, J., Tarasawa, B., Johnson, A., Ruzek, E., & Liu, J. (2020). Projecting the potential impact of COVID-19 school closures on academic achievement. *Educational Researcher, 49*(8), 549–565. https://doi.org/10.3102/0013189x20965918

Kuhfeld, M., Tarasawa, B., Johnson, A., Ruzek, E., & Lewis, K. (2020). Learning during COVID-19: Initial findings on students' reading and math achievement and growth. *NWEA.* https://www.nwea.org/uploads/2020/11/Collaborative-brief-Learning-during-COVID-19.NOV2020.pdf

Lewis, K., & Kuhfeld, M. (2022). Progress toward pandemic recovery: Continued signs of rebounding achievement at the start of the 2022–23 school year. *NWEA*. https://www.nwea.org/uploads/2022/12/CSSP-Brief_Progress-toward-pandemic-recovery_DEC22_Final.pdf

Macek, M. (2023). Michigan test results show big post-COVID learning loss. *Mackinac Center for Public Policy*. https://www.mackinac.org/blog/2023/michigan-test-results-quantify-covid-era-learning-loss

Mahnken, K. (2023). NAEP scores "flashing red" after a lost generation of learning for 13-year-olds.

Maldonado, J. E., & De Witte, K. (2021). The effect of school closures on standardised student test outcomes. *British Educational Research Journal, 48*(1), 49–94. https://doi.org/https://doi.org/10.1002/berj.3754

Mangrum, M. (2021, August 2). Tennessee student performance plunged during the pandemic; under 30% of students on grade level in key areas. *The Tennessean*. https://www.tennessean.com/story/news/education/2021/08/02/tennessee-student-performance-plunged-during-covid-pandemic/5382615001/

Mangrum, M. (2022, June 14). Tennessee student reading scores "largely back to pre-pandemic levels," state data shows. *The Tennessean*. https://www.tennessean.com/story/news/education/2022/06/14/state-data-tennessee-student-reading-scores-improving-after-covid/7621835001/

Maryland State Board of Education. (2023). Spring 2022 English language arts and mathematics assessment results Part 2. https://marylandpublicschools.org/stateboard/Documents/2023/0124/MCAPAssessmentResultsPart2.pdf

Maryland State Department of Education. (2020). Maryland together: Maryland's recovery plan for education. State Board Update. http://marylandpublicschools.org/stateboard/Documents/2020/0901/Maryland-Recovery-Plan-Education-Student-Engagement.pdf?fbclid=IwAR061A3MKqXJDGtbBS06h1EJQORwNUQtSjEsO-j2S_XmtbY-jXYfRdBxRsw

Melzer, E. (2023). A researcher wants to study the effect of Denver's reform policies. The superintendent has qualms. *Chalkbeat*. https://co.chalkbeat.org/2023/6/14/23761289/denver-education-reform-policies-research-request-parker-baxter-study-marrero-state-board

Michigan Board of Education. (2023). 2023 state test scores improve in many grades in math, science, social studies, and English language arts. https://www.michigan.gov/mde/news-and-information/press-releases/2023/08/31/2023-mstep

Moscoviz, L., & Evans, D. K. (2022). Learning loss and student dropouts during the covid-19 pandemic: A review of the evidence two years after schools shut down. Center for Global Development. https://www.cgdev.org/sites/default/files/learning-loss-and-student-dropouts-during-covid-19-pandemic-review-evidence-two-years.pdf

National Academy of Education. (2021). Educational assessments in the COVID-19 era and beyond. National Academy of Education. https://naeducation.org/wp-content/uploads/2021/02/Educational-Assessments-in-the-COVID-19-Era-and-Beyond.pdf

National Assessment of Educational Progress (NAEP). (2017). 2017 NAEP mathematics & reading assessments. National Center for Education Statistics, Institute of Education Sciences, US Department of Education. https://www.nationsreportcard.gov/reading_math_2017_highlights/

National Assessment of Educational Progress (NAEP). (2019). An overview of NAEP. National Center for Education Statistics, Institute of Education Sciences, US Department of Education. https://nces.ed.gov/nationsreportcard/subject/about/pdf/naep_overview_brochure_2021.pdf

National Assessment of Educational Progress (NAEP). (2022a). Civics score declines for the first time; score unchanged compared to 1998. National Center for Education Statistics, Institute of Education Sciences, US Department of Education. https://www.nationsreportcard.gov/highlights/civics/2022/

National Assessment of Educational Progress (NAEP). (2022b). Reading and mathematics scores decline during COVID-19 pandemic. National Center for Education Statistics, Institute of Education Sciences, US Department of Education. https://www.nationsreportcard.gov/highlights/ltt/2022/

National Assessment of Educational Progress (NAEP). (2023a). NAEP long-term trend assessment results: Reading and mathematics. National Center for Education Statistics, Institute of Education Sciences, US Department of Education. https://www.nationsreportcard.gov/highlights/ltt/2023/

National Assessment of Educational Progress (NAEP). (2023b). NAEP report card: Mathematics. U.S. Department of Education. Institute of Education Sciences, National Center for Education Statistics, National Assessment of Educational Progress (NAEP). https://www.nationsreportcard.gov/mathematics/districts/scores/?grade = 4

National Assessment of Educational Progress (NAEP). (2023c). Scores decline again for 13-year-old students in reading and mathematics. U.S. Department of Education. Institute of Education Sciences, National Center for Education Statistics, National Assessment of Educational Progress (NAEP). https://www.nationsreportcard.gov/highlights/ltt/2023/

National Assessment of Educational Progress (NAEP). (2023d). Trial Urban District Assessment (TUDA). U.S. Department of Education, Institute of Education Sciences, National Center for Education Statistics, National Assessment of Educational Progress (NAEP). https://nces.ed.gov/nationsreportcard/tuda/

National Assessment of Educational Progress (NAEP). (2023e). What are the differences between long-term trend NAEP and main NAEP? National Center for Education Statistics, Institute of Education Sciences, US Department of Education. https://nces.ed.gov/nationsreportcard/about/ltt_main_diff.aspx

National Association of School Psychologists. (2020). The pandemic's impact on special education evaluations and SLD identification. National Association of School Psychologists. https://www.nasponline.org/resources-and-publications/resources-and-podcasts/covid-19-resource-center/return-to-school/the-pandemics-impact-on-special-education-evaluations-and-sld-identification

National Center for Education Statistics. (2019). The nation's report card: Reading 2019 state snapshot reports. https://nces.ed.gov/nationsreportcard/subject/publications/stt2019/pdf/2020014AL4.pdf

National Center for Education Statistics. (2021). Students with disabilities. U.S. Department of Education, Institute of Education Sciences. https://nces.ed.gov/programs/coe/indicator/cgg

New Jersey Department of Education. (2023). NJ school performance report. https://rc.doe.state.nj.us

NWEA. (2023). The MAP suite. https://www.nwea.org/the-map-suite/

OECD. (2023). PISA 2022 results: Factsheets. OECD. https://www.oecd.org/publication/pisa-2022-results/country-notes/united-states-a78ba65a/#chapter-d1e11

Oxner, R. (2021, June 28). Texas students' standardized test scores dropped dramatically during the pandemic, especially in math. *The Texas Tribune*. https://www.texastribune.org/2021/06/28/texas-staar-test-results/

Patrinos, H. A., Vegas, E., & Carter-Rau, R. (2022). An analysis of COVID-19 student learning loss [Policy Research working paper no. WPS 10033]. http://documents.worldbank.org/curated/en/099720405042223104/IDU00f3f0ca808cde0497e0b88c01fa07f15bef0

Ponce, A. (2021). Educational recovery now: LA's children and schools need a comprehensive plan. https://gpsnla.org/wp-content/uploads/2021/03/EdRecoveryNow_Final_3-29-21.pdf

Reed, D. K., Ma, J., & Gerde, H. K. (2023). Resiliency and vulnerability in early grades writing performance during the COVID-19 pandemic. *Assessing Writing*, *57*, 100741. https://doi.org/10.1016/j.asw.2023.100741

Reilly, K. (2022). L.A. was the only big district to improve student scores this year. Here's how they did It. *Time*. https://time.com/6225894/los-angeles-schools-improvement-pandemic-learning-naep/

Rose, S., Badr, K., Fletcher, L., Paxman, T., Lord, P., Rutt, S., . . . Twist, L. (2021). Impact of school closures and subsequent support strategies on attainment and socio-emotional wellbeing in Key Stage 1. Research Report. *Education Endowment Foundation*. https://files.eric.ed.gov/fulltext/ED620409.pdf

Shepard, L. (2020). Testing students this spring would be a mistake. *Education Week*. https://www.edweek.org/teaching-learning/opinion-testing-students-this-spring-would-be-a-mistake/2020/12

Shoair, O. A., Smith, W. J., Abdel Aziz, M. H., Veronin, M. A., Glavy, J. S., & Pirtle, S. J. (2023, June 21). Pharmacy students' perceptions and attitudes toward face-to-face vs. virtual team-based learning (TBL) in the didactic curriculum: A mixed-methods study. *Medical Education Online*, *28*(1), 2226851. https://doi.org/10.1080/10872981.2023.2226851

St. George, D. (2023, June 21). National test scores plunge, with still no sign of pandemic recovery. *The Washington Post*. https://archive.ph/ycTWT#selection-389.0-406.0

Strunk, K. O., Hopkins, B. G., Kilbride, T., Imberman, S. A., & Yu, D. (2023). The path of student learning delay during the COVID-19 pandemic: Evidence from Michigan. Education Policy Innovation Collaborative, College of Education, Michigan State University. https://epicedpolicy.org/wp-content/uploads/2023/05/Benchmark_WP2_StudentOutcomes_May2023.pdf

Strupp, J. (2023). NJ post-COVID school test scores down, absences and troubles up. *App*. https://www.app.com/story/news/education/education-trends/2023/04/06/nj-data-shows-test-scores-down-troubles-up-in-2021-2022-school-year/70085396007/

Tennessee Department of Education. (2023). 2023 state assessment. https://tdepublicschools.ondemand.sas.com/state/assessment

U.S. Department of Education. (2023). Every student succeeds act (ESSA). https://www.ed.gov/essa?src = rn

U.S. Department of Education. (2021). https://www2.ed.gov/policy/elsec/guid/stateletters/dcl-assessments-and-acct-022221.pdf

Vazquez Toness, B. (2023). Millions of kids are missing weeks of school as attendance tanks across the US. *Associated Press*. https://projects.apnews.com/features/2023/missing-students-chronic-absenteeism/index.html

Waters, L. (2023). Exclusive: First peek at last spring's statewide test scores. *NJ Education Report*. https://njedreport.com/exclusive-first-peek-at-last-springs-statewide-test-scores/

WLRN. (2021). Test scores drop for Florida students, with sharpest decline in math scores. *WLRN Florida*. https://www.wlrn.org/news/2021-07-29/test-scores-drop-for-florida-students-with-sharpest-decline-in-math-scores

World Bank. (2023). Learning recovery to acceleration: A global update on country efforts to improve learning and reduce inequalities. *World Bank*. http://documents.worldbank.org/curated/en/099071223174514721/P179960038bed500a08dfc0489b6fa2254a

World Bank, The Bill & Melinda Gates Foundation, FCDO, UNESCO, UNICEF, & USAID. (2022). Guide for learning recovery and acceleration: Using the RAPID framework to address COVID-19 learning losses and build forward better. Washington, DC, World Bank. https://thedocs.worldbank.org/en/doc/e52f55322528903b27f1b7e61238e416-0200022022/related/Guide-for-Learning-Recovery-and-Acceleration-06-23.pdf

*Young, D. (*2021, May*)*. S FUSD lost touch with 8,800 students during the pandemic. *The San Francisco Bay View National Black Newspaper*. https://sfbayview.com/2021/05/sfusd-lost-touch-with-8800-students-during-the-pandemic/

4

Crisis of Education Remediation Plans

The words of Thomas Kane, economist and professor of education at the Harvard Graduate School of Education and director for the Center for Education Policy Research, provide valuable framing and perspective on the crisis of remediation plans:

> As a researcher, I did find the size of the [learning] losses startling—all the more so because I know that very few remedial interventions have ever been shown to produce benefits equivalent to 22 weeks of additional in-person instruction. . . . The achievement loss is far greater than most educators and parents seem to realize. The only question now is whether state and local governments will recognize the magnitude of the educational damage and make students whole. (Kane, 2022)

The Scope of the Challenge

Remediation of disrupted learning is a major concern for the educational system and for clinicians, who may be asked to evaluate students for eligibility for participation in remediation programs, make disability determinations, or estimate educational experience. At present, the true crisis of remediation plans is that there is no single coordinated plan to close the gap of lost educational experiences for millions of students.

Some researchers have expressed concerns that the return to classrooms has been more of a return to "business as usual," without acknowledgment of what Asadullah et al (2023) called a "major cognitive trauma." The Secretary-General of the United Nations termed the crisis an "education catastrophe" and the most severe disruption of global education systems in history (UNESCO, 2020). UNESCO (2023) has continued to raise concerns that millions of children have prematurely exited educational systems, further complicating efforts in remediation.

Neurodevelopment in the Post-Pandemic World. Molly Colvin, Jennifer Linton Reesman, and Tannahill Glen, Oxford University Press. © Oxford University Press 2024. DOI: 10.1093/9780197762660.003.0004

The World Bank RAPID program (World Bank et al., 2022) details major learning loss interventions, including targeted instruction, high-dosage tutoring, and extended instructional time. These interventions will be reviewed in the present chapter, in addition to ways in which schools and educational systems are evolving in light of the faltering remediation plans, budgetary crises, attenuated learning gains, and altered developmental progress in students since the onset of the pandemic.

As noted in Chapter 3, Goldhaber et al. (2022) described the "implied scale of recovery effort," which refers to translating decreases in learning gains into interventions required to make up losses. In stark terms, the authors describe the scale of the fiscal need, estimating that high-poverty schools that remained remote for longer periods could offer high-intensity tutoring to every student and still not make up for declines in achievement, which, if not reversed, has implications for future earnings and even gross domestic product (GDP). Goldhaber et al. (2022) also attempted to put a price tag on the cost for recovery of learning loss, estimating the percentage of a school year required to make up for the attenuated gains. They cautioned that the estimate would likely be conservative: for instance, to make up for a quarter of an academic year's learning would probably cost more than a quarter of the district's annual budget, because a district would need to pay overtime or would experience smaller gains with certain types of interventions. They found that surprisingly, higher income, longer remote schools would face the greatest budget shortfalls, since federal aid was based on poverty level rather than learning loss; higher income, longer remote schools lost an estimated 27% of a year's learning, but received less than 15% of the annual budget in aid.

Time is another factor: older students will leave the system before interventions and supports are fully implemented, or they will leave the system before their needs for additional support are ever recognized. This is reminiscent of the findings of outcomes after Massive Resistance school closures in Virginia: older students were more likely to simply leave the educational system to seek employment and thus missed academic remediation opportunities.

Figure 4.1, from the World Bank, outlines the various possibilities for educational recovery following the period of disrupted education. As with many neurodevelopmental conditions in which achievement gaps widen with time, the cohort of children that experienced the most disruption is at risk for developing the greatest distance between their progress and that

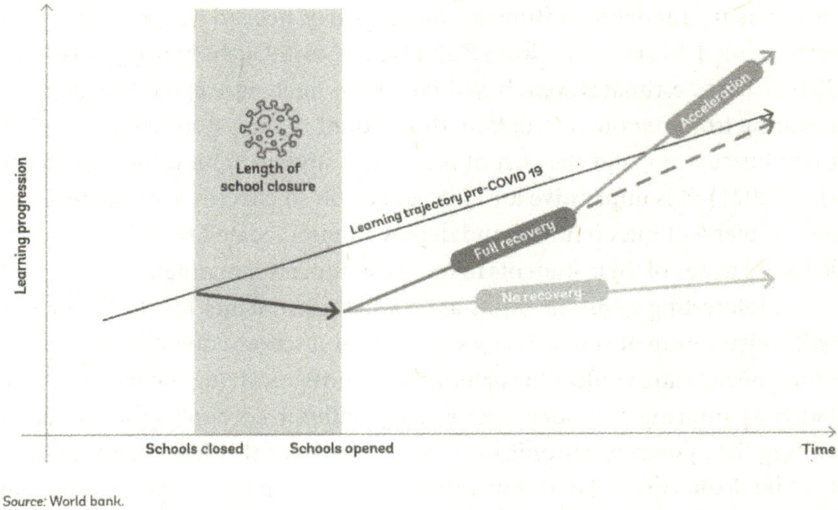

Figure 4.1. Illustration of learning recovery and acceleration trajectories. (Data from the World Bank.)

of peers with less disrupted education. Note that this depiction of potential trajectories represents typically developing students, and it does not necessarily represent the trajectories of at-risk children and those with disabilities, which would demonstrate further gaps from typically developing peers.

Between 2020 and 2021, Congress passed stimulus bills providing almost $190 billion to the Elementary and Secondary School Emergency Relief (ESSER) Fund. States were directed to distribute at least 90% of these funds to local educational agencies (U.S. Department of Education, 2021). These stimulus bills included the Coronavirus Aid, Relief and Economic Security Act (CARES); Coronavirus Response and Relief Supplemental Appropriations Act (CRRSA); and the American Rescue Plan Act, all of which have funded ESSER. Funding requirements for states and local educational agencies included provisions that states reserve 5% of their funds to address learning loss, 1% for afterschool activities, and 1% for summer learning programs. Local educational agencies (LEAs) were required to reserve no less than 20% of funding received to address the issue of learning loss (Office of Elementary and Secondary Education and Department of Education, 2021).

Despite large sums of money directed to districts, with relatively rapid timelines for expenditure, there is concern that funds are insufficient: modeling estimates for funding needed to remediate the documented losses range from $325 billion to $930 billion (Pan & Sass, 2020). These estimates were based on factors such as average learning loss resulting from remote instruction, the amount of time students spent in remote instruction, and the cost of increasing student achievement (Guryan et al., 2021). It is imperative for LEAs to be able to effectively evaluate, scale, and implement interventions and deploy funds allocated for addressing the learning needs of their students in the most impactful manner.

An interesting question arises as to whether students lost to the system will impact estimates of efficacy of remedial interventions; for instance, if outcome measures reflect the gains of only those receiving the interventions (such as tutoring, summer school, etc.) without accounting for students exiting the system or chronically absent, results of this historic investment may be artificially inflated. Put simply, the makeup of school districts may have been altered fundamentally, with the most at-risk and vulnerable students exiting the system, rendering comparisons more complicated and potentially inappropriate due to sampling bias.

High-Dosage Tutoring

High-dosage tutoring is an especially intensive and costly remedial intervention. Economist Thomas Kane wrote that to significantly increase learning progress at the scale of the post-pandemic crisis, a "trained tutor working with one to four students at a time, three times a week for a whole year—is one of the few interventions with a demonstrated benefit that comes close, producing an average gain equivalent to 19 weeks of instruction," which would represent about half an academic year's worth of instruction (Kane, 2022).

High-dosage tutoring was identified prior to the onset of widespread educational disruption as the most empirically supported remediation method, after school closures from natural disaster. This type of approach to tutoring is referred to variably as high-dosage, high-intensity, or high-impact tutoring. The approach generally involves regular meetings with a trained teacher or tutor, in person, for several hours per week on a one-on-one or small group basis. The technique has been found to improve student achievement after widespread disruption to education following Hurricane Katrina (McGuire, 2023) among other upheavals.

In both the United States and in the Netherlands, high-dosage tutoring interventions demonstrated strikingly similar outcomes when provided and evaluated in a randomized controlled trial. A single year of a high-dosage math tutoring program in the Netherlands was associated with gains of about 0.28 standard deviation (de Ree et al., 2023). By comparison, a 0.28 standard deviation is approximately one decile and is described as a large effect when compared to other educational interventions. These gains approximate a doubling effect in the average math test score gain compared to students that did not receive the tutoring intervention, and they did not appear to be the result of tutors teaching specifically to the test. These findings mirrored studies in the United States at about the same time (Guryan et al., 2021), showing high-dosage tutoring significantly reduced the achievement gap in math between high- and low-income students. A sample math intervention included tutoring during school hours, each tutor working with a pair of students for the duration of the school year, in four 1-hour sessions per week. Two of the sessions replaced math instruction and were meant to shadow the math curriculum being presented, and two of the tutoring sessions took place at a time where the student did not miss core academic instruction during the day (de Ree et al., 2023).

Another study, a randomized controlled trial of a similar high-impact tutoring program (Saga Education), found similar results with a 0.16 to 0.37 standard deviation increase in math performance for students receiving the high-impact, in-school tutoring (Guryan et al., 2021) where students worked in small groups with a trained tutor for one class period every day. Findings from the two studies suggest high-dosage tutoring, when provided on a regular basis in small groups led by highly trained tutors, can yield results that are particularly striking in math, and they support the notion that the achievement gap between high- and low-income students can be closed with appropriate support. Notably, these high-impact tutoring intervention studies were carried out several years prior to the period of widespread pandemic-related educational disruption.

In contrast, analysis of the impact of high-dosage tutoring that has been provided following prolonged pandemic-related educational disruption has been mixed, at best. Careful analysis and review of data published by various school systems implementing high dosage tutoring indicates that many school systems are administering this intervention in ways not considered in earlier research, such as tutoring outside of the school day, virtually, or in other ways that differed significantly from existing research on intervention that yielded impressive effects.

Tennessee is the highest-profile state attempting high-dosage tutoring statewide through a range of programs, including the Tennessee Accelerating Literacy and Learning Corps (TN ALL Corps). For Tennessee, the percentage of children from low-income households that scored "below basic" on annual proficiency tests rose from 2019 to 2021, and it was even higher in 2022 (Barshay, 2022). The remediation program is estimated to provide high-dosage tutoring to 150,000 Tennessee students, in which one to three students work with a trained tutor for 30–45 minutes per session, two to three times per week, during the school day. Similar to other trends, attendance concerns have plagued the tutoring sessions as well, particularly for tutoring sessions that are scheduled before or after school. It is reasonable to query whether the impact of tutoring will be easily measured if attendance concerns plague the programs.

Worryingly, data from Maryland's largest school system (Montgomery County, Maryland) indicated that for second-grade students who received an intervention referred to as "high-dosage tutoring," the percentage of students meeting grade-level expectations for reading fluency actually decreased by 51.5%. Kindergarten and first-grade students had similar declines—a decrease of 33.5% of students meeting grade-level expectations for those who received high-dosage tutoring (McGuire, 2023). In math, the district demonstrated slightly better outcomes, with an increase of 9.6% of students meeting grade-level expectations in math for those who received high-dosage tutoring. Once again, the techniques applied are rather different from the well-researched high-dosage tutoring delivered in previous randomized controlled trials: tutoring was provided to students outside of school hours, by existing staff members. Thus, while the district was reporting staffing shortages for regular school, it was faced with staffing an additional program. The reach of the intervention was also extremely limited. In a district of approximately 160,000 students, only 5,146 received high-dosage tutoring outside of the school day, approximately 3% of the student body (McGuire, 2023).

Disappointingly, when districts have turned to tutoring in remediation planning, programs have often been virtual and/or optional (Institute of Educational Sciences, 2023; St. George, 2023), with actual high-dosage tutoring only offered to select students at 37% of public schools. Self-paced, often virtual, tutoring was offered in 21% of public schools surveyed in December 2022. Online tutoring programs vary widely in terms of their structure, format, expertise of tutors, and accessibility for students with disabilities and those in areas where unreliable Internet access may preclude use of full features of the tutoring program. In some examinations of the impact of online tutoring, statistically insignificant effects have been found (Kraft et al., 2022). This is consistent with other examinations of effectiveness that have found no statistically significant difference between students receiving online tutoring and those in a comparison group in Montgomery County, Maryland (McGuire, 2023). Nationwide estimates indicate only a fraction of students in need of high-dosage tutoring were receiving it, with the National Center for Education Statistics (Institute of Educational Sciences, 2023) indicating that approximately 1 in 10 students were receiving high-dosage tutoring.

The National Assessment of Educational Progress (NAEP) described in Chapter 3, commonly referred to as the "Nation's Report Card," includes questions about whether students attended tutoring during the school day (or after school), and how often. Remarkably, data from this survey indicated that in 2022 fewer students in fourth and eighth grade were receiving tutoring compared to 2019, with 5% fewer fourth and eighth graders attending schools that offered teacher-led math tutoring (National Assessment of Educational Progress [NAEP], 2023). Similarly, and equally concerning, the percentage of children who had never received math tutoring rose from 2019 to 2022. Despite significant resources invested inproviding tutoring to those most in need, fewer children nationwide were receiving tutoring according to large-scale nationally representative samples.

While high-dosage tutoring has been lauded for its potential, others have pointed out the importance of factors that may inhibit the effectiveness of such programs. As described in Chapter 2, absenteeism is an important early indicator of academic difficulty, and it has dramatically increased since the period of prolonged pandemic-related educational disruption. It may be that decreasing absenteeism is a multifaceted challenge (described in greater detail in Chapter 10) that needs to be ameliorated in order for any educational intervention to have a measurable impact, as the students that are at greatest risk of feeling disconnected from the educational environment, and with chronic attendance problems, are in many cases precisely those who need the program most.

Summer Instruction and the Extended School Year

Historical perspective on the efficacy of summer programs and extended-school-year initiatives is not especially promising. Looking back to studies of students impacted by school shutdowns of the Massive Resistance, alternative instruction programs demonstrated only small effects. After 1 year of Free School programming, achievement scores remained lower than the national average (Heaton, 2008). The state of Virginia continues to fund a program to provide scholarships to the direct descendants of those impacted by the school shutdowns during Massive Resistance, in recognition of the ongoing negative impact of disruption and deprivation of education (Commonwealth of Virginia, 2023).

Callen et al. (2023) analyzed the impact of summer school programs as a potential remediation for pandemic-era learning losses. They evaluated data from the Road to Recovery project, a partnership among the Center for Analysis of Longitudinal Data in Education Research, the American Institutes for Research, and the NWEA designed to help school districts identify which remediation efforts are most effective or most unhelpful. Summer academic programming is intensive: best practices for these programs have been identified, and they include a minimum of 25 hours of mathematics instruction and 34 hours of language arts instruction (Schwartz et al., 2018).

Summer school as a learning recovery strategy after disruption related to COVID-19 does have some measurable support: a 2022 examination of eight U.S. districts serving 400,000 students indicated a positive impact for summer school on math achievement (Callen et al., 2023). In reading, unfortunately, the same analysis found results to be "statistically indistinguishable from zero" in all but one of the districts examined (Callen et al., 2023). These effects are in line with research prior to the pandemic: a multisite, randomized control trial of summer learning programs found math achievement improvements following summer intervention, but none in reading (Augustine et al., 2016). Informatively, attendance was identified as a challenge to optimal efficacy of the programming. A related study found a positive impact on math achievement after the first summer of intervention, but no benefits after the second summer, during which attendance declined, with less than a third of the sample attending the program (Schwartz et al., 2018). These findings underscore the importance of addressing absenteeism, given its impact on remediation and intervention program outcomes. Higher rates of summer school participation have been identified for programs with extended operating hours (from 8 a.m. to 5:30 p.m., or 9 a.m. to 4 p.m.), promoted as a summer "camp" with learning and enrichment as opposed to "summer school" (Callen et al., 2023). Part of the appeal of summer programs includes their voluntary nature, which can avoid the political challenges associated with creating a required extension of the school year for all. However, the voluntary participation may inadvertently serve to widen inequality of achievement gains further, in the absence of dedicated outreach and marketing to students most in need of intervention.

Overall, the authors estimated the summer programs conferred a small benefit (2%–3% improvement) in math (Callen et al., 2023). These modest returns on investment have prompted other researchers to posit that if districts want to recover learning losses in math, they would need to send "every student to summer school for two to three years in a row" *just to return to pre-pandemic math levels* for their district (Lynch et al., 2023). Kane and Reardon (2023), in a *New York Times* opinion piece, discussed the enormity of need, stating that even if the accelerated pace of 2021–2022 learning suggested by early data (Callen et al., 2023) were maintained, it would take an additional *4 years* for students to reach pre-pandemic achievement—not factoring in any impact of the cessation of ESSER funds for tutoring and remediation. Kane and Reardon advised schools to partner with organizations that already have summer and after-school programs (e.g., summer camps, sports programs, and museums) to add an academic program; they also suggested reaching far outside the usual after-school programming to consider weekend and "13th year" tutoring and remediation. While these policy ideas appear as solid solutions, there has been little appetite for the adoption of such policy proposals, or even discussion of them in depth at the state or local level, let alone national level.

In the Los Angeles Unified School District (LAUSD), the district and teachers' union reached an agreement for a smaller scale option: they added additional instructional days to the academic calendar. In the 2022–2023 school year, the district added four additional instructional days; the added days, termed "Acceleration Days," remained *optional*. LAUSD added three additional, voluntary days to the 2023–2024 and 2024–2025 academic years, for an optional Winter Recess Academy to provide additional instruction, enrichment, meals and supervision for students (City News Service, 2023). The cost for the first two acceleration days offered was reported to be $36 million; officials later reported the actual cost was $11.6 million, though this has not been officially confirmed (Blume, 2023a). The explanation for the lower cost may lie in the details of attendance rather than any fiscal responsibility: for the first acceleration days, only 40% of those registered attended, although some children attended without previously registering (Blume, 2023b). Of the nearly 420,000 students enrolled in LAUSD, approximately 33,000 attended the two spring acceleration days, and 40,000 attended acceleration days during the winter break (Jones, 2023). Thus, at best estimate between 8% and 9% of LAUSD students participated in the optional added days—even after efforts to boost participation included personal invitations to students identified as high-need, webinars, and events at schools meant to increase awareness of the additional days (Harter, 2023).

The small amount of time added to the LAUSD school calendar and its voluntary nature contrast with the existing literature on the positive impact of increasing instructional time to the school day, or adding days to the school year. Pre-pandemic, both techniques were associated with increases in math and reading, for example, adding 10 (or more) additional days to the school calendar (Aucejo & Romano, 2016). When comparing the impact of extending the school calendar by 10 days or reducing absences by the same amount—the impact and improvement on gains in reading and math achievement scores is greater when absences are reduced. For math, extension of the school calendar is estimated to increase gains in test scores by 1.7% compared to an estimated 5.5% increase for a similar decrease in absenteeism (Aucejo & Romano, 2016). The authors conclude that interventions to reduce absenteeism are the more effective intervention than extension of the school year (Aucejo & Romano, 2016). For the lowest performing students, it becomes more challenging to catch up after an absence, and attendance patterns will likely have different impacts on high versus lower achieving students. These findings, again, have implications for the importance of reducing absenteeism: if the lowest performing students are targeted to increase attendance, improvements in overall math and reading achievement would be greater than extending the school year. These findings are of importance to policymakers in considering the best use of limited resources to improve student outcomes.

Due to the scale of the crisis, it will be imperative for policymakers to consider the use of a "both/and" approach, instead of a "pick one" approach to make measurable learning gains. This will require analysis of costs, human and economic, and possibly a commitment to making these mandatory and available to all students in need. Still, it remains unclear whether school districts will be able to implement individualized intensive remediation on such a large scale; implementation is also likely to vary due to staffing challenges and long wait lists for such programs (Natanson et al., 2021). For example, by Fall 2023, New Jersey had recruited only 10% of planned tutors for its high-dosage tutoring initiative (Waters, 2023a). While an effective intervention may not be dependent on the difficult task of recruiting highly skilled specialists, it most certainly will be costly: one California reading tutoring project staffed by community members was shown to result in reading gains—but required a 2-month training period, stipends for tutors, childcare, meals, and transportation (Jacobson, 2023). While these expenses are undoubtedly necessary for the implementation of a community-based program, scaling the cost to a national level is almost incalculable.

Finite resources, financial and human, may preclude optimal implementation of empirically supported remediation plans. This calls into question the ability of leaders, however sincere, to adhere to promises of historic investment in children's education to make up for devastating losses experienced in academic progress.

Implementation Strains

Fahle et al. (2023) concerningly suggested that large-scale remediation, for instance, through accelerated learning, is not feasible after such a broad and sustained shock to learning progress, because it is so difficult to coordinate resumption or adjustment of course content across thousands of teachers and millions of students, compared to a shock to learning that may have been caused in an isolated area due to a particularly challenging influenza year or a poor teaching team. Michigan, for instance, did not have a statewide tutoring program funded until 2023, despite some of the nation's largest declines in learning gains (Lohman, 2023). Remediation programs were highly variable in quality and empirical support and availability. Funding for tutoring through the newly approved program is dependent on meeting strict guidelines, Lohman notes, and even then, funds would not be available until early 2024.

Kogan (2023), in an analysis of Ohio student scores from Spring 2023, documented increased pace of learning compared to pre-pandemic growth, but persistence of gains was more tenuous. Kogan also found English/language arts (ELA) score growth that was slower compared to the previous year, and no evidence for accelerated math learning for middle-school students. Thus, some promising initial results may not persist and long-term follow-up, and ongoing analysis of effectiveness will be necessary.

Other strains to the system have compromised optimal follow-through on promises of special education support and services, such as extended school year (ESY) services. Staffing shortages have strained districts' ability to offer ESY services, which differ from traditional remediation services. ESY services are provided to students whose individualized educational program (IEP) team has determined that ESY services are necessary to prevent a decline or regression that would occur without such instruction, or that the services are needed in an area of critical life skills. One district faced such significant staffing shortages in Summer 2022 that it was forced to cancel ESY services for approximately 175 students (Peetz, 2022), providing families with less than a week's notice that their children would not be able to participate in the services already deemed necessary for the child. Staffing challenges have persisted into 2023 (Espey, 2023a). Lack of adequate personnel (related to both a system-wide staffing crisis and the massive scale of need) has been identified as a likely factor in less good outcomes for various interventions, including tutoring, small group interventions, external programs, virtual learning, and extensions of the school year (Callen et al., 2023). Teacher shortages were a serious concern prior to the pandemic, but they may have been exacerbated by various factors, including staff fatigue, mental health concerns, and student fights (Kamenetz, 2021).

Remediation of chronic absenteeism has been a focus of researchers and school administrators and, as noted, is a major factor in both the study and implementation of remediation strategies. Articles in the press have detailed school staff and community volunteer efforts to personally reach students through home visits and social supports, such as vouchers for food purchases for students in low-income households (Fortin, 2022). Attendance Works, a nonprofit organization dedicated to reducing chronic absenteeism even before the pandemic, lists pre-pandemic research on evidence-based interventions for reducing absenteeism, such as engaging influential third parties, home visits, and increasing school-based health clinics (see https://www.attendanceworks.org/research/evidence-based-solutions/). The organization, along with FutureEd, an independent think tank at Georgetown University, published a three-tiered model for increasing attendance, with a baseline school-wide effort to instill the importance of attendance (such as recognizing superior attendance and clearly defining class start times). The second tier details early intervention for students already missing at least

10% of classes. The third and most intensive tier targets those missing 20% or more of classes, and it typically involves case management (Turner, 2023). Gottfried, Page, and Edwards (Gottfried et al., 2022) also described a three-tiered strategy for reducing absenteeism, with a first tier designed to address basic needs, such as transportation and communications, a second tier detailing targeted early warning identification and mentorship, and a third tier involving community partnerships (e.g., schools and intervention teams that work to reward engagement rather than "punishing" it with suspension).

Liu and Lee (2022) studied growth rates of chronic absenteeism to identify students at most risk. Their findings led them to suggest targeting interventions with students with more unexcused absences, students of color and those from low-income households, and those who report disengagement from school culture. Even with such interventions described and available, school systems writ large and nationwide appear to be grappling with unprecedented rates of chronic absenteeism, with very few districts reporting improvement in chronic absenteeism and many reporting double-digit percentage increases since 2019 (Vazquez Toness, 2023). Chronic absenteeism appears to be a persistent issue that can undercut the success of remediation intervention programs. It was not present to the concerning degree seen now, prior to the pandemic.

The Fiscal Cliff: Implications of Time-Limited Funds and Dwindling Enrollments

ESSER funding infused school systems with significant funds, but many school systems chose to fund or retain permanent positions. While this at face value appears to be a sound fiscal decision (more staff, smaller staff-to-student ratios), the longer term trajectory is unsustainable because of the time-limited funding and the absence of a plan for a replacement. Public schools that invested in longer term fiscal commitments, such as an increase in district staff, may face difficult decisions about what programs or staff to cut once time-limited funds have ended. This has been referred to as a "fiscal cliff": budget needs will eventually outstrip incoming funding, and pandemic-related school closures have dramatically hastened the moment.

Examples are numerous. Minneapolis public schools committed nearly $30 million of its ESSER funding to add 400 positions to create "interventionist triads." Simultaneously, the district estimated that by the end of the

2024–2025 school year it will have exhausted its general fund balance and entered statutory operating debt, which can be compared to bankruptcy (Winter, 2023). In California, more recently, in response to the expiration of federal pandemic funding and declines in enrollment, the LAUSD announced a hiring freeze and potential closures of some schools (Chapman, 2023). San Francisco schools are facing similar financial strain, with a forecast budget deficit of more than $400 million; notably, the district used pandemic aid to help pay for previous spending (Tucker, 2023). Similarly, schools in Denver, Colorado, have predicted a budget deficit for at least the 2025–2026 school year. Coupled with local trends that indicate a declining enrollment by 1,000 students per year, Denver school leadership proposed closing 10 schools, which the school board refused (Seaman, 2023). In short, many districts are rapidly approaching the projected "fiscal cliff," due to a combination of the end of pandemic relief funding, declines in enrollment, and other budgetary pressures (Fensterwald & Yuxuan, 2024).

Some school systems used ESSER dollars to create a parallel school system on a virtual basis, such as the K–12 virtual academy in Montgomery County Public Schools, complete with its own administrators and teachers that provide instruction and support solely to the virtual academy (Montgomery Public Schools, 2022). After the first year of the program, state-level leaders expressed concerns about the developmental appropriateness of a virtual kindergarten, so kindergarten was excluded from the option. Funding and sustainability for this program have been proposed to continue into the 2025 operating budget, despite rapidly declining enrollment (Montgomery Public Schools, 2022). At the time of this writing, outcomes for this wholly virtual offering lagged behind in-person schooling on standardized math and reading assessments at every grade level assessed (Montgomery Public Schools, 2022). Formal reporting of outcomes for this program was repeatedly delayed and indicates that chronic absenteeism was higher for virtual academy students compared to in person (Wilson & Wade, 2023). The school system concluded, based on their analysis, that in-person instruction yielded better outcomes than virtual instruction, particularly for elementary-aged students.

Other school systems remain in a precarious economic position with enrollment declines. Some of the higher need schools have spent their ESSER funds at a slower pace than lower poverty districts, resulting in an even steeper decline in funding and contraction of budgets (Roza & Silberstein, 2023). Complicating matters are concerns from watchdog agencies that enrollment was misreported to state agencies. As noted in Chapter 2, the Office of the Inspector General for Education released a report in 2022 showing nearly 3,000 instances in which Maryland students were found eligible for state funding but did not meet the attendance or enrollment requirements. Almost a third of those students did not have documented attendance at any point during the school year (Pagnucco, 2023). The combination of forces, including the end of federal pandemic-relief funds, falling enrollments in many districts, and decrease in state-level revenues, has presented what some call a "perfect storm" of financial chaos for school systems struggling to continue to remediate long-term needs of students (Roza & Silberstein, 2023). It is anticipated that many districts will have to wrestle with decisions that could directly impact already-marginalized groups, including decisions about reductions in staff and closing of schools.

Despite the threat of a fiscal cliff at a time when students are experiencing increased need, there are some developing options. Nonprofit organizations have stepped in with grant monies and commitment to study outcomes of different tutoring initiatives rolled out across the United States. Accelerate, an initiative associated with the America Achieves nonprofit education advocacy organization, awarded $10 million in research grants to study tutoring initiatives to determine which in-school interventions are the most cost-effective, financially sustainable, and empirically supported (Belsha, 2023). Accelerate recently announced federal funding initiatives of $50 million, with commitments to allocate these funds to literacy interventions, support for new tutors, and efforts to combat chronic absenteeism (U.S. Department of Education, 2023). The organization's grantees range from school districts to tutoring services. Funded programs include the following: an in-person tutoring program for students in the lowest quintile, a program to use existing teachers in high-need schools, and training for paraprofessionals in early literacy tutoring.

Resetting Benchmarks for Academic Progress: The "New Normal"

Since the pandemic-related school closures, several policies have arisen in response to what some have termed the "new normal" for academic achievement. Most have focused on revising cutoffs for determining proficiency, changing or eliminating access to advanced math courses, grade retention, and reclassifying what constitutes successful completion of academic demands.

Proficiency thresholds or benchmarks may have been adjusted for national and/or state testing. Although the NAEP is a national exam, states set their own proficiency threshold scores (Center for Education Policy Research [CEPR] at Harvard University & Educational Opportunity Project [EOP] at Stanford University, 2023). This has already occurred in some states in response to pandemic-era declines in test scores. In 2022, New York State's Board of Regents reset required proficiency benchmarks in response to steep declines in proficiency scores (Moore, 2023). According to a Board of Regents Technical Advisory Committee Co-Chair Marianne Perie, "Yes, there's learning loss between 2019 and 2022, but in some ways we don't want to keep going backwards . . . we're at this new normal. So for New York, we are saying the new baseline is 2022." There is room for genuine debate on this approach: supporters describe the risk of low achievement scores leading to school closures, but critics note that such changes create the perception that test scores do not measure ability and reflect external (non-student) factors.

In Massachusetts, public school students must meet the competency determination (CD) standard to graduate from high school (Massachusetts Department of Elementary and Secondary Education, 2023), and the state's website notes: "Some students in the classes of 2021–2025 may score in the Not Meeting Expectations level, but their scaled score is high enough to earn the CD in the subject." For students graduating in the classes of 2021 or 2022, CD is attained by reaching a specified passing score on the Massachusetts Comprehensive Assessment tests, or they may demonstrate "successful completion of a relevant high school course" instead (Massachusetts Department of Elementary and Secondary Education, 2023).

Similarly, in New Jersey, student growth percentiles are measured using consecutive years of test results. However, New Jersey student assessment was canceled in the 2019–2020 year and again in 2020–2021. Thus, the state's student growth percentiles simply are not available for 2019 through 2022 (Strupp, 2023). This is concerning because New Jersey has exhibited increased rates of chronic absenteeism, jumping from 10% in 2018–2019 to 18% in 2021–2022 (Rotuno-Johnson, 2023), and New Jersey was among the states with the longest school closures (Jordan, 2023), factors now known to be associated with greater alteration of learning progress. A different method of calculating growth was substituted with the approval of the New Jersey Department of Education, one based on relative school improvement (comparison to other schools versus a traditional change score), and weighs *growth* more heavily than it does *proficiency* (New Jersey Department of Education, 2023).

In 2022, the New Jersey Graduation Proficiency Assessment (NLGPA) was introduced to indicate whether graduating students are proficient in tenth-grade English language arts and math (Geometry and Algebra I) (Waters, 2023b). Waters reported that when more than half of students failed at least one of the sections, the State Board of Education lowered passing scores and altered labels, so that passing means that one is "high school graduation ready" rather than "college career ready." Following the changes, in 2023, ELA pass rates rose by 40%, and more than half of test takers passed the math portion.

More recently, the Board of Ohio's largest school district, Columbus County, voted to lower academic goals for reading proficiency, after already lowering them once before during the pandemic, in 2021. The goal of having 55% of third graders reading at proficiency was reset to 40.5% (Ferenchik, 2023).

Illinois achievement test scores in 2022 were sharply lower than in 2019, and only about a quarter of the state's students met or exceeded proficiency expectations in math, but graduation rates were at the highest levels in 12 years (Smylie, 2022). This seemingly contradictory result may reflect the increase in passing grades and the moratorium on failing students during the pandemic rather than increased achievement (Flaherty, 2020).

Washington, DC, schools developed the Bold Performance Schools initiative to recognize successful urban schools serving a high-poverty student population, with greater numbers of at-risk children compared to other schools. According to Empower K-12 (2023), because only 11% of at-risk students met or exceeded learning expectations in ELA or math in 2022, the district lowered the cutoff for schools to meet the criteria for high performance, and they plan for a longer term reset of the cutoffs: they chose a lower cutoff of 5 percentage points higher than average (for other similar schools) cutoff for 2022, raising that level to 7.5 percentage points in 2023 and 10 percentage points in 2025—after that, schools will only use post-pandemic test scores to calculate expected proficiency rates, in effect, creating a "new normal."

Some efforts to stem declining achievement scores have generated controversy. Cambridge Public Schools in Massachusetts removed advanced math courses in middle school immediately prior to the pandemic to mitigate racial and ethnic disparities. However, pandemic-related school closures precluded implementing a new math program, and compounding the issue, pandemic-era learning losses are now cited as the reason why advanced math classes cannot be reinstated (Huffaker, 2023). This practice highlights the longer term nature of complications arising from school closures: reduced curriculum material resulted from decreased class time when schools were closed, which likely contributed to learning losses. California received media attention for a similar reimagining of math education. Critics describe the effort as a dilution of curriculum that uses lowered standards to cloak poor achievement scores, while advocates describe the plan as one that will reduce achievement gaps (Blume & Watanabe, 2023). As Conrad (2023) notes, the California Mathematics Framework, after a decade of implementation in the San Francisco Unified School District, has little empirical support, but risks becoming an "off-ramp" from more advanced math courses. The California and Cambridge schools' experience suggests curriculum changes may be a factor for the foreseeable future. This is unsurprising, given the precipitous drops in math performance reviewed in Chapter 3.

In Oregon, students had to demonstrate proficiency in nine different "essential skills" that included reading, writing, math, critical thinking, technology usage, and civic and community engagement (Miller, 2021). The requirement to demonstrate proficiency was present from 2012 through 2019, and students could demonstrate proficiency by passing a standardized test or submission of work samples. In 2020, schools were permitted to skip standardized tests, and the requirement for demonstration of the essential skills was suspended in 2020 and 2021. State lawmakers in the summer of 2021 signed legislation requiring a review of graduation requirements for the state and suspension of the essential learning skill requirement (Miller, 2021). At the time of this writing, the Oregon Department of Education had not made public any plans to reverse course, and the assessment of essential skill policy remained suspended.

Grade retention is another aspect of remediation plans, as rates of students with failing grades increased during the pandemic. However, retaining students exhibiting learning losses and absenteeism may introduce new problems, negatively impacting graduation rates and reducing opportunities for enriched instruction (Borter & O'Brien, 2021). Accelerated instruction, instead of grade retention, is advocated by some groups, such as the National Association of School Psychologists (National Association of School Psychologists, 2011), but states vary, either enforcing pandemic-related grade retention (Sitrin,

2021) or preventing grade retention by altering grading systems (Geduld, 2023). Tennessee passed the Tennessee Learning Loss Remediation and Student Acceleration Act (2021) that would retain third-grade students who did not pass a state-based reading test. While on its surface, the act provided significant consequences for those students who did not pass the test, it also provided significant support and opportunity to demonstrate proficiency as well as the opportunity to appeal a test finding before a decision of retention in third grade was made. However, in that first year, 86% of appeals of retention decisions were approved. In 2023, about one quarter of third-grade test takers were exempt from retention due to disability or emerging English fluency (Gilreath, 2023). Alternatives to retention included participation in a 4-week summer reading camp with agreement to attend 90% of scheduled days, or commitment to taking tutoring throughout the fourth-grade year (Styf, 2023). The question of whether to retain a student was already a complex decision prior to the onset of the pandemic and became a much more challenging decision for parents, schools, and policymakers after children returned to school buildings with varying levels of skill within a single classroom.

The concept of grading for equity has been embraced by numerous school systems, especially when the 2020–2021 school year was marked by dramatic increases in failing grades, and district leaders sought solutions to a mounting crisis. The idea, based on the book *Grading for Equity* (Feldman, 2018), involves giving students more time to make up work, allowance for retaking tests, and excluding factors from grading practices such as attendance, late work, or even behavior. Advocates emphasize the need to avoid penalizing marginalized students and point to disparities in outcomes related to traditional grading systems; for instance, a student from a home with economic hardship may not be able to reach school on time due to lack of transportation, and homework may take a back seat to the need to work for money for the family. Critics, while recognizing they initially may have been in favor of the promise in these practices (Randazzo, 2023), note unintended consequences such as reduced incentive to attend class or to avoid "failing" a class. The practice has not been accepted in all areas and remains a topic of heated debate in some (Espey, 2023b).

Implications of the "New Normal" and Failed Remediation

Establishing a "new normal" and the patchwork nature of existing remediation plans are critically relevant to the practice of neuropsychology, as they directly impact the reliability of pre-pandemic normative data (a topic covered in detail in Chapter 9). Current practice involves stratification of normative groups by, among other factors, level of education. The practice of dramatically changed grading systems, or failure to document curriculum requirements, could mean that 12 years of education is no longer generalizable across groups. For instance, it would be unsound to assume "12 years of education" means the same thing for students who remained in person with no alterations to grading or graduation practices to those from areas with prolonged virtual education and unexpectedly high graduation rates in the face of high chronic absenteeism rates (Geduld, 2023). This also has implications for research, as groups or outcomes may be stratified in part by education level.

The quality of remediation plans is an issue that has received scant attention, with increased attention toward the need for a fast-paced rollout of high-quality programs. This has led to an influx of online and other virtual resources for tutoring. Some school districts have relied on a combination of virtual and in-person resources as a means of offering remediation to students in need. Available data indicate limited support for their efficacy and utility, with some districts reporting limited uptake and use of available tutoring resources.

Even more concerningly, a massive-scale remediation plan has not been developed, likely due at least in part to lack of parental awareness of the need or availability of such programming. Parents appear to be broadly unaware of the reduced gains their own children have made, and thus they are less alarmed about learning loss (Polikoff & Houston, 2022). Kane and Reardon (2023) echoed this sentiment, explaining their efforts to make public their data on learning loss; further, they referred to the idea that schools can simply make up unfinished learning gains as "magical thinking" and suggested public officials create a communications plan to inform parents and recruit families for extended learning opportunities.

National parent surveys (Silver et al., 2022) indicated that in Spring 2022, fewer than half of parents believed their child's school offered tutoring or summer school. This dearth of information for parents contributes to an ineffective and troubling cycle: education leaders see low uptake and participation in voluntary remediation programs, and subsequently they are less likely to justify the enormous funding and personnel efforts needed to execute successful and meaningful interventions.

One means of increasing uptake of remediation programming could be the use of local school communications reviewing the impacts of educational disruption and highlighting availability of resources to parents and families, with full transparency of scores and comparisons to pre-pandemic status. Another option could be the return of regularly scheduled and meaningful parent–teacher conferences, in which the most personalized feedback can be provided. In the first 2 years of the pandemic, conferences were virtual or even discontinued in many districts. In New York City Public Schools, for instance, parents and family members were unable to enter school buildings for any events until February 10, 2023 (Amin, 2023), due to COVID-19 vaccination policies. Strong family and school partnerships are associated with positive outcomes across educational and social-behavioral domains (Reinke et al., 2019), and efforts to revitalize strong parent involvement may be an underutilized method of improving uptake and awareness of school-based remediation efforts (Jacobson, 2023).

Clinicians should be aware of remediation and retention plans in their region, evaluate the intensity and quality of interventions, and consider providing advocacy for their patients as needed. Clinicians and policymakers are encouraged to critically evaluate interventions and be aware of evidence-based practice for remediation. It is important to know if districts offer interventions, including crucial elements of empirically supported remediation efforts. It is as important to be able to identify unsupported programs as successful ones. Stakeholders will need to voice support for effective interventions and demand data to support alternative methods. An informed citizenry and transparent educational system can determine the extent to which prolonged educational disruption will alter the trajectory of development of a generation.

References

Amin, R. (2023). COVID vaccine mandate dropped for city employees, visitors to NYC public schools. *Chalkbeat.* https://ny.chalkbeat.org/2023/2/6/23588165/ny-vaccine-mandate-covid-vWoStors-schools-employees-adams

Asadullah, M. N., Bouhlila, D. S., Chan, S. J., Draxler, A., Ha, W., Heyneman, S. P., . . . Yemini, M. (2023). A year of missed opportunity: Post-Covid learning loss—A renewed call to action. *International Journal of Education Development, 99*, 102770. https://doi.org/10.1016/j.ijedudev.2023.102770

Aucejo, E. M., & Romano, T. F. (2016). Assessing the effect of school days and absences on test score performance. *Economics of Education Review, 55*, 70–87. https://doi.org/https://doi.org/10.1016/j.econedurev.2016.08.007

Augustine, C. H., McCombs, J. S., Pane, J. F., Schwartz, H. L., Schweig, J., McEachin, A., & Silver-Evans, K. (2016). *Learning from summer: Effects of voluntary summer learning programs on low-income urban youth*. Santa Monica, CA: RAND Corporation.

Barshay, J. (2022). Proof points: Early data on "high-dosage" tutoring shows schools are sometimes finding it tough to deliver even low doses. *The Hechinger Report*. https://hechingerreport.org/proof-points-early-data-on-high-dosage-tutoring-shows-schools-are-sometimes-finding-it-tough-to-deliver-even-low-doses/

Belsha, K. (2023). It's often hard to tutor students during the school day. A new initiative seeks to change that. *Chalkbeat*. https://www.chalkbeat.org/2023/4/26/23698377/accelerate-tutoring-school-day-states-covid

Blume, H. (2023a, January 25). At $611 a day per students, some question if L.A. schools' extra learning days are worth it. *The Los Angeles Times*.

Blume, H. (2023b, April 12). LAUSD pitched students an expensive experiment to get higher grades. Most turned it down. *The Los Angeles Times*. https://www.latimes.com/california/story/2023-04-12/lausd-launches-two-more-controversial-acceleration-days-this-time-on-the-down-low

Blume, H., & Watanabe, T. (2023, July 12). California math overhaul focuses on equity amid low test scores. *The Los Angeles Times*. https://www.latimes.com/california/story/2023-07-12/california-math-overhaul-focuses-on-equity-amid-low-test-scores#:~:text = California%20education%20officials%20on%20Wednesday,5.8%20million%20public%20school%20students.

Borter, G., & O'Brien, G. (2021). Another danger for kids in the age of COVID: Failing grades. *Reuters*. https://www.reuters.com/article/us-health-coronavirus-usa-students-insig/another-danger-for-kids-in-the-age-of-covid-failing-grades-idUSKBN2BL1BF

Callen, I., Carbonari, M. V., DeArmond, M., Dewey, D., Dizon-Ross, E., Goldhaber, D., . . . McDonald, A. (2023). Summer school as a learning loss recovery strategy after COVID-19: Evidence from summer. *CALDER Working Paper No. 291-0823*.

Center for Education Policy Research (CEPR) at Harvard University, & Educational Opportunity Project (EOP) at Stanford University. (2023). The Education Recovery Scorecard. Cambridge, MA: Harvard University. https://www.google.com/url?q = https://educationrecoveryscorecard.org/about/&sa = D&source = docs&ust = 1691605260375231&usg = AOvVaw1oMJwa1q5fu7maYAAFnDI3

Chapman, B. (2023). Carvalho: "Not out of the woods yet"— LAUSD enacts targeted freeze as federal aid expires. *LA School Report*. https://www.laschoolreport.com/carvalho-not-out-of-the-woods-yet-lausd-freezes-hiring-as-federal-aid-expires/?utm_source = The%2074%20Million%20Newsletter&utm_campaign = e0eff8ed0e-EMAIL_CAMPAIGN_2023_04_25_02_50_COPY_01&utm_medium = email&utm_term = 0_-60f9be30e7-%5BLIST_EMAIL_ID%5D

City News Service. (2023). LAUSD to add instructional days over next two school years. *City News Service*. https://www.foxla.com/news/lausd-to-add-instructional-days-over-next-two-school-years

Commonwealth of Virginia. (2023). Brown v. Board of Education Scholarship Committee. http://brownscholarship.virginia.gov/

Conrad, B. (2023). California's math misadventure is about to go national. *The Atlantic*. https://www.theatlantic.com/ideas/archive/2023/10/california-math-framework-algebra/675509/

de Ree, J., Maggioni, M., Pelle, B., Rossignoli, D., Ruijs, N., & Walentek, D. (2023). Closing the income-achievement gap? Experimental evidence from high-dosage tutoring in Dutch primary education. *Economics of Education Review, 94*(102383. https://doi.org/https://doi.org/10.1016/j.econedurev.2023.102383

Empower K-12. (2023). 2023 Bold Performance Schools Report. https://www.empowerk12.org/research-source/2023-bold-performance-report

Espey, E. (2023a). Montgomery County summer school shifts to invitation-only. *MoCo 360 Media*. https://moco360.media/2023/05/25/montgomery-county-summer-school-shifts-to-invitation-only/

Espey, E. (2023b). Some MCPS grading policies incentivize absenteeism, teachers say. *MoCo 360 Media*. https://moco360.media/2023/07/24/some-mcps-grading-policies-incentivize-absenteeism-teachers-say/#:~:text = The%2050%25%20rule%20requires%20teachers,according%20to%20current%20MCPS%20policy.

Fahle, E. M., Kane, N. T. J., Patterson, T., Reardon, S. F., Staiger, D. O., & Stuart, E. A. (2023). School district and community factors associated with learning loss during the COVID-19 pandemic. Cambridge, MA: Center for Education Policy Research, Harvard University.

Feldman, J. (2018). *Grading for equity: What it is, why it matters, and how it can transform schools and classrooms* (1st ed.). Thousand Oaks, CA: Corwin Press.

Fensterwald, J., & Yuxuan, X. (2024). California education issues to watch in 2024—and predictions. *EDSource*. https://edsource.org/2024/california-education-issues-to-watch-in-2024-and-predictions-of-what-might-happen/703252

Ferenchik, M. (2023, December 17). Will lowering reading standard goals hurt Columbus City Schools third graders? *The Columbus Dispatch*. https://www.dispatch.com/story/news/education/2023/12/17/will-lowering-reading-standard-goals-for-columbus-twill-lowering-reading-standard-goals-hurt-columbu/71878288007/

Flaherty, C. (2020). Pass-fail hardball. *Inside Higher Ed*. https://www.insidehighered.com/news/2020/11/30/students-seek-pass-fail-options-again-fall-light-covid-19

Fortin, J. (2022, April 20). More pandemic fallout: The chronically absent student. *The New York Times*. https://www.nytimes.com/2022/04/20/us/school-absence-attendance-rate-covid.html

Geduld, A. (2023). NYC's rising graduation rates bucked national trends. A little-known grading policy may hold clues. *Chalkbeat*. https://ny.chalkbeat.org/2023/7/10/23777035/nyc-schools-pandemic-learning-grading-policy-nx-failing-courses-college-readiness

Gilreath, A. (2023). Tennessee law could hold back thousands of third graders in bid to help kids recover from the pandemic. *The Hechinger Report*. https://hechingerreport.org/tennessee-law-could-hold-back-thousands-of-third-graders-in-bid-to-help-kids-recover-from-the-pandemic/

Goldhaber, D., Kane, T. J., McEachin, A., Morton, E., Patterson, T., & Staiger, D. O. (2022). The consequences of remote and hybrid instruction during the pandemic. Cambridge, MA: National Bureau of Economic Research.

Gottfried, M., Page, L., & Edwards, D. (2022). District strategies to reduce student absenteeism. *EdResearch for Recovery*. https://annenberg.brown.edu/sites/default/files/EdResearch_for_Recovery_Brief_22.pdf

Guryan, J., Ludwig, J., Bhatt, M. P., Cook, P. J., Davis, J. M. V., Dodge, K., . . . Fryer, R. G. (2021). Not too late: Improving academic outcomes among adolescents. Vol. 28531. Cambridge, MA: National Bureau of Economic Research.https://www.nber.org/system/files/working_papers/w28531/w28531.pdf

Harter, C. (2023). Thousands of LAUSD students show up for school—during spring break. *Daily Breeze*. https://www.dailybreeze.com/2023/04/04/thousands-of-lausd-students-show-up-for-school-during-spring-break/

Heaton, P. (2008). Childhood educational disruption and later life outcomes: Evidence from Prince Edward County. *Journal of Human Capital*, *2*, 154–187.

Huffaker, C. (2023, July 14). Cambridge schools are divided over middle school algebra. *The Boston Globe*. https://archive.ph/p3Sp4#selection-1465.0-1465.56

Institute of Educational Sciences. (2023). School Pulse Panel. *Institute of Educational Sciences*. https://ies.ed.gov/schoolsurvey/spp/

Jacobson, L. (2023). Oakland study finds parents as effective as teachers in tutoring young readers. *The 74 Million*. https://www.the74million.org/article/oakland-study-finds-parents-as-effective-as-teachers-in-tutoring-young-readers/

Jones, C. (2023). 33,000 students show up for voluntary "acceleration days" in L.A. Unified. *EdSource*. https://edsource.org/updates/33000-students-show-up-for-voluntary-acceleration-days-in-l-a-unified

Jordan, P. (2023). New study: Kids who scored worst on NAEP missed the most school before the test. *The 74 Million*. https://www.the74million.org/article/new-study-kids-who-scored-worst-on-naep-missed-the-most-school-before-the-test/

Kamenetz, A. (2021). Parents are scrambling after schools suddenly cancel class over staffing and burnout. *NPR*. https://www.npr.org/2021/11/23/1057979170/school-closures-mental-health-days-families-childcare-thanksgiving-break

Kane, T. (2022, May). Kids are far, far behind in school. *The Atlantic*. https://www.theatlantic.com/ideas/archive/2022/05/schools-learning-loss-remote-covid-education/629938/?utm_source = apple_news

Kane, T., & Reardon, S. (2023, May 11). Pandemic learning losses were very steep. They don't have to be permanent. *The New York Times*. https://archive.is/2023.05.11-110838/https:/www.nytimes.com/interactive/2023/05/11/opinion/pandemic-learning-losses-steep-but-not-permanent.html#selection-351.0-351.74

Kogan, V. (2023). Student achievement and learning acceleration on spring 2023 Ohio state tests. Columbus, OH: The Ohio State University. https://glenn.osu.edu/sites/default/files/2023-08/Spring2023_OST_1.pdf

Kraft, M. A., List, J. A., Livingston, J. A., & Sadoff, S. (2022). Online tutoring by college volunteers: Experimental evidence from a pilot program. *AEA Papers and Proceedings*. https://doi.org/10.1257/pandp.20221038

Liu, J., & Lee, M. (2022). Beyond chronic absenteeism: The dynamics and disparities of class absences in secondary school. EdWorkingPaper: 22-562. Annenberg Institute at Brown University. https://doi.org/10.26300/z1fp-0b98

Lohman, I. (2023). Michigan school tutoring funds not likely until spring state officials say. *Bridge Michigan*. https://www.bridgemi.com/talent-education/michigan-school-tutoring-funds-not-likely-until-spring-state-officials-say

Lynch, K., Lee, M., & Loeb, S. (2023). An investigation of Head Start preschool children's executive function, early literacy, and numeracy learning in the midst of the COVID-19 pandemic. *Early Childhood Research Quarterly*, *64*, 255–265. https://doi.org/https://doi.org/10.1016/j.ecresq.2023.04.002

Massachusetts Department of Elementary and Secondary Education. (2023). Massachusetts graduation requirements and related guidance. https://www.doe.mass.edu/mcas/graduation.html

McGuire, E. (2023). Briefing: Tutoring interventions in Montgomery County public schools. https://www.montgomerycountymd.gov/council/Resources/Files/agenda/cm/2023/20230216/20230216_EC1.pdf

Miller, E. (2021). A closer look at Oregon's decision to drop high school graduation "essential skill" requirements. *Oregon Public Broadcasting*. https://www.opb.org/article/2021/09/20/examining-oregon-decision-to-drop-high-school-essential-skill-requirements/

Montgomery Public Schools. (2022). Budget Question and Answer https://ww2.montgomeryschoolsmd.org/departments/budget/archiveDetail.aspx?id = 506

Moore, K. (2023. NYS changes minimum scores for student proficiency in math, English. *Times Union*. https://www.timesunion.com/news/article/new-york-lowers-bar-student-math-english-17841120.php

Natanson, H., St George, D., & Stein, P. (2021, May 23). DC area school systems trying to staff summer programs. *The Washington Post*. https://www.washingtonpost.com/local/education/dmv-summer-school-teacher-shortage/2021/05/23/c6bd0b4e-ba43-11eb-a5fe-bb49dc89a248_story.html

National Assessment of Educational Progress (NAEP). (2023). NAEP long-term trend assessment results: Reading and mathematics. National Center for Education Statistics, Institute of Education Sciences, US Department of Education. https://www.nationsreportcard.gov/highlights/ltt/2023/

National Association of School Psychologists. (2011). Grade retention and social promotion (Position Statement). https://www.nasponline.org/research-and-policy/policy-priorities/position-statements

New Jersey Department of Education. (2023). Understanding the 2021–22 ESSA Academic Progress (Growth) Measure: Relative School Improvement Measure (RSIM). https://www.nj.gov/education/title1/accountability/rsim.shtml

Office of Elementary and Secondary Education and Department of Education. (2021). American Rescue Plan Act Elementary and Secondary School Emergency Relief Fund. Department of Education. https://www.federalregister.gov/documents/2021/04/22/2021-08359/american-rescue-plan-act-elementary-and-secondary-school-emergency-relief-fund

Pagnucco, A. (2023, June 26). State Inspector General: MCPS reports incorrect enrollment. *Montgomery Perspective.* https://montgomeryperspective.com/2023/06/26/state-inspector-general-mcps-reports-incorrect-enrollment/

Pan, W., & Sass, T. (2020). Potential remediation strategies in the wake of COVID-19 school closures: A review of the literature. *Georgia Policy Labs Reports.* Atlanta, GA. https://doi.org/10.57709/30728953

Peetz, C. (2022). Staffing shortages push MCPS summer school program students online. *MoCo 360 Media.* https://moco360.media/2022/06/30/staffing-shortages-push-mcps-summer-school-program-students-online/

Polikoff, M., & Houston, D. (2022). Experts say kids are far behind after COVID; Parents shrug. Why the disconnect? *The 74.* https://www.the74million.org/article/experts-say-kids-are-far-behind-after-covid-parents-shrug-why-the-disconnect/

Randazzo, S. (2023, April 26). Schools are ditching homework, deadlines in favor of "equitable grading." *The Wall Street Journal.* https://www.wsj.com/articles/schools-are-ditching-homework-deadlines-in-favor-of-equitable-grading-dcef7c3e

Reinke, W. M., Smith, T. E., & Herman, K. C. (2019). Family-school engagement across child and adolescent development. *School Psychology, 34*(4), 346–349. https://doi.org/10.1037/spq0000322

Rotuno-Johnson, M. (2023). New NJ school performance reports show student struggles post-COVID. *Patch.* https://patch.com/new-jersey/across-nj/new-nj-school-performance-reports-show-student-struggles-post-covid

Roza, M., & Silberstein, K. (2023). The ESSER fiscal cliff will have serious implications for student equity. *The Brookings Institution.* https://www.brookings.edu/articles/the-esser-fiscal-cliff-will-have-serious-implications-for-student-equity/

Schwartz, H. L., McCombs, J. S., Augustine, C. H., & Leschitz, J. T. (2018). *Getting to work on summer learning: Recommended practices for success* (2nd ed.). Santa Monica, CA: RAND Corporation. https://doi.org/10.7249/RR366-1

Seaman, J. (2023, January 12). Denver public schools facing $9 million budget shortfall, expected to be in the red for years. *The Denver Post.* https://www.denverpost.com/2023/01/12/denver-public-schools-budget-deficit/

Silver, D., Saavedra, A., & Polikoff, M. (2022). Low parent interest in COVID-recovery interventions should worry educators and policymakers alike. *Brookings.* https://www.brookings.edu/articles/low-parent-interest-in-covid-recovery-interventions-should-worry-educators-and-policymakers-alike/

Sitrin, C. (2021). "Parents are powerless": Students face being held back after a year of remote learning. *Politico.* https://www.politico.com/news/2021/04/22/repeat-school-year-482336

Smylie, S. (2022). Illinois test scores highlight pandemic fallout with declines in math, reading. *Chalkbeat.* https://www.chalkbeat.org/chicago/2022/10/27/23425426/illinois-school-report-card-2022-reading-math-covid/

St. George, D. (2023, June 21). National test scores plunge, with still no sign of pandemic recovery. *The Washington Post.* https://archive.ph/ycTWT#selection-389.0-406.0

Strupp, J. (2023). NJ post-COVID school test scores down, absences and troubles up. *App.* https://www.app.com/story/news/education/education-trends/2023/04/06/nj-data-shows-test-scores-down-troubles-up-in-2021-2022-school-year/70085396007/

Styf, J. (2023). Tennessee approves 7,800 appeals of third-grade reading retention law. *The Center Square*. https://www.thecentersquare.com/tennessee/article_c6012b78-271e-11ee-9444-f77748ec9c03.html

The Tennessee Learning Loss Remediation and Student Acceleration Act. (2021). http://www.capitol.tn.gov/Bills/112/Bill/SB7002.pdf

Tucker, J. (2023, December 27). S.F. public schools facing a $420 million deficit. Here's how it got so bad. *San Francisco Chronicle*. https://www.sfchronicle.com/bayarea/article/sfusd-deficit-budget-staff-cuts-18562068.php

Turner, A. (2023). A call to action on early childhood learning disparities in marginalized communities. *Pearson Clinical Assessments*. https://www.pearsonassessments.com/professional-assessments/blog-webinars/blog/2023/06/a-call-to-action-on-early-childhood-learning-disparities-in-marginalized-communities.html?utm_source = MHA-PromoStory_C3973&utm_medium = email&utm_campaign = 7010N000000Cr7kQAC&utm_content=&mc_sid = 704100427

U.S. Department of Education. (2021). Chronic absenteeism in the nation's schools. https://www2.ed.gov/datastory/chronicabsenteeism.html

U.S. Department of Education. (2023). Fact sheet: Biden-Harris administration announces new actions to build on work to accelerate learning and improve student achievement. https://www.ed.gov/news/press-releases/fact-sheet-biden-harris-administration-announces-new-actions-build-work-accelerate-learning-and-improve-student-achievement?utm_content=&utm_medium = email&utm_name=&utm_source = govdelivery&utm_term=

UNESCO. (2020). UN Secretary-General warns of education catastrophe, pointing to UNESCO estimate of 24 million learners at risk of dropping out. https://www.unesco.org/en/articles/un-secretary-general-warns-education-catastrophe-pointing-unesco-estimate-24-million-learners-risk-0

UNESCO. (2023). 244M children won't start the new school year. Paris: UNESCO.

Vazquez Toness, B. (2023). Millions of kids are missing weeks of school as attendance tanks across the US. *Associated Press*. https://projects.apnews.com/features/2023/missing-students-chronic-absenteeism/index.html

Waters, L. (2023a). Education commissioner concedes state tutoring programs are falling short of projected goals. *NJ Education Report*. https://njedreport.com/education-commissioner-concedes-state-tutoring-programs-are-falling-short-of-projected-goals/

Waters, L. (2023b). First peek at last spring's statewide test scores. *NJ Education Report*. https://njedreport.com/exclusive-first-peek-at-last-springs-statewide-test-scores/

Wilson, H., & Wade, J. (2023). Montgomery County public schools Montgomery Virtual Academy (MVA) program. https://ww2.montgomeryschoolsmd.org/departments/sharedaccountability/reports/2023/Virtual%20Academy%20FINAL.pdf

Winter, D. (2023, June 12). Minneapolis school district on the brink of insolvency, state involvement. *Minnesota Reformer*. https://minnesotareformer.com/2023/06/12/minneapolis-school-district-on-the-brink-of-insolvency-state-involvement/

World Bank, The Bill & Melinda Gates Foundation, FCDO, UNESCO, UNICEF, & USAID. (2022). Guide for learning recovery and acceleration: Using the RAPID framework to address COVID-19 learning losses and build forward better. Washington, DC: World Bank.

5

Disrupted Delivery of Special Education Services and Accommodations

While educational disruption during the COVID-19 pandemic affected *all* students, it was particularly detrimental for many children with disabilities. For those who have developmental delays, medical conditions, or social and emotional difficulties, the public schools represent a primary access point for much-needed services and family support. At the beginning of the COVID-19 pandemic, more than 7 million children were receiving special education services regulated under the Individuals with Disabilities Education Act (IDEA; National Center for Education Statistics, 2021). The labyrinthine system that regulates eligibility and delivery of those services was severely disrupted, leading to delays in the identification of children in need of support, changes in service delivery, and in some cases, suspension of ongoing supports.

The full scope of the impact on these vulnerable children is yet unknown, but there is emerging evidence for concern. Diamond and Merrick (2022) wrote that disability research related to pandemic disruption "is just beginning." The authors noted that although early intervention for children with atypical development is the standard of care, data from the Centers for Disease Control (CDC) and the Association of University Centers on Disabilities (AUCD) (Centers for Disease Control and Prevention [CDC], 2022) indicate evaluation and intervention services were severely impacted during the pandemic, with fewer children evaluated, and delivery of hybrid services negatively impacting the breadth and depth of required evaluation services. In this chapter, we discuss how services for children with disabilities or developmental risk factors were disrupted at all ages.

Special Education 101

In the United States, the federal government guarantees each child access to a free and appropriate public education (FAPE). The universal right to public

Neurodevelopment in the Post-Pandemic World. Molly Colvin, Jennifer Linton Reesman, and Tannahill Glen, Oxford University Press. © Oxford University Press 2024. DOI: 10.1093/9780197762660.003.0005

education emerged following a long and hard-fought battle by civil and disability rights activists, ultimately leading to the passage of the landmark Rehabilitation Act of 1973. Prior to this federal legislation, children with disabilities were routinely barred from public school education or offered substandard educational opportunities. Only one in five U.S. children with disabilities were educated in 1970 (U.S. Department of Education, 2023a). Judith Heumann, a leader in the fight for the passage of the Rehabilitation Act, was not permitted to attend school in the 1950s because she used a wheelchair for mobility after contracting polio in 1949 (Heumann, n.d.). As a result of her efforts and those of many others, Section 504 of the Rehabilitation Act now requires institutions receiving federal funds, including public schools, to provide reasonable accommodations to support inclusion (U.S. Department of Education, n.d.-a).

To this day, a plan that lists accommodations for a student with a physical or cognitive disability is known as a Section 504 plan or "504 plan." Accommodations provided by Section 504 may include modifications to the physical environment (e.g., access to an elevator for a child with mobility limitations), daily routine (e.g., opportunity for a child with attention-deficit/hyperactivity disorder [ADHD] to stand or move in the classroom), or curriculum (e.g., access to spell-check or extended time on testing for a child with dyslexia). Groups of individuals who should be protected from discrimination were later specified in the Americans with Disabilities Act (ADA), which was first passed in 1990 and revised in 2008. The ADA also recognizes that cognitive and physical disabilities may be permanent or temporary (U.S. Department of Justice Civil Rights Division, n.d.).

In addition to accommodations, the current special education system includes specialized instruction from school personnel. Learning services may target specific academic (e.g., reading, writing, math) or cognitive (e.g., language) skills. Other services aim to support students' mental and physical health with counseling, social skills training, occupational therapy, physical therapy, and/or school-based nursing. Services may be provided either informally (e.g., through response-to-intervention [RTI]) and/or formally through the special education system (U.S. Department of Education, 2023a).

The framework for determining eligibility for special education services is outlined by IDEA. Initially passed by Congress in 1990, IDEA extended the Education for all Handicapped Children Act (EHA) that was first passed in 1975 (U.S. Department of Education, 2023a). IDEA intends to provide equal access to educational opportunities for children with disabilities between birth and young adulthood.

If a child is found eligible, then special education service delivery is formalized as part of an individualized education program (IEP). An IEP may also include accommodations, and a child who needs both accommodations and services should have an IEP (i.e., accommodations that would be included in a 504 plan are included in the IEP) (U.S. Department of Education, n.d.-b). For example, a child with a language disorder may receive the *service* of speech and language therapy from a speech and language pathologist, and the *accommodation* of having extra time to respond to a teacher's question. Similarly, a child with dyslexia may receive reading *services* from a special education teacher, and the *accommodation* of not being asked to read aloud in front of her peers. A deaf child may receive instruction in American Sign Language, or sign language interpretation *services*, and the *accommodation* of closed captioning on video-based instruction.

A key IDEA principle—highly relevant to the pandemic-era educational disruption—is classroom placement in the least restrictive environment (LRE). There is a presumption that the general education classroom in a child's local school is the LRE. For example, there must be evidence that a child's math skills are below grade-based expectations and interfering with educational access before they will be found eligible for pull-out math instruction with the special education teacher. There must be evidence that the child is not making effective progress before they can receive services that reduce their time in the regular education setting. The intent of this principle is to allow for children with disabilities to be "mainstreamed" as much as possible, even if it requires the school to provide support services to do so (U.S. Department of Education, n.d.-b).

As such, LRE also requires evidence that the existing interventions are not meeting a child's needs before services are intensified, or the child is offered an alternative educational setting. Special education services cannot be offered preemptively to children who are "at risk" or to prevent an emerging gap between the student's skills and those of their peers; the gap must first exist before services will be initiated. However, in 2004 when IDEA was reauthorized, public schools were permitted to allocate federal funds to response-to-intervention (RTI) programs designed to meet the needs of struggling students who do not reach the threshold for impairment, before they receive a school-based evaluation to determine eligibility for special education services (e.g., reading recovery group) (U.S. Department of Education, 2011).

School-based psychoeducational evaluations are required to determine eligibility and can be requested by teachers and school staff or by parents. Evaluations may be performed by school-based assessment teams, except when a school district or parent has requested that a neuropsychologist or psychologist perform an independent educational evaluation (IEE) (U.S. Department of Education, 2017b). The school-based assessment team usually does not offer clinical diagnoses or comprehensive treatment plans (e.g., whether therapy, medication, or further medical evaluation may be needed), as the purpose and intention of the evaluation center on educational needs. Interpretation of test results is usually limited to identifying that a child's functioning is below age-based expectations (see Table 5.1).

In other words, psychoeducational evaluations typically identify that a developmental delay exists, but they may not tell you *why* there is a developmental delay. This is often a point of confusion for parents and clinical providers when they review psychoeducational evaluations and IEPs. IEPs identify one of 13 disability classifications as the basis for special education service eligibility (U.S. Department of Education, n.d.-b). In some cases, these disability classifications align with clinical diagnoses (e.g., autism spectrum disorder is an IDEA disability classification and a clinical diagnosis), but having the disability classification does not necessarily mean that a clinical diagnosis has been made. This is why many effective school-based evaluation teams will encourage the parent to follow up with their pediatrician and/or a developmental specialist if problems are identified (see Table 5.2).

For clinicians and parents, it is important to understand that a clinical diagnosis *does not automatically qualify a child for special education services.* The school must still perform an evaluation to find that the clinical condition is a disability limiting the child's school performance. For example, if a psychologist finds that a child has anxiety or depression, then the school must also determine the condition is impacting functioning in school before services can be offered (e.g., school-based counseling, placement in a therapeutic classroom). In the case of learning disabilities, evidence for a clinical syndrome (e.g., developmental dyslexia) must be paired with evidence that it significantly impacts academic performance before the child will be found eligible for intervention.

Nonetheless, psychoeducational evaluations are critical in identifying the presence of an underlying neurodevelopmental disorder. They often include

Table 5.1 Key Terms Related to Special Education Services in the United States

Term	Definition
Free and appropriate public education (FAPE)	The principle established by the Rehabilitation Act of 1973 and regulated by IDEA that all children in the United States, including those with disabilities, are entitled to a free public education that appropriately meets their needs.
Least restrictive environment	The principle established by the Rehabilitation Act of 1973 and regulated by IDEA that children should be placed in the regular education environment unless there is evidence that they cannot access the curriculum and/or are not making effective academic progress.
Evaluation	An evaluation is performed by the public school system to identify a child's strengths and weaknesses and to determine whether the child has a disability that requires special education services.
Individualized education program (IEP)	A formal plan, written by the special education team in accordance with IDEA regulations that specifies (1) a child's disability classification, (2) targets for intervention with measurable progress goals, (3) service delivery frequency and intensity, both within and outside of the regular education setting, and (4) accommodations.
504 plan	A formal plan, written by the 504 coordinator or special education team in accordance with ADA regulations that specifies academic accommodations that the child requires to access the regular education classroom.
Early childhood special education (ECSE)	Services provided to toddlers and preschoolers (age 3 to 5) as part of an individualized education program (IEP). These may include occupational therapy, physical therapy, speech and language therapy, and applied behavior therapy (ABA) therapy.
Early intervention services	Services provided to infants and toddlers (birth to age 3) that are regulated at the state level. These are often provided in the child's home and may include occupational therapy, physical therapy, speech and language therapy, ABA therapy, and other family support.
Individuals with Disabilities Education Act (IDEA)	IDEA was passed by Congress in 1990, extending the Education for all Handicapped Children Act (EHA) first passed in 1975. IDEA aims to provide equal access to educational opportunities for children with disabilities and provides a framework for determining eligibility for special education services.
Individualized Family Services Plan (IFSP)	A written plan that specifies the early intervention services that a family receives.
Response to intervention (RTI)	A multitier approach to the early identification and support of struggling students, prior to finding eligibility for special education services and accommodations.

Table 5.2 IDEA Disability Classifications and Possible Corresponding Clinical Conditions or DSM-5 Diagnoses (IDEA, 2017)

IDEA Disability Classification	Possible Clinical Conditions or DSM-5 Diagnosis
Specific learning disability	Specific learning disorder (DSM-5) Developmental dyslexia Developmental dysgraphia Developmental dyscalculia
Other health impairment	Attention-deficit/hyperactivity disorder (ADHD) Tourette syndrome Epilepsy Cancer, including brain tumors Diabetes AsthmaCardiac conditions HemophiliaKidney disease Sickle cell anemia
Autism spectrum disorder	Autism spectrum disorder
Emotional disturbance	Anxiety (e.g., generalized anxiety disorder, specific phobia, etc.) Obsessive-compulsive disorder Depression Bipolar disorder Schizophrenia/schizoaffective disorder
Speech or language impairment	Language disorder Speech sound disorder Social communication disorder Stuttering
Visual impairment, including blindness	Multiple clinical conditions
Deafness	Multiple clinical conditions
Hearing impairment	Multiple clinical conditions
Deaf-blindness	Multiple clinical conditions
Orthopedic impairment	Cerebral palsy Muscular dystrophy Amputations Congenital abnormalities Multiple clinical conditions (e.g., poliomyelitis)
Intellectual disability	Multiple clinical conditions
Traumatic brain injury	Traumatic brain injury (TBI)
Multiple disabilities	Multiple clinical conditions

Source: From U.S. Department of Education and Individuals with Disabilities Education Act (2017) Sec. 300.8 (c)(4). Available at: https://sites.ed.gov/idea/regs/b/a/300.8.

comprehensive and standardized assessment of cognitive (e.g., intellectual functioning, speech, and language), academic (e.g., reading, writing, and math achievement), psychological (e.g., anxiety, attention, social skills), and physical (e.g., fine motor skills, gross motor skills) development. Once eligible for an IEP, reevaluation is then performed every 3 years. Examination of serial psychoeducational evaluations can provide critical data about an individual child's developmental progress during childhood and adolescence; the relevance of pandemic-related alterations in development to these evaluations is clear, and measuring individual and group progress through successive grades has become a major focus of learning loss research.

The remainder of this chapter will focus on delays and disruptions in early intervention services, special education services, and accommodations, as well as avenues for remedy for those who have experienced those disruptions.

Disruption to Early Intervention Services

Beginning in 1986, the EHA was extended to provide services to infants and toddlers with developmental delays or disabilities, thus launching early intervention (EI) services, which were later integrated into IDEA (Ramey & Ramey, 1998). In fall 2019, 3.7% of infants and toddlers in the United States—over 420,000 children under age 3 years—were receiving EI services (Office of Special Education and Rehabilitative Services, 2023), which have long been associated with improved developmental outcomes (Ramey & Ramey, 1998). Effective early childhood interventions (birth to age 5 years) have also been associated with a positive return on monetary investment (i.e., in the long run, the government spends less money on individual supports), and this may be especially true for younger and at-risk children (Karoly et al., 2005).

EI services are provided by individual states to improve functioning in five developmental areas: physical, cognitive, communication, social/emotional, and adaptive development. Specific services may include speech and language therapy, occupational therapy, physical therapy, or parent counseling. Children may also receive medical and nursing services, including access to assistive devices (e.g., hearing aids, mobility devices) (U.S. Department of Education, 2017a). For children who have autism spectrum disorders (ASDs), EI also often provides access to much-needed behavioral therapy, including applied behavior analysis (ABA) (Commonwealth of Massachusetts, n.d.; U.S. Department of Education, 2017a).

By Fall 2020, the number of infants and toddlers receiving EI services had dropped for the first time in at least the 10 preceding years. Only 3.2% of children under 3 years old were receiving EI services, which corresponds to 60,000 fewer children than in the year before. Even more worrisome was that the greatest decline in service delivery was for younger children. In Fall 2019, 6.2% of 2-year-olds were receiving EI services—by Fall 2020, only 5.3% were receiving services (Office of Special Education and Rehabilitative Services, 2023). The most recent available U.S. Department of Education data indicated that the number of children receiving EI services rebounded in 2021–2022, but it still remained lower than the numbers served in 2019 (Office of Special Education Programs, 2023), suggesting that many infants and toddlers who needed services did not receive them during the first 2 years of the COVID-19 pandemic.

There were likely multiple contributing factors to the drop in EI service delivery. First, there was a decline in referrals for evaluations that are needed to establish eligibility for EI services. Pediatricians are a primary source of these referrals, but preventative care visits dropped steeply in the first few months of the pandemic (Schweiberger et al., 2021). In a national survey, referrals for EI services fell in 45 states, dropping by 25% or more in half (24) of those states (Gillispie, 2021).

Second, even if a referral was made, evaluations to determine eligibility for EI services were delayed. While some diagnoses will automatically qualify a child for EI services (e.g., deafness, Down syndrome, prematurity), eligibility criteria are set by individual states, with varying thresholds for "at-risk" children (U.S. Department of Education, 2022b). In many states, these required evaluations were suspended during the early stages of the COVID-19 pandemic. In a national survey of professionals who typically provide evaluations to determine eligibility for EI or preschool special education services, half (51%) reported that evaluations were paused at least temporarily during 2020 and 2021 (Steed et al., 2023).

There is emerging evidence that disruptions to EI services during the COVID-19 pandemic exacerbated preexisting economic disparities. Although EI services fall under the umbrella of IDEA, they are administered at the state level. Children in states with the fewest economic resources (lower state median income) have fewer children receiving EI services, including during the COVID-19 pandemic. For example, in fall 2020, 10%

of children under 3 years received EI services in Massachusetts (state with a high median income), while only 1% received services in Arkansas or Hawaii. COVID-19 relief funding provided some additional support for EI services, but this was not equally distributed across states, especially when cost of living is considered (Friedman-Krauss & Barnett, 2023).

Racial disparities in the provision of EI services also became more pronounced. In Fall 2020, White children were more likely than Black, Hispanic, and Asian children to receive EI services (Friedman-Krauss & Barnett, 2023). In a national survey of EI state coordinators during the first year of the COVID-19 pandemic, EI referral rates had dropped in five states for families identifying as Black, Latino, or with limited English proficiency. EI service delivery rates had dropped for Black children and those from families with limited English proficiency in five states, for Latino children in seven states, and for families with low incomes in four states (The Education Trust, 2021). Combined, the cumulative impact of these inequities is likely to manifest as even greater racial and economic disparities in long-term outcomes for the cohort of children who had early developmental concerns during the COVID-19 pandemic.

Even when services were available, the way that they were delivered was often altered. EI services have traditionally been provided in the home setting, with only a small number of children receiving EI services in a community-based setting. There was a decline in community-based EI services (4% drop) during the early phase of the COVID-19 pandemic (Friedman-Krauss & Barnett, 2023). In Fall 2020, most EI services (92.7%) were still provided in the child's home. However, home service delivery methods (i.e., in person, virtual) were not reported (Office of Special Education and Rehabilitative Services, 2023) (Table 5.3). A CDC study of those providing EI services indicated that like public school instruction, care quickly integrated telehealth, with more than half (57%) reporting the transition to hybrid services (Centers for Disease Control and Prevention [CDC], 2022), which may have still been counted as home-based services.

As was the case for the transition to hybrid education for school-age children, there were limited preexisting studies of the efficacy of telehealth EI services. Research had primarily focused on extending access of EI services to rural families, with some finding qualitative support for telehealth EI (Ashburner et al., 2016; Cason, 2009; Cason et al., 2012). However, studies comparing developmental outcomes by service delivery method were limited, and states had only just begun to discuss statewide policies for telehealth

Table 5.3 U.S. Department of Education's Report on the Number of Infants and Toddlers Receiving Early Intervention Services From Fall 2011 to Fall 2020

	Total Served under Part C (Birth through age 2)			
Year	**In the 50 States, DC, PR, and the Four Outlying Areas**	**In the 50 States and DC**	**Resident Population Birth through Age 2 in the 50 States and DC**	**Percentage of resident population birth through age 2 served under Part C in the 50 States and DC**
2011	336,895	331,636	11,937,319	2.8
2012	333,982	329,859	11,904,557	2.8
2013	339,071	335,023	11,886,860	2.8
2014	350,581	346,394	11,868,245	2.9
2015	357,715	354,081	11,913,185	3.0
2016	372,896	369,672	11,957,307	3.1
2017	388,694	386,155	11,936,322	3.2
2018	409,315	406,582	11,752,545	3.5
2019	427,234	424,318	11,534,695	3.7
2020	363,387	361,462	11,361,919	3.2

Percentage was calculated by dividing the number of infants and toddlers birth through age 2 served under IDEA, Part C, on the state-designated data collection date in the year by the estimated U.S. resident population birth through age 2 for that year and then multiplying the result by 100.

Source: U.S. Department of Education, ED*Facts Metadata and Process System* (E*MAPS*), OMB #1820-0557: IDEA Part C Child Count and Settings Collection, 2011–20. U.S. Department of Commerce, U.S. Census Bureau. Intercensal Estimates of the Resident Population by Single Year of Age and Sex for States and the United States: April 1, 2011 to July 1, 2020, 2011–20.

Data for 2011 were accessed in Fall 2012. Data for 2012 were accessed in Fall 2013. Data for 2013 were accessed in Fall 2014. Data for 2014 were accessed in Fall 2015. Data for 2015 were accessed in Fall 2016. Data for 2016 were accessed in Fall 2017. Data for 2017 were accessed in Fall 2018. Data for 2018 were accessed in Fall 2019. Data for 2019 were accessed in Fall 2020. Data for 2020 were accessed in Fall 2021. For actual IDEA data used, go to https://www2.ed.gov/programs/osepidea/618-data/state-level-data-files/index.html.

From the U.S. Department of Education, Office of Special Education and Rehabilitative Services and Office of Special Education Programs (2023) 44th Annual Report to Congress on the Implementation of the Individuals with Disabilities Education Act, 2022. Washington, DC.

EI services (e.g., Cole et al., 2016). Thus, when the Department of Education suspended typical compliance regulations during the COVID-19 pandemic, states were permitted to independently choose how to modify EI service delivery. Without guidance or prior research, the way that early intervention services were provided by telehealth during the COVID-19 pandemic was likely highly variable, with yet unknown efficacy.

Even when states returned to in-person EI services, eligible infants and toddlers were sometimes unable to secure them due to staffing shortages. Even into 2023, some eligible children in Rhode Island were still not receiving their legally protected supports or services (Sherman & Machado, 2023), including those with significant developmental delays and those without language by 3 years of age. State officials confirmed that families could seek recourse under the courts, but this begs the question: what relief would come to families under the law, if what they were seeking was immediate access to interventions? What would be the point of due process or relief under the courts and IDEA when critical developmental windows had already been missed?

Disruption to Special Education and Head Start Services for Preschoolers

Under IDEA, when children reach the age of 3 years, special education services may be continued through the public school system. The transition from EI typically involves the initiation of an IEP, which may remain in effect throughout the rest of formal schooling so long as a student continues to meet eligibility criteria. Between the ages of 3 and 5 years (kindergarten entry), services are known as early childhood special education services (ECSE) (U.S. Department of Education, 2023b).

During the COVID-19 pandemic, fewer 3-year-olds transitioned from EI to ECSE services, suggesting that there were many preschoolers who lost access to needed developmental services. In Fall 2020, 56.2% of 3-year-olds exiting EI services were found eligible for ECSE services compared to 60.3% who had transitioned in Fall 2019 (Office of Special Education and Rehabilitative Services, 2023; U.S. Department of Education, 2023c). During the pandemic, significantly more Black children were lost during this transition process than White or Hispanic/Latino children (Friedman-Krauss & Barnett, 2023). This loss of these younger students mirrors the stunning report by Vazquez Toness and Lurye (2023) about older students lost to the system.

There were also declines in the number of preschoolers receiving ECSE services. In Fall 2019, 6.7% (793,542) children between the ages of 3 and 5 years were receiving special education services. One year later, the number of enrolled children had declined for the first time since at least 2011, to 6.2% (739,739) children (Office of Special Education and Rehabilitative Services,

2023). Data from the 2021–2022 school year had been recently released at the time of this writing and indicated continuation of this downward trend (U.S. Department of Education, 2023c), suggesting that many children did not receive needed developmental services during the COVID-19 pandemic.

The location of service delivery also changed. In Fall 2019, 11.3% of children were receiving ECSE services *outside* of a regular early childhood program or separate classroom (10.4% in Fall 2018). By Fall 2020, that number had increased to 15.6% of children—so fewer preschoolers were receiving special education services in a formal school setting (Office of Special Education and Rehabilitative Services, 2023; Office of Special Education Programs, 2023). Again, preschool children identifying as Black, African American, and Asian were less likely to be receiving ECSE services than prior to the pandemic. As with EI services, there were also likely economic disparities; children in higher income states were more likely to receive ECSE services even prior to the pandemic (Friedman-Krauss & Barnett, 2023).

Head Start is another federally funded program designed to promote early childhood development for vulnerable preschool children. Started in 1965, Head Start provides services for children under age 5 years whose families meet the federal low-income guidelines. Early Head Start serves infants and toddlers, while Head Start serves 3- and 4-year-olds. Services may be provided in a center, in the child's home, or in a daycare setting (Office of Head Start, 2023).

There is extensive research showing that children who received Head Start services are more likely to have better educational and developmental outcomes. Importantly, Head Start programs reach a significant number of children who do not receive special education services; nationally, only 13% of Head Start children and 12% of Early Head Start children are also eligible for IDEA-regulated services (Friedman-Krauss et al., 2022). In 2022, Head Start was funded to serve 833,000 children and families (U.S. Department of Health & Human Services, 2023).

At the beginning of the COVID-19 pandemic, a national survey of Head Start providers found that 73% had difficulty providing virtual services because families did not have reliable technology or Internet access. More than half also reported difficulty recruiting and hiring staff (Shaw et al., 2023). Prior to the pandemic, 40% of eligible children were enrolled, but it is estimated that only 30% of eligible children received Head Start services in the first year of the pandemic. Specifically, 33% (257,000) fewer children attended Head Start programs and 10% (22,000) fewer children attended Early Head Start. Enrollment declined sharply, with state-based variability.

Head Start enrollment declined by more than 40% in six states (Illinois, Mississippi, New Mexico, Nevada, South Carolina, and Oklahoma), and Early Head Start enrollment declined in all but seven states (Friedman-Krauss et al., 2022). To combat these challenges, the federal COVID-19 relief fund included $2 billion for Head Start programming (U.S. Department of Health & Human Services, 2021).

For the children who did participate in Head Start programs during the pandemic, outcomes data are relatively limited and somewhat mixed. There was some promising data indicating that children engaged in virtual Head Start programs still made gains in cognitive and academic skill development (Groom-Thomas et al., 2021). However, another study suggested that those participating in in-person programming made more progress in the acquisition of early academic skills (Lynch et al., 2023).

Research on the efficacy of Head Start programming during the pandemic will need to account for a prolonged recovery period. Many Head Start programs struggled to quickly regain their footing after the onset of the COVID-19 pandemic. Staffing shortages remain a challenge. In Massachusetts, which serves 11,000 children through Head Start programs, three programs have closed due to staffing. In the city of Boston alone, there were 400 children on the waiting list for Head Start slots in Fall 2023 (DeCosta-Klipa, 2023). Nationally, even in October 2023, 14% of Head Start classrooms remained closed and 55% of programs had applied for a change in scope of services since 2020 (National Head Start Association, 2023).

Combined, these data strongly suggest that vulnerable children are entering the public school system without the same benefit of services aimed to promote early childhood development that were available prior to the COVID-19 pandemic. This is particularly concerning, given that many children also delayed entry to kindergarten, and that program enrollment continues to lag, even years after the beginning of the COVID-19 pandemic. Given the extensive evidence showing better outcomes from participation in these programs, we should brace for more negative long-term developmental and sociological outcomes.

Disruption to Special Education Services in School-Aged Children

In 2019–2020, 14% of school-aged students—more than 7 million students—received special education services under IDEA, with learning disorders as the largest classification category (National Center for Education Statistics, 2021). In the 10 years prior to Fall 2019, the number of school-aged children receiving special education services steadily increased. This upward trend then halted: in Fall 2019, 9.7% (6,374,498) of school-aged children were receiving services under IDEA; this number remained static in Fall 2020 (9.7%, 6,370,821). At the time of this writing, data had been recently released for the 2020–2021 school year, suggesting perhaps a slight increase in school-aged children receiving services (U.S. Department of Education, 2023c).

Critically, this lack of expected increase in the number of school-aged children receiving services likely reflects fewer children being identified as having a learning disability, which is also the IDEA disability category that has the most students. Across the 13 IDEA disability categories, the percentage of students receiving services in Fall 2020 was stable compared to 2019, *except for* specific learning disability, where the number of students decreased from 3.6% to 3.3%, the lowest percentage of students with this classification in the previous 10 years (Office of Special Education and Rehabilitative Services, 2023).

These statistics highlight a critical point in examining educational disruption: eligibility for a learning disability classification under IDEA requires formal assessment of academic skills, which was often deferred during the COVID-19 pandemic. In cases where testing occurred, *interpretation of low test scores may have been seen as an indicator of learning loss, rather than an indicator of a learning disability.*

Delays in official reporting can complicate accurate estimation of impacts of school closures. At the time that this book was being written (Fall 2023), the U.S. Department of Education's most recent Annual Report to Congress only reported data on IDEA service delivery through Fall 2020. However, there are reasons to suspect lower numbers of children receiving special education services. When public schools transitioned to remote instruction in Spring 2020, scheduled initial evaluations and reevaluations were postponed. By Fall 2020, nearly 2,000 children and families were waiting for psychoeducational evaluations in Boston alone (Cohan, 2020). Some districts also reported fewer referrals for psychoeducational evaluations. In New York City, during the 2020–2021 school year, there was a 57% decline in referrals to determine eligibility for special education services. For Black students, referral rates declined by 66% (Zimmerman, 2021).

Altogether, the available data point to a decline in eligibility for special education services among the most vulnerable children after the onset of the

COVID-19 pandemic. Younger children, those with learning disabilities, and those from historically marginalized racial and ethnic groups were less likely to receive special education services. Compounding these factors, children who receive special education services are also more likely to live in households with fewer socioeconomic resources. Two thirds of children who receive special education services also have special health care needs, and 39% have health care coverage through Medicaid or the Children's Health Insurance Program (CHIP), which is only available to those families with lower household incomes (Williams & Musumeci, 2022). Altogether, some of the children who most needed special education services were the ones who were least likely to receive it during the COVID-19 pandemic.

Vanishing Accommodations and Interventions

In Spring 2020, in response to confusion about provision of special education services when schools transitioned to virtual learning, the U.S. Department of Education (DOE) indicated that public school districts were still legally obligated to provide special education services and accommodations under remote learning during the pandemic. However, the DOE also gave schools discretion in how to implement services and accommodations, acknowledging that remote learning may impede schools' ability to provide services in the typical manner (U.S. Department of Education, 2020). The DOE published a supplement in March 2020, confirming that provision of special education services remotely would be an acceptable interpretation of federal law, stating "We remind schools they should not opt to close or decline to provide distance instruction, at the expense of students, to address matters pertaining to services for students with disabilities" (Individuals with Disabilities Education Act [IDEA], 2020). In short, schools were informed they should not avoid shutting down or transitioning to virtual instruction out of concern they could not provide special education services.

As a result of DOE guidance, there was variability in the implementation of Section 504 plans and IEPs beginning in Spring 2020. While some services were easier to adapt for remote instruction (e.g., speech and language therapy, reading instruction), there are no studies demonstrating efficacy of such interventions, particularly over a prolonged period for children and adolescents who have developmental disabilities. Unfortunately, service delivery requiring greater in-person interaction (e.g., applied behavior analysis, occupational therapy, physical therapy, Braille instruction, orientation and mobility training) was significantly impacted by social distancing requirements and the physical closure of school buildings.

Many parents of children with developmental disabilities despaired about the lack of access to services. In interviews with these parents during the COVID-19 pandemic, Sonnenschein et al. (2022) identified three main themes: (1) special education and related service hours decreased during virtual learning; (2) children were unable to participate in virtual learning without significant adult support; and (3) parents often were unable to provide their children with assistance due to other commitments, including work and childcare. For the youngest children, and for children with sensory disabilities, or other disabilities that required one-on-one support to engage in learning, distance or virtual means of attempting to provide education were woefully inadequate. Most of the difficulties these families reported experiencing (e.g., limited access to services) were unique to children with disabilities (Sonnenschein et al., 2022). A majority (74%) of parents and caregivers of children with intellectual and developmental disabilities reported lost access to at least one therapy or education service during the pandemic (Jeste et al., 2020). School service loss was compounded by disrupted access to private and community-based services (e.g., physical therapy in an outpatient rehabilitation setting; Cankurtaran et al., 2021).

During the pandemic and the period of educational disruption, schools had difficulty providing specialized, virtual educational technology to children with sensory disabilities. For instance, children with visual impairment lost access to in-person orientation and mobility training services as well as tactile feedback needed to promote learning and Braille literacy (Battistin et al., 2021). In the rush to provide computers and tablets to children to access virtual-based instructional models, children with low vision struggled to access monitors that provided sufficient visual access if they needed materials enlarged, and they may have lost access to materials that would provide enlarged printing services during home-based instruction. Deaf or hard-of-hearing (D/HH) students often did not have computer-assisted real-time transcription (CART) and/or access to sign language interpretation during distance learning. Systematic critical literature reviews of access to online instruction for D/HH students identified several factors that hindered access, including difficulties having full access to sign language interpreters during video-based instruction and limitations with participating in discussion in which multiple individuals used sign language as cues for turn taking (Schafer et al., 2021).

In 2020, one of the popular video conferencing platforms being used by schools to provide live instruction did not offer free live captioning for D/HH users until a lawsuit was filed on their behalf. The lawsuit filing posited that the video conferencing platform, Zoom, had violated Title III of the Americans with Disabilities Act (see Kane et al. v. Zoom Video Communications Inc. et al., 2020). At the time of the lawsuit filing, there was also a petition on the website Change.org that garnered 80,000 signatures, asking for Zoom to make captions freely available. Following the filing of this lawsuit, the video conferencing platform slowly rolled out availability to automatic captions to all free account holders and users that requested them via a form. The platform finally made the captioning feature available to all users in Fall 2021 when most schools had returned to in-person instruction on a more regular basis. Disability advocates pointed out the fact that it was disappointing to see a technology company with the capability to provide accessibility of virtual communication delay the accessibility features. This difficulty represented much of the challenges of accessibility within virtual and disrupted education: accessibility options were not made readily available without significant public pressure (Metraux, 2021).

For students who were involved in the juvenile justice system and identified as having disabilities or special education needs, there was an abrupt and profound cessation of accessible educational services. Students who were enrolled in an alternative high school program within the District of Columbia jail were provided with paper packets of work and limited access to any digital instructional materials, and zero in-person instruction for well over a year. This practice only ended when an injunction ordered the public schools to begin providing instruction in June 2021, following filing of a class action lawsuit on behalf of incarcerated students (Stein, 2021). In the initial filing, it was asserted that students did not receive live virtual instruction or any of the additional services identified within their IEP, including mental health counseling. In September 2023, a settlement was reached in which affected students were to receive significant compensatory education packages based on how much time each student was denied instruction (Lumpkin, 2023). The funds can be used for tutoring, classes, college courses, or vocational programs.

Seeking Remedy for Disruption

A variety of lawsuits seeking remedy for the disruption of special education are working their way through the courts. The failure to provide legally mandated services for students with disabilities resulted in subsequent U.S. DOE Office of Civil Rights investigations and settlement agreements in two large school districts (Los Angeles Unified School District and Fairfax County Public Schools). Both investigations found (and settlement agreements concurred) that these districts failed to provide a free and appropriate public education to qualified students with disabilities, in violation of Section 504 (U.S. Department of Education, 2022a, 2022c). As a result of these settlement agreements, school teams that oversee Section 504 plan implementation and IEPs were tasked with determining whether students received mandated accommodations or interventions, and if the child would be found eligible for compensatory services. By September 2023, Fairfax County Public Schools reported they had reviewed 96% of children with IEPs for their eligibility for compensatory services and found approximately 20% of the students were eligible for compensatory services (Gelman, 2023).

In 2022, the DOE concluded that the Los Angeles Unified School District had not only failed to track service delivery but had also informed parents that the district was not obligated to provide compensatory services (Esquivel & Gomez, 2022). For students with disabilities, virtual instruction may not have been provided in an accessible format, and assistance or accessible technology was simply not provided (Shakespeare et al., 2021).

Blume (2021) described how a California court ordered schools to provide distance learning comparable to in-person special education programs made available before the pandemic. To prioritize in-person classes, California legislation deemed virtual instruction was lesser in quality than live teaching. The upshot was that students with moderate to severe support needs not only experienced a lapse in special education services in 2020, but when schools reopened, the only remote education available was entirely inadequate; families only had the choice of a "general education" curriculum, without special education services, or a "home and hospital" curriculum, comprising only 5 hours per week of instruction. Virtual coursework was offered as a type of independent study format, and it was not made available to some preschool students or some students with disabilities. Thus, students with the most need experienced an even greater duration and magnitude of disruption in comparison to their peers in general education. This created a distressing dilemma for parents of children with multiple medical disabilities: children were no longer able to access a reasonable virtual means of schooling at a time when children with certain medical conditions (children with tracheostomies or chronic lung disease) were being advised by their medical providers to avoid in-person schooling.

As described earlier, compensatory education services refer to special education and related aids and services provided to remedy any educational or other deficits that resulted from schools failing to provide students with a disability (with an IEP or Section 504 plan) the evaluations or services to which they were entitled to during the COVID-19 pandemic. Recoupment services, in contrast, differ in their aim and definition: they are "needed services to address learning loss and/or lack of progress toward IEP goals and objectives resulting from school facility closures" (Los Angeles Unified School District, 2022). Recoupment services are an additional means of providing educational support to directly address learning loss or lack of progress toward educational goals that resulted from school and facility closures (Los Angeles Unified School District, 2022).

Class action lawsuits filed in Fairfax County, Virginia, in 2022 allege bias against those seeking relief: it was reported 83% of hearing officers assessing due process complaints in Northern Virginia have never ruled in parents' favor in the past decade (Arundel, 2022a, 2022b). In 2023, the federal government opened an investigation into the Virginia Department of Education and their guidance offered to local educational agencies about pandemic special education (Jacobson, 2023). The basis for some of these complaints includes specific actions in which children with disabilities were excluded from the in-person learning hubs that opened to allow children to receive supervision during the online school offered. Other potentially discriminatory practices included a lack of provision services in the manner or amount prescribed and agreed to in an IEP. It was alleged the state gave conflicting instructions to local educational agencies that appeared to allow for reduced special education services to be provided, in part due to the pandemic and associated public health emergency.

The case of *Perez v. Sturgis Public Schools* was decided by the Supreme Court in March of 2023 (Luna Perez v. Sturgis Public Schools, 2023) and appears to open a door for children with disabilities and their families seeking relief under ADA. The unanimous ruling indicated students with disabilities who have exhausted the IDEA administrative hearings process may pursue relief in federal court (including monetary damages) under the

ADA. Previous rulings had prohibited individuals with disabilities from seeking relief under the ADA, although the IDEA process for relief may preclude relief on a timeline relevant to families seeking help, dissuading many from even attempting to seek relief.

In a related vein, although not specific to students with disabilities, George Washington University settled a suit by four former students who claimed the university violated its agreement with students when remote education was adopted (Shaffer v. George Washington University, 2020). The four students were to receive $10,000 each in tuition reimbursement, with the remaining funds from the $5.4 million settlement going to students who incurred costs for Spring 2020 virtual education. The university denied all wrongdoing and liability in the formal agreement. The agreement is clearly a very limited instance of remedy-seeking for the claimed harms of educational disruption, but one that may have implications for other cases across the country and perhaps even over time, as impacts of prolonged virtual learning develop.

Even while historic settlement agreements and compelling legal arguments lay out steps to ensure that students with disabilities receive appropriate compensatory education or recoupment services within the public schools, much of this hinges on development of an administrative process to oversee review of student IEP and Section 504 plans, with oversight from the district and reporting to the federal government (see Adams & Associates, 2020).

At the time of this writing, there is no evidence to suggest that the actions of the school systems that are subject to litigation were outliers. Further, multiple alternative resolution processes are available for families of students with disabilities to settle complaints, so the true scope of special education disruption is likely to be much greater in breadth and impact than is publicly reported. Finally, many cases of disruptions or absence of service provision likely went unreported, uninvestigated, and subsequently unremedied.

Despite evidence of special education disruption, litigation of special education disputes does not appear to have materialized in the way that many predicted it might (Arundel, 2022a). There are several possible explanations. The Council of Parent Attorneys and Advocates (COPAA) conducted a survey in October–November of 2021 and found that only 25% of parents were informed by their school district about compensatory services. There was a chasm between what federal regulations required and what parents experienced in the return to more typical school routines. Another explanation is that litigation remains a costly and time-consuming means of accessing relief, and vulnerable families' appetites for this was likely to be low as families were managing more immediate needs. Also, the baseline rate of success for families prevailing in a due process complaint varies. At baseline in Maryland, families prevail just 20% of the time (Espey, 2023). Families in California prevailed in approximately 15% of due process complaints that reached a hearing from 2008 to 2019 (Adams & Associates, 2020). In Virginia, a class action lawsuit filed against the Virginia Department of Education and Fairfax County School Board alleged that between 2010 and 2021, parents prevailed at a much lower rate, less than 1.5% of the time (Moyer & Harden, 2022). This low rate of success, combined with this high cost of retaining counsel and engaging in the due process complaint steps, has likely contributed to low rates of relief seeking via adversarial means or traditional IDEA conduits.

Some school districts that remained virtual for a prolonged period of time demonstrated a reduced amount of spending on special education litigation in 2022–2023 compared with 2021–2022 (Espey, 2023). Public relations for the district proclaimed this as a positive sign for the district, that fewer families were filing due process complaints. Advocates interviewed were more inclined to interpret the decline as evidence more families were giving up and choosing to withdraw complaints instead of undertaking the costly and time-consuming process of filing a complaint with little chance of prevailing. Clearly, even at baseline rates prior to educational disruption in the pandemic, families were faced with difficult chances of prevailing at a due process hearing and were left with few other means of seeking relief for their children with disabilities.

Assessing the Disruption Impact

In considering whether children and adolescents are making appropriate developmental progress due to interventions, neuropsychologists, school psychologists, and others providing developmental services or making eligibility determinations will need to know whether and how services and accommodations have been implemented since Spring 2020. Students who have not received appropriate services and accommodations may be eligible for compensatory services, and these should be implemented as soon as possible to mitigate learning losses.

Evaluation of the impact of the pandemic on reading achievement by D/HH students enrolled at a school for the deaf, in which the students experienced 17 months of remote learning, demonstrated a negative impact of pandemic related closures on reading. Kuntze et al. (2023) examined Measures of Academic Performance (MAP) scores, evaluated longitudinally from 2016 through 2021. They found a somewhat protective effect of what they termed as tenure; that is, students who had been at the school for the deaf for a longer period of time had higher performance compared to students who joined the school as older students and had less time at the specialized school. These authors suggest a diminishing effect of the pandemic across semesters over time and note significant demographic effects. This particular analysis found Hispanic students' reading performance was "greatly" impacted and performance of Black and Asian students was more negatively affected by pandemic disruptions.

A survey of parents of children with autism spectrum disorder (ASD) indicated greater negative effects of the pandemic and educational disruption than parents of neurotypical children (Genova et al., 2021). Stressors endorsed by parents of children with ASD included more concerns about disruption of routine, whereas parents of neurotypical children were more likely to report concerns with social isolation. These authors concluded that children with autism were at much greater risk of negative outcome directly related to widespread educational disruption.

Vibert et al. (2023) conducted a large-scale study of 1,075 North American/European youth with neurodevelopmental disorders (NDDs) and ASD, evaluating pandemic-related changes in mental health symptoms and access to services. A major aim of the study was to examine protective and risk factors for symptom changes and heterogeneity of clinical outcomes in the NDD/ASD population. Investigators identified four categories of symptom change and special services provision: about half of those youth had no major changes in symptoms or services. Twenty percent experienced *broad symptom worsening*, about a quarter of youth experienced *modified services*, and 6% *lost services*. Greater intellectual impairment was a predictor of falling in the *lost services* subgroup.

Interestingly, the authors found that worries about COVID-19 infection and new reports of child COVID-19 infections in the participant's area were not the most influential predictors of subgroup membership, ranking well behind pre-pandemic level of services, government stringency (reflecting stricter government COVID-19 policies), and lifestyle stress.

Case Illustration: Sarah

Sarah, a 9-year-old child in fourth grade, presented for evaluation to a neuropsychologist. Her teachers noted concerns with progress in reading comprehension. Sarah was diagnosed with ADHD in first grade, prior to the period of disrupted education and local school closures in the spring of 2020. Her school developed and implemented a Section 504 plan that provided her with additional check-ins from a teacher's aide, more frequent reminders and redirection to task, and accommodations related to organizational check-ins related to work completion. While Sarah had some reading difficulties in first grade and she was placed into a smaller reading group at school, her Section 504 team at the time felt that she would be making progress and they could monitor and provide additional support if needed. Family history was noteworthy for several extended family members with a learning disability in reading, and Sarah's mother recalled that she had received some sort of intervention for reading while she was in elementary school.

Sarah's transition to virtual learning during the fall of her second-grade year was very challenging. She was unable to interact with virtual classes without parent one-on-one support, and she frequently would play with stuffed animals or with a handheld game console if her parents left the room to attend to her older siblings or to their own work. Her school followed a hybrid schedule that involved in-person learning for 2 days per week, virtual learning for 2 days per week, and a fifth day that was designated as at-home learning. Parents reported that on in-person learning days, her teacher occasionally taught remotely from home while an aide monitored the class in the classroom. In school, there were also restrictions on how many children Sarah could interact with, and what they could play at recess since physical objects that could be shared between students were prohibited. Sarah returned to full-time in-person instruction during third grade; however, school attendance records noted that Sarah had missed 23 days of in-person instruction due to quarantine or COVID-19 exposure.

Sarah's neuropsychological evaluation findings indicated average intellectual functioning and age-appropriate skills across most cognitive domains, except those related to phonological processing, which fell below age-based expectations. There were also weaker academic skills. Single-word reading was within the below average range, and her performance on a reading comprehension task fell within the low average range. While reading was effortful for her, Sarah enjoyed looking through books and reported that her favorite time of day was when her parents read a story to her before bed or when the teacher read aloud in the classroom. Math-based problem-solving skills were noteworthy for difficulties with word problems, despite average math calculation skills. Parent and teacher ratings continued to indicate clinically significant symptoms of ADHD, predominantly inattentive presentation.

Given Sarah's history, evaluation, and ratings, the neuropsychologist provided a diagnosis of a learning disability in reading in addition to confirming her previous ADHD diagnosis. Recommendations were provided that included sharing the results with her school team and to convene her Section 504 Plan team and consider Sarah's potential eligibility for an IEP.

When the school meeting occurred, Sarah's classroom teacher and the special educator explained that, compared to her classmates, Sarah's performance was not significantly different from her classmates. They provided school-based educational testing showing that Sarah was behind pre-COVID age- and grade-based expectations in reading, but her performance was comparable to peers within her class, school, and even district. The school-based team explained that they did not feel that Sarah was eligible for an IEP. The team agreed that Sarah remained eligible for accommodations included in her current Section 504 Plan for ADHD, and they agreed that she should get some small group reading instruction with her classroom teacher. They planned for a reading specialist to reassess her reading skills in the classroom prior to the end of the school year.

Ultimately, Sarah's parents (at the urging of one of the extended family members with a history of a learning disability in reading) contacted a local special education advocate for support in navigating the situation with her school, and a second meeting was held and with the support of the advocate, who helped the family to gather and present class-based assessment data that indicated concern with her reading from prior to the school closures in 2020, and also presented the school with a list of the ways in which Sarah did not receive the accommodations and supports listed in her Section 504 plan during the extended period of virtual and hybrid instruction. Following the involvement of an advocate, Sarah's parents were offered compensatory educational services, and the school agreed to provide Sarah with an IEP under the federal classification of learning disability. Her parents identified a school-approved provider of a phonologically based reading intervention, and Sarah began after-school work with this reading interventionist three times per week, in addition to working with the reading specialist at school on a daily basis.

Sarah's case illustrates how disrupted special education support and services delayed the recognition and remediation of a learning disability. Prior to the prolonged and disrupted school closures, her school team had identified that she was a student with a disability (i.e., ADHD) that required accommodations to access her curriculum. When she was no longer provided with these accommodations, and the mechanism of instruction shifted to virtual, she struggled with accessing the curriculum. Sarah's case demonstrates that even children with household advantage (high education, fluent in English speaking, stable health insurance, and resources to obtain a private neuropsychological evaluation and support from an educational advocate) may have enormous difficulty accessing services to which they are legally entitled. It is not a great leap to predict that, for those without resources, seeking redress for failures of service provision may be nearly insurmountable in a system already overwhelmed by need. A final point is that schools may be disincentivized from rapidly identifying children with disabilities and ensuring adherence to legal mandates to provide support services: schools are experiencing a staffing crisis, and fiscal cliffs loom for many, and, as in Sarah's case, many children that are "behind" in their academics. Will disability definitional and eligibility criteria within the educational system fail to identify and aid students at the critical time and age when intervention services—for reading disabilities in particular—are the most effective?

References

Adams & Associates. (2020). California special education law: Hearing decisions by administrative law judge. https://www.californiaspecialedlaw.com/wiki/hearing-decision-statistics/hearing-decisions-by-administrative-law-judge/

Arundel, K. (2022a). Remote learning special ed litigation lower than expected. *K-12 Dive*. https://www.k12dive.com/news/remote-learning-special-ed-litigation-lower-than-expected/621949/

Arundel, K. (2022b). Virginia lawsuit claims bias in special education rulings. *K-12 Dive*. https://www.k12dive.com/news/virginia-lawsuit-claims-bias-in-special-education-rulings/632535/

Ashburner, J., Vickerstaff, S., Beetge, J., & Copley, J. (2016). Remote versus face-to-face delivery of early intervention programs for children with autism spectrum disorders: Perceptions of rural families and service providers. *Research in Autism Spectrum Disorders*, *23*, 1–14. https://doi.org/https://doi.org/10.1016/j.rasd.2015.11.011

Battistin, T., Mercuriali, E., Zanardo, V., Gregori, D., Lorenzoni, G., Nasato, L., & Reffo, M. E. (2021). Distance support and online intervention to blind and visually impaired children during the pandemic COVID-19. *Research in Developmental Disability*, *108*, 103816. https://doi.org/10.1016/j.ridd.2020.103816

Blume, H. (2021, November 5). Court order reinstates distance learning for group of disabled students. *Los Angeles Times.*

Cankurtaran, D., Tezel, N., Yildiz, S. Y., Celik, G., & Unlu Akyuz, E. (2021). Evaluation of the effects of the COVID-19 pandemic on children with cerebral palsy, caregivers' quality of life, and caregivers' fear of COVID-19 with telemedicine. *Irish Journal of Medical Sciences, 190*(4), 1473–1480. https://doi.org/10.1007/s11845-021-02622-2

Cason, J. (2009). A pilot telerehabilitation program: Delivering early intervention services to rural families. *International Journal of Telerehabilitation, 1*(1), 29–38. https://doi.org/10.5195/ijt.2009.6007

Cason, J., Behl, D., & Ringwalt, S. (2012). Overview of states' use of telehealth for the delivery of early intervention (IDEA Part C) services. *International Journal of Telerehabilitation, 4*(2), 39–46. https://doi.org/10.5195/ijt.2012.6105

Centers for Disease Control and Prevention (CDC). (2022). Impact of the COVID-19 pandemic early identification of developmental delays and disabilities and opportunities for improvement: A summary of findings from the Act Early Response to COVID-19 needs assessment. https://www.cdc.gov/ncbddd/actearly/pdf/Impact-COVID-DevelopDisabil-508.pdf

Cohan, A. (2020, October 19). Nearly 2,000 Boston students awaiting special education assessments due to coronavirus backlog. *Boston Herald.* https://www.bostonherald.com/2020/10/19/nearly-2000-boston-students-awaiting-special-education-assessments-due-to-backlog/

Cole, B., Stredler-Brown, A., Cohill, B., Blaiser, K., Behl, D., & Ringwalt, S. (2016). The development of statewide policies and procedures to implement telehealth for Part C service delivery. *International Journal of Telerehabilitation, 8*(2), 77–82. https://doi.org/10.5195/ijt.2016.6206

Commonwealth of Massachusetts. (n.d.). Birth to three years old. *Mass.gov.* https://www.mass.gov/info-details/birth-to-three-years-old

DeCosta-Klipa, N. (2023). 4 things to know about Head Start's recent challenges in Massachusetts. *WBUR.* https://www.wbur.org/news/2023/11/09/head-start-massachusetts-child-care-waitlist-newsletter

Diamond, G., & Merrick, J. (2022). Editorial: Children's neurodevelopment in the post-COVID era: From hospital to community. *Frontiers in Pediatrics, 10*, 976884. https://doi.org/10.3389/fped.2022.976884

The Education Trust. (2021). The impact of COVID-19 on early intervention: How states can support our youngest learners. https://edtrust.org/wp-content/uploads/2014/09/The-Impact-of-COVID-19-on-Early-Intervention-How-States-Can-Support-Our-Youngest-Learners-May-2021.pdf

Espey, E. (2023). MCPS outside spending for special education litigation cut in half. *MoCo 360 Media.*

Esquivel, P., & Gomez, M. (2022, April 28). LAUSD failed students with disabilities during pandemic, federal investigation finds. *Los Angeles Times.* https://www.latimes.com/california/story/2022-04-28/lausd-failed-disabled-students-under-remote-learning-during-pandemic-investigation-finds

Friedman-Krauss, A. H., & Barnett, W. S. (2023). The state(s) of early intervention and early childhood special education: Looking at equity. *National Institute for Early Education Research.* https://nieer.org/policy-landscapes/special-education-report

Friedman-Krauss, A. H., Barnett, W. S., & Duer, J. K. (2022). The State(s) of Head Start and Early Head Start: Looking at Equity. *National Institute for Early Education Research.* chrome-extension://efaidnbmnnnibpcajpcglclefindmkaj/https://nieer.org/wp-content/uploads/2022/12/HS_FullReport.pdf

Gelman, S. (2023, September). Fairfax Co. schools still owes students with disabilities thousands of learning hours from the pandemic. *WTOP News.* https://wtop.com/fair

fax-county/2023/09/fairfax-co-schools-gets-extension-to-arrange-compensatory-services-meetings/

Genova, H. M., Arora, A., & Botticello, A. L. (2021). Effects of school closures resulting from COVID-19 in autistic and neurotypical children. *Frontiers in Education, 6*. https://doi.org/10.3389/feduc.2021.761485

Gillispie, C. (2021). The impact of COVID-19 on early intervention: Survey of states. Our youngest learners. *Education Trust and National Center for Learning Disabilities*. URL: https://edtrust.org/wp-content/uploads/2014/09/The-Impact-of-COVID-19-on-Early-Intervention-Survey-of-States-May-2021.pdf

Groom-Thomas, L., Kalogrides, D., Lee, M., Loeb, S., & Lynch, K. (2021). Acelero learning: Annual report. Annenberg Institute at Brown University. https://annenberg.brown.edu/sites/default/files/Acelero%20Report%202021.pdf

Individuals with Disabilities Education Act (IDEA). (2017). US Department of Education. https://sites.ed.gov/idea/regs/b/a/300.8

Individuals with Disabilities Education Act (IDEA). (2020, March 21). Supplemental fact sheet addressing the risk of COVID-19 in preschool, elementary and secondary schools while serving children with disabilities. https://sites.ed.gov/idea/idea-files/supplemental-fact-sheet-addressing-risk-covid-19-preschool-elementary-secondary-schools-serving-children-disabilities-march-21-2020/

Jacobson, L. (2023). "Everybody is frustrated": Feds probe Virginia handling of special education. *The 74 Million*. https://www.the74million.org/article/everybody-is-frustrated-feds-probe-virginias-handling-of-special-education/

Jeste, S., Hyde, C., Distefano, C., Halladay, A., Ray, S., Porath, M., . . . Thurm, A. (2020). Changes in access to educational and healthcare services for individuals with intellectual and developmental disabilities during COVID-19 restrictions. *Journal of Intellectual Disability Research, 64*(11), 825–833. https://doi.org/https://doi.org/10.1111/jir.12776

Judy Heumann. (n.d.). Judy Heumann. *Knowbility*. https://knowbility.org/instructors/judy-heumann

Kane et al. v. Zoom Video Communications Inc et al. (2020). United States District Court, Eastern District of New York.

Karoly, L. A., Kilburn, M. R., & Cannon, J. S. (2005). *Early childhood interventions proven results, future promise* (1st ed.). Santa Monica, CA: RAND Corporation.

Kuntze, M., Branum-Martin, L., & Scott, J. (2023). Pandemic effects on the reading trajectories of deaf and hard of hearing students: A pilot analysis. *Reading and Writing, 36*(2), 429–448. https://doi.org/10.1007/s11145-022-10365-4

Los Angeles Unified School District. (2022). COVID-19 compensatory education plan. Los Angeles, CA: Author https://www.lausd.org/compedplan

Lumpkin, L. (2023, September 25). D.C. settles suit over failure to provide special ed to jailed students. *The Washington Post*.

Luna Perez v. Sturgis Public Schools. (2023). 143 S.Ct. 859.

Lynch, K., Lee, M., & Loeb, S. (2023). An investigation of Head Start preschool children's executive function, early literacy, and numeracy learning in the midst of the COVID-19 pandemic. *Early Childhood Research Quarterly, 64*, 255–265. https://doi.org/https://doi.org/10.1016/j.ecresq.2023.04.002

Metraux, J. (2021). The problem with Zoom addin g free captions after getting called out. *Gizmodo*. https://gizmodo.com/the-problem-with-zoom-adding-free-captions-after-getting-1846353898

Moyer, J., & Harden, J. (2022, October 30). Disabled kids fighting school placements "almost always lose," Va. suit says. *The Washington Post*. https://www.washingtonpost.com/education/2022/10/30/virginia-idea-school-placement-disability/

National Center for Education Statistics. (2021). Students with disabilities. U.S. Department of Education, Institute of Education Sciences. https://nces.ed.gov/programs/coe/indicator/cgg

National Head Start Association. (2023). The Head Start and Early Head Start workforce is in crisis. https://nhsa.org/resource/confronting-head-starts-workforce-crisis/

Office of Head Start. (2023). Head Start Services. U.S. Department of Health & Human Services (HHS), Administration for Children and Families (ACF). https://www.acf.hhs.gov/ohs/about/head-start

Office of Special Education and Rehabilitative Services. (2023). 44th annual report to Congress on the implementation of the Individuals with Disabilities Education Act, 2022. Washington, DC: OSEP

Office of Special Education Programs. (2023). OSEP fast facts: OSEP releases two new fast facts on IDEA Section 618 data collected on children with disabilities served under IDEA in the time of the COVID-19 pandemic. Washington, DC: OSEP. https://sites.ed.gov/osers/category/covid-19/

Ramey, C. T., & Ramey, S. L. (1998). Early intervention and early experience. *American Psychology, 53*(2), 109–120. https://doi.org/10.1037//0003-066x.53.2.109

Schafer, E. C., Dunn, A., & Lavi, A. (2021). Educational challenges during the pandemic for students who have hearing loss. *Language, Speech, and Hearing Services in Schools, 52*, 889–898.

Schweiberger, K., Patel, S. Y., Mehrotra, A., & Ray, K. N. (2021). Trends in pediatric primary care visits during the coronavirus disease of 2019 pandemic. *Academy of Pediatrics, 21*(8), 1426–1433. https://doi.org/10.1016/j.acap.2021.04.031

Shaffer v. George Washington University. (2020). United States District Court District of Columbia.

Shakespeare, T., Ndagire, F., & Seketi, Q. E. (2021). Triple jeopardy: Disabled people and the COVID-19 pandemic. *Lancet, 397*(10282), 1331–1333. https://doi.org/10.1016/s0140-6736(21)00625-5

Shaw, S., Franchett, A., LaForett, D., Maxwell, K., & Bultinck, E. (2023). Head Start's response to the COVID-19 pandemic. OPRE Report#2023-025. Washington, DC: Office of Planning, Research, and Evaluation, Administration for Children and Families US Department of Health and Human Services.

Sherman, E., & Machado, S. (2023, March 9). "Heartbreaking": Dozens of RI children with special needs not receiving education. https://www.wpri.com/target-12/heartbreaking-dozens-of-providence-children-with-special-needs-not-receiving-education/

Sonnenschein, S., Stites, M. L., Grossman, J. A., & Galczyk, S. H. (2022). "This will likely affect his entire life": Parents' views of special education services during COVID-19. *International Journal of Education Research, 112*, 101941. https://doi.org/10.1016/j.ijer.2022.101941

Steed, E. A., Stein, R., & Charlifue-Smith, R. (2023). Initial evaluation practices to identify young children with delays and disabilities during the COVID-19 pandemic. *Journal of Early Intervention, 45*(3), 264–284. https://doi.org/10.1177/10538151221127909

Stein, P. (2021, June 18). Judge gives D.C. 15 days to provide incarcerated students with their legally mandated special education-services. *The Washington Post.*

U.S. Department of Education. (2011). IDEA memo: OSEP Memo 11-07 response to intervention (RTI). https://sites.ed.gov/idea/idea-files/osep-memo-11-07-response-to-intervention-rti-memo/

U.S. Department of Education. (2017a). Individuals with Disabilities Education Act, Sec. 303.13: Early intervention services. https://sites.ed.gov/idea/regs/c/a/303.13

U.S. Department of Education. (2017b). Sec. 300.502 independent educational evaluation. https://sites.ed.gov/idea/regs/b/e/300.502

U.S. Department of Education. (2020). Supplemental fact sheet addressing the risk of COVID-19 in preschool, elementary and secondary schools while serving children with disabilities. https://www2.ed.gov/about/offices/list/ocr/frontpage/faq/rr/policyguidance/Supple%20Fact%20Sheet%203.21.20%20FINAL.pdf

U.S. Department of Education. (2022a). Fairfax County Public Schools resolution agreement. https://www2.ed.gov/about/offices/list/ocr/docs/investigations/more/11215901-b.pdf

U.S. Department of Education. (2022b). Individuals with Disabilities Education Act, Part 303 (Part C)—Early intervention program for infants and toddlers with disabilities. https://sites.ed.gov/idea/regs/c

U.S. Department of Education. (2022c). Los Angeles Unified School District Resolution Agreement OCR Docket No. 09-21-5901. https://www2.ed.gov/about/offices/list/ocr/docs/investigations/more/09215901-b.pdf

U.S. Department of Education. (2023a). A history of the Individuals with Disabilities Education Act. https://sites.ed.gov/idea/IDEA-History

U.S. Department of Education. (2023b). Individuals with Disabilities Education Act: 2023 early childhood transition questions and answers. *Office of Special Education Programs*. https://sites.ed.gov/idea/idea-files/2023-early-childhood-transition-questions-and-answers/

U.S. Department of Education. (2023c). OSEP fast facts: IDEA Section 618 data collected on children with disabilities served under IDEA, Part B during the time of the COVID-19 pandemic. https://sites.ed.gov/idea/osep-fast-facts-idea-b-section-618-data-covid19-pandemic

U.S. Department of Education. (n.d.-a). About IDEA: Rehabilitation Act. https://sites.ed.gov/idea/about-idea/#Rehab-Act

U.S. Department of Education. (n.d.-b). IDEA topic areas: Individualized education programs (IEP). https://sites.ed.gov/idea/topic-areas/#IEP

U.S. Department of Health & Human Services. (2021). FY 2021 American rescue plan funding increase for Head Start programs. ACF-PI-HS-21-03. *Office of Head Start*. https://eclkc.ohs.acf.hhs.gov/policy/pi/acf-pi-hs-21-03

U.S. Department of Health & Human Services. (2023). Head Start program facts: Fiscal year 2022. *Office of Head Start*. https://eclkc.ohs.acf.hhs.gov/data-ongoing-monitoring/article/head-start-program-facts-fiscal-year-2022#:~:text = Since%20its%20inception%20in%201965,and%20family%20child%20care%20homes

U.S. Department of Justice Civil Rights Division. (n.d.). The Americans with Disabilities Act (ADA) protects people with disabilities from discrimination. *ADA.gov*. https://www.ada.gov/

Vazquez Toness, B., & Lurye, S. (2023). Thousands of kids are missing from school. Where did they go? *T. A. Press*. https://projects.apnews.com/features/2023/missing-children/index.html

Vibert, B., Segura, P., Gallagher, L., Georgiades, S., Pervanidou, P., Thurm, A., . . . Di Martino, A. (2023). CRISIS AFAR: An international collaborative study of the impact of the COVID-19 pandemic on mental health and service access in youth with autism and neurodevelopmental conditions. *Molecular Autism*, *14*(1), 7. https://doi.org/10.1186/s13229-022-00536-z

Williams, E., & Musumeci, M. (2022). The intersection of Medicaid, special education service delivery, and the COVID-19 pandemic. *Kaiser Family Foundation*.

Zimmerman, A. (2021). NYC special education referrals plunge 57% from pre-pandemic levels. *Chalkbeat*. https://ny.chalkbeat.org/2021/11/18/22789162/special-education-referral-drop-nyc

6

Delayed Evaluation, Diagnosis, and Treatment of Childhood Disorders

The COVID-19 pandemic and related societal and educational disruption resulted in significant delays in evaluation, diagnosis, and treatment of childhood disorders. Parents are often the first to recognize that a child may be on a different developmental trajectory. While many parents report being aware of differences in a child from an early age, some parents only report their concerns to teachers or health care providers when they see their child in the community. When parents notice differences in their child's behavior at the playground, at the neighborhood block party, or when heading off to school, their accumulated observations often propel them to seek help. In other words, social comparison often provides critical confirmatory evidence.

Opportunities for social comparison were severely restricted by the COVID-19 pandemic, especially during the early lockdown phases, with many families extending social isolation due to fears about virus exposure, especially before children were eligible for vaccination. During this time, there was also limited access to educators, medical providers, childcare providers, and others who might confirm parents' suspicions or even first identify developmental concerns. As discussed in prior chapters, many teachers only observed their children over screens, children were less likely to see their pediatricians for well-child visits (Schweiberger et al., 2021), and daycare enrollment plummeted (National Center for Education Statistics, 2023). There were simply fewer people beyond the immediate family who had opportunities to interact with children and identify potential areas of concern.

At the same time, parents' increased exposure to their children during the COVID-19 pandemic provided more opportunities to observe differences that confirmed any preexisting concerns. For instance, we saw many children for attention-deficit/hyperactivity disorder (ADHD) evaluations prompted by parents who observed distractibility and disengagement with

Neurodevelopment in the Post-Pandemic World. Molly Colvin, Jennifer Linton Reesman, and Tannahill Glen, Oxford University Press. © Oxford University Press 2024. DOI: 10.1093/9780197762660.003.0006

virtual learning. There were also learning disorder evaluations prompted by parents who witnessed their child struggle to learn to read or to form letters during virtual schooling.

Unfortunately, even in cases where parents were seeking help for their child, further assessment and intervention were often still delayed, due to lack of access to services. These delays, when combined with changes in educational instruction and community involvement, have significantly complicated the identification and diagnosis of neurodevelopmental disorders. Clinically, the impact of delayed intervention is already apparent and will likely have long-term implications.

Learning Disorders

Learning disorders are brain-based neurodevelopmental disorders that impact skill acquisition, specifically academic skills. Up to 10% of youth in the United States are clinically diagnosed with a specific learning disorder that impacts the development of reading, writing, or math abilities (Altarac & Saroha, 2007). The most common clinical syndromes underlying learning disorder diagnoses include dyslexia (reading), dysgraphia (writing), and dyscalculia (math). Although not as well-characterized or researched, additional learning disorder syndromes may include nonverbal learning disorder (NLD; Margolis et al., 2020) and slow processing speed (Braaten et al., 2020).

Like most neurodevelopmental disorders, there are early developmental signs and symptoms of learning disorders, including hypotonia, fine or gross motor delays, and/or language delays. Learning disorders may co-occur (e.g., a child may have diagnoses of both dyslexia and dysgraphia) and are more likely in the context of other neurodevelopmental disorders (e.g., autism spectrum disorder, ADHD), medical conditions (e.g., prematurity), and neurological conditions (e.g., seizure disorders) (Colvin, Forchelli, et al., 2022; Colvin, Reesman, et al., 2022). There is a strong genetic component to learning disorders; heritability may explain a significant proportion of the variance in reading, math, or spelling outcomes (Fletcher & Grigorenko, 2017; Grigorenko et al., 2020; Willcutt et al., 2010).

Developmental dyslexia is the best characterized learning disorder. It has been associated with atypical activity throughout the language network in the brain's left hemisphere. Common symptoms include difficulties with phonological processing associated with delayed reading skill acquisition. Early warning signs include speech and language delays, especially articulation difficulties (Peterson & Pennington, 2015). It is strongly heritable, occurring in 68% of identical twins and in 50% of those who have an affected parent or sibling.

While the impact of learning disorders is often lifelong, reflecting intrinsic differences in neuronal wiring, the magnitude of the impact may be mitigated by early intervention. Those with specific learning disorders in reading, math, or writing may have difficulty achieving equivalency with their peers, but early intervention in each of these areas has been shown to be effective (Fletcher & Grigorenko, 2017; Grigorenko et al., 2020). Indeed, effective reading intervention has also been associated with changes in neural activity within the brain, such that the dyslexic's brain patterns look more typical after appropriate instruction (Gabrieli, 2009). As will be discussed in greater detail in Chapter 8, early intervention capitalizes on the brain's increased receptivity to input and also corrects maladaptive processes before they have a chance to undermine the development of more complex skills.

New Challenges in Clinical Learning Disorder Diagnosis Using DSM-5 Criteria

Despite considerable evidence that specific learning disorders can be at least partially *identified* by clinical history, signs, and symptoms, it is not how they are clinically *diagnosed*. Using *Diagnostic and Statistical Manual of Mental Disorders, Fifth Edition* (DSM-5) diagnostic criteria, clinical diagnosis of a learning disorder requires evidence that a child's skills are significantly below grade-based expectations despite at least 6 months of remediation, and that academic difficulties cannot be accounted for by psychosocial adversity or inadequate instruction (American Psychiatric Association, 2013). Learning disorders are thus unique in the DSM-5 nosology in that they only require a measured deficit using standardized assessment tools, and that remediation must have been attempted prior to diagnosis.

Since the beginning of the COVID-19 pandemic, the clinical diagnostic criteria for learning disorders have been particularly hard to satisfy. Many children faced significant psychosocial adversity, which will be described in more detail in Chapter 7. As discussed in Chapter 5, academic instruction and the provision of response to intervention (RTI) or special education services aimed to provide remediation to struggling students was disrupted and/or substantially altered. When psychoeducational evaluations or reading assessments were performed, there was less certainty in the degree to which low scores on standardized academic achievement measures might indicate a learning disorder because of normative data drift or alterations in test administration, for example (Colvin, Reesman, et al., 2022). The following case illustrates a now common clinical diagnostic problem:

Luke was an 8-year-old in Fall 2021 when he presented with reading concerns. He had a clear history of early language delays, including articulation difficulties, for which he had received early intervention (EI) services. There was a strong family history of dyslexia. He had struggled with reading since kindergarten, and had received RTI reading services. Evaluating him to determine eligibility for special education services had been discussed when he was in first grade, but this was delayed by the transition to remote instruction in Spring 2020. He also stopped receiving RTI reading services in March 2020. In Spring 2021, Luke's family moved after his mother left her job because she had to stay home with his younger siblings after their daycare closed. Now at a new school in third grade, Luke's teachers told his mother that all students were behind in their reading skills and that RTI reading services were not available due to staffing shortages.

Luke's neuropsychological profile was highly consistent with developmental dyslexia. Overall intellectual functioning fell in the average range, and there were multiple indicators of difficulties with phonological processing (e.g., reduced phonemic fluency and rapid naming) and auditory working memory. When he struggled on a letter sequencing task, he verbalized feeling frustrated by his lack of automaticity with the alphabet. Word reading, nonword decoding, and spelling skills were all significantly below age-based expectations, clustering at the first-grade level.

While the neuropsychological profile provides clear evidence of the clinical syndrome of developmental dyslexia, he did not fully meet DSM-5 diagnostic criteria for a Specific Learning Disorder with Impairment in Reading. His academic achievement scores in reading were significantly below grade-based expectations, but he had not had 6 months of remediation services and had experienced significant psychosocial and educational disruption.

In clinical practice since the COVID-19 pandemic, we have addressed this challenge by clearly differentiating between the clinical syndrome (e.g., dyslexia, dysgraphia, dyscalculia) and learning disorder diagnosis, articulating the reasons a clinical syndrome is likely, as well as the reasons we cannot offer a formal clinical learning disorder diagnosis. This requires consideration and documentation of the clinical history, including the onset and course of clinical signs and symptoms, as well as educational access and remediation efforts, and psychosocial history (Colvin, Reesman, et al., 2022). From a practical perspective, identification of the clinical syndrome has often been sufficient to support intervention, especially through private services (e.g., tutoring provided by parents). However, we have seen cases where school-based services have been denied, at least in part because there is not a clinical diagnosis.

In cases that are not as straightforward as Luke's, there is now increased risk of two types of diagnostic errors related to learning disorders when clinicians adhere to strict DSM-5 diagnostic criteria requiring evidence from academic achievement data in the absence of other clinical factors. *False-negative errors* occur when low academic achievement scores are incorrectly attributed to other factors when there is a learning disorder. *False-positive errors* occur when low academic achievement scores are incorrectly attributed to a learning disorder when they were related to other factors. The associated clinical risk of diagnostic error is higher in the case of the false-negative error, as this will potentially delay much-needed interventions. However, false-positive errors may also entail a cost of unnecessary intervention and the inaccurate integration of a learning disorder within a child's and family's identity (Colvin, Reesman, et al., 2022).

Complicating matters further, medical insurance does not cover neuropsychological evaluations that are solely requested to identify the presence of a learning disorder, even though other neurodevelopmental disorders are considered eligible (e.g., autism spectrum disorder). The rationale for this is that learning disorders can be assessed and diagnosed by the school. However, as discussed earlier, school evaluations usually do not offer clinical diagnoses. They may identify that a child has a reading disorder, but they will not diagnose the clinical syndrome of developmental dyslexia, which may be present even if the child's reading scores are within grade-based expectations, especially in early grades. The result is that many families pay high out-of-pocket fees for evaluations to diagnose a learning disorder, and intervention is delayed until there is significant everyday interference (Colvin, Forchelli, et al., 2022).

New Challenges in Learning Disability Classification Under the Individuals with Disabilities Education Act

Schools have faced similar decision-making challenges related to the Individuals with Disabilities Education Act (IDEA) criteria for a learning disability, which overlap with DSM-5 criteria. IDEA classification for a learning disability also requires that *there must be evidence of a learning difficulty using standardized academic achievement measures*, that *difficulties must persist following intervention*, and that learning difficulties *cannot be* accounted for by "environmental, cultural, or economic factors, or to lack of appropriate instruction" (U.S. Department of Education, 2019). In cases like Luke, who will primarily receive reading intervention services through school, ineligibility for IDEA classification with a learning disability is potentially catastrophic.

In Spring 2020 when most schools were engaged in remote instruction, the National Association of School Psychologists (NASP) recognized this challenge, writing that "even if schools return to in-person instruction in the fall, it will be almost impossible to rule out a lack of appropriate instruction as a causal factor in learning difficulties." Their recommendation was that remediation efforts "be applied across entire classrooms before individual students are identified as having a learning disability" (National Association of School Psychologists, 2020).

Following this advice almost certainly resulted in delayed identification of children with true learning disorders. Blanket remediation efforts may have been helpful for typically developing children who needed to "catch up" from lost instruction, but not for children with learning disorders who require specialized interventions for remediation. Perhaps related to this, NASP also recommended prioritizing the evaluation of students who demonstrated learning difficulties prior to the pandemic, but this approach would also miss younger children who may have entered school during the pandemic, at precisely the time when their challenges should have come to clinical attention.

Compounding this problem, there is a significant challenge of interpreting academic achievement data. As reviewed in Chapter 3, academic achievement test scores have declined as a result of pandemic-related educational disruption. As noted by Luke's teacher, there are many more children who have low academic achievement scores who presumably do not have a learning disorder. It is currently much more difficult to differentiate between students who have low scores due to missed instruction and students who have low scores due to learning disorders. This will inevitably result in delayed identification of children with learning disorders and delayed initiation of the specialized services that they need to access the regular education curriculum.

Not surprisingly, the rate of children being identified as having a learning disability has dropped. As described earlier, in the Fall 2020, the percentage of students receiving services across the 13 IDEA disability classifications was stable, *except* for specific learning disability. The number of students in this category decreased from 3.6% to 3.3%, the lowest percentage of students with learning disabilities in the previous 10 years (Office of Special Education and Rehabilitative Services, 2023) (Table 6.1).

Table 6.1 U.S. Department of Education's Report on the Percentage of the Population Ages 5 Through 21 Served Under IDEA, Part B, by Year and Disability Category: Fall 2011 Through Fall 2020

Disability	2011	2012	2013	2014	2015	2016	2017	2018	2019	2020
All disabilities below	8.2	8.2	8.3	8.5	8.7	8.8	9.2	9.2	9.5	9.1
Autism	0.6	0.7	0.7	0.8	0.8	0.9	0.9	1.0	1.1	1.1
Deaf-blindness	#	#	#	#	#	#	#	#	#	#
Emotional disturbance	0.5	0.5	0.5	0.5	0.5	0.5	0.5	0.5	0.5	0.5
Hearing impairment	0.1	0.1	0.1	0.1	0.1	0.1	0.1	0.1	0.1	0.1
Intellectual disability	0.6	0.6	0.6	0.6	0.6	0.6	0.6	0.6	0.6	0.6
Multiple disabilities	0.2	0.2	0.2	0.2	0.2	0.2	0.2	0.2	0.2	0.2
Orthopedic impairment	0.1	0.1	0.1	0.1	0.1	0.1	0.1	0.1	#	#
Other health impairment	1.1	1.1	1.2	1.3	1.3	1.4	1.5	1.5	1.6	1.6
Specific learning disability	3.4	3.4	3.4	3.4	3.4	3.5	3.5	3.6	3.6	3.3
Speech or language impairment	1.5	1.5	1.5	1.5	1.5	1.5	1.5	1.6	1.6	1.7
Traumatic brain injury	#	#	#	#	#	#	#	#	#	#
Visual impairment	#	#	#	#	#	#	#	#	#	#

Source: From the U.S. Department of Education, Office of Special Education and Rehabilitative Services and Office of Special Education Programs (2023) 44th Annual Report to Congress on the Implementation of the Individuals with Disabilities Education Act, 2022. Washington, DC.

Percentage was non-zero but less than 0.05 or 5/100 of 1 percent.

[a] States' use of the developmental delay category is optional for children and students ages 3 through 9 and is not applicable to students older than 9 years of age. Because the category is optional and the exhibit presents percentages that are based on the estimated U.S. resident population ages 5 through 21, the developmental delay category is not included in this exhibit. For information on the percentages of the population ages 5 (school age) through 9 reported under the category of developmental delay and States with differences in developmental delay reporting practices, see Exhibits B-2 and B-3 in Appendix B.

Potential Long-Term Costs

There is an enormous potential cost of delayed identification of learning disorders. Students with learning disabilities are 2–3 times more likely to become involved with the criminal justice system, making them a significant proportion of children who become ensnared in the school-to-prison pipeline. Indeed, among incarcerated youth, 39% have been identified as having a specific learning disability (Mallett, 2017).

There are also significant economic costs to the delayed identification and inadequate treatment of learning disorders. Those with learning disorders are more likely to have limited employment opportunities and lower economic security as an adult (National Center for Learning Disabilities, 2014). As discussed in greater detail in Chapter 5, school districts may also need to pay for compensatory special education services if children with learning disabilities did not receive required services and accommodations to ensure free and appropriate education (FAPE) during the COVID-19 pandemic.

In addition to these payments, the Supreme Court recently ruled that students could seek financial compensation for having been discriminated against under the Americans with Disabilities Act (ADA) if they do not receive the services outlined in individualized education programs (IEPs) (Luna Perez v. Sturgis Public Schools, 2023). Previously, claims of denial of educational access due to disability were limited to relief under IDEA and due process, which can be a lengthy process, and in many jurisdictions relief is challenging to find, depending on state laws regarding who bears the burden of proof and the method for adjudicating the disputes. Seeking relief under the ADA and the courts opens up another avenue for parents to access relief if their children with disabilities experienced discrimination when education was disrupted.

Compounding economic costs, there are potentially increased mental health risks for children with learning disorders who do not receive adequate support. Learning disabilities in childhood are associated with a higher risk of psychiatric disorders, both in childhood and in adulthood. While this risk may reflect shared genetic risk (i.e., specific genes may confer risk of both learning and psychiatric disorders) (Willcutt & Pennington, 2000), psychiatric difficulties may also be secondary to the cumulative experience of living with a learning disorder, especially one that is untreated (Tsatsanis et al., 1997). Clinically, we often see school-related anxiety, lower self-esteem, and decreased social confidence in children who have learning disorders.

Other Neurodevelopmental Disorders

Postponed early intervention and school-based assessments, as well as changes in the academic curriculum and decreased opportunities to observe students during periods of remote learning, also likely contributed to delayed identification and intervention of other neurodevelopmental disorders. While data from early in the COVID-19 pandemic shows stability in the numbers of children in disability classifications other than specific learning disability, it is important to remember that classification does not mean that there has been a clinical diagnosis, and that schools are often at the front lines of recognizing that there are developmental delays or challenges. There are now emerging data to suggest that there were disruptions in the process of identifying children with autism spectrum disorder (ASD), ADHD, and language disorder, which may compound the potential costs related to learning disabilities.

Autism Spectrum Disorder

Impairment in social communication is the hallmark of an ASD. Salient challenges include trouble initiating and fostering peer relationships and recognizing others' perspectives and emotions. In addition, there may be repetitive behaviors and routines, narrow interests or fixations, and strong sensory aversions and preferences. There is considerable variability among individuals with ASD in symptom presentation and functional independence. There are also higher rates of global developmental delay (intellectual disability) and other cognitive, neurodevelopmental, and psychiatric disorders, including ADHD, language disorders, anxiety, and learning disorders (American Psychiatric Association, 2013; Lord et al., 2020).

ASD signs and symptoms are usually present within the first year or two of life, but the mean age of diagnosis in the United States is 4 years old (Lord et al., 2020). Prior to the COVID-19 pandemic, there were extensive efforts to identify and diagnose ASD earlier, given overwhelming data showing that evidence-based interventions are most effective when delivered before age 4 years (Fuller & Kaiser, 2020). The American Academy of Pediatrics (AAP) currently recommends autism screening of all children at ages 18 and 24 months but also states that children should be referred for intervention as soon as delays are noticed (Hyman et al., 2020).

During the COVID-19 pandemic, many of these ASD screenings did not occur. There were significantly fewer ASD screenings by pediatricians in the spring and summer of 2020 (Wallis et al., 2022), likely in part reflecting decreased numbers of well-child visits (Schweiberger et al., 2021). Even into late 2020, the numbers of ASD screenings remained significantly below pre-pandemic levels (Shaw et al., 2023), which corresponded to fewer ASD diagnoses in all of 2020 (Shaw et al., 2023). Not surprisingly, in our clinical practices, we are now seeing more children presenting later for ASD evaluation and diagnosis, leaving us with shorter windows of optimal intervention.

The need to adjust autism evaluation processes to maintain safety protocols compounded the negative impact of delayed referrals. There are numerous specialized assessment tools that are highly sensitive and specific to ASD, but many of these require direct in-person and face-to-face interaction between a child and examiner. One of the more commonly used performance-based measures is the Autism Diagnostic Observation Schedule (ADOS), which includes a set of activities designed to elicit a child's play-based skills (e.g., imaginary play, using toys as intended), social communication skills (e.g., turn taking, ability to understand metaphorical language, sensitivity to social bids and others' experiences), and frequency of repetitive behaviors (Lord et al., 2020).

In-person administration of the ADOS-2 was limited during the COVID-19 pandemic. Social distancing requirements and masking made it difficult to assess whether a child was appropriately responding to the examiner and/or attending and responding to facial expressions and communication cues. Because of these limitations, many clinics, including one of ours (Dr. Colvin at MGH), turned to telehealth for assessments of young children needing ASD evaluations (Jang et al., 2022). One promising tool that became more widely used is the TELE-ASD-PEDS, which was designed for telehealth autism evaluations of children under age 36 months. The examiner guides the parents through a series of tasks that are designed to assess the same diagnostic domains as the ADOS-2 (Corona et al., 2020). While the TELE-ASD-PEDS may be insufficient in complex diagnostic cases, it has shown promise as a first-line screening tool even beyond the COVID-19 pandemic (Wagner et al., 2021), potentially allowing for faster identification of patients, especially those in areas where there are relatively few providers.

Perhaps the biggest challenge to ASD assessments since the start of the COVID-19 pandemic has been the need to account for how changes in the environment may have impacted the development of social communication skills. Many infants and toddlers had fewer opportunities for socialization than their pre-pandemic peers. A recent meta-analysis examining infant development during the pandemic found that there were higher rates of communication skill delay compared to a pre-pandemic cohort (Hessami et al., 2022). As a result, it can be harder to know whether observed social communication delays are fully attributable to autism.

Clinically, this manifests as less diagnostic certainty, particularly for children with mild or complex presentations, as illustrated in the following case:

David is a nearly 4-year-old boy who presented to his pediatrician for a well-child examination after 18 months of being lost to clinical care during the COVID-19 pandemic. He has a history of speech and language delays and was referred for an early intervention evaluation by his pediatrician when he was 24 months old (Winter 2020). However, the evaluation never occurred, and he did not receive any early intervention services.

David is an only child who lives with his parents and maternal grandmother, who has been a primary caregiver as both parents work full-time. Because his grandmother's chronic health conditions increased her risk of complications if she were to have COVID-19, the family was relatively isolated during the COVID-19 pandemic. David did not have any regular interactions with peers in the community. There were no babysitters or regular extended family gatherings.

David recently began attending preschool and his teachers have raised concerns about language delays and atypical play skills. David often prefers to play alone, and can usually be found at the train table, but he sometimes likes to build with blocks. When his peers attempt to engage him in play or share his toys, he often rebuffs their overtures and can sometimes become physically aggressive if his belongings are disturbed. He also seems to be easily overwhelmed in busy or crowded environments and might cover his ears until things calm down. He is also a somewhat picky eater; he has a somewhat restricted range of acceptable foods and resists trying new things.

David's history is notable for several signs and symptoms of ASD, including social communication delays, difficulties relating to peers, and sensory sensitivities. There are also concerns about language delays, behavioral rigidity, and restricted interests. However, his exposure to others, particularly same-aged peers, was severely limited during the COVID-19 pandemic. This raises at least a possibility that the observed difficulties reflect lack of practice or exposure to an environment where he could develop age-appropriate social communication skills.

Given these circumstances, it would be entirely reasonable to defer ASD diagnosis so that we can see how David responds to regular engagement with preschool. Presumably, if his challenges are related to lack of exposure, he may "catch up" relatively quickly with more opportunities to engage with peers. However, the risk of delaying an ASD diagnosis is relatively high, as he is at an age when the efficacy of early intervention will likely be lower if service initiation continues to be deferred.

Even if David was diagnosed with ASD, the COVID-19 pandemic delayed initiation of interventions for young children who were diagnosed with ASD. Applied behavior analysis (ABA) is an intensive behavioral therapy that focuses on shaping behavior and communication skills by reinforcing desired actions. ABA is tailored to the individual child and is typically provided by a trained therapist in the child's home, school, and/or community for hours each week (Lord et al., 2020). Prior to age 3 years, ABA services and other needed interventions (e.g., speech and language therapy, occupational therapy, physical therapy) are offered through EI. As discussed in Chapter 5, after a child's third birthday, services are provided under IDEA, and typically formalized in an IEP.

Because of the service intensity that is required, and the growing number of children diagnosed with ASD, there were often long waiting lists for ABA even prior to the COVID-19 pandemic. In many areas of the United States, wait times only increased after 2020, in part reflecting the challenges of delivering this type of intervention while maintaining social distancing guidelines (Miller & Gold, 2022). Altogether, the path to ASD evaluation and intervention has been much longer than seen prior to the COVID-19 pandemic.

Attention-Deficit Hyperactivity Disorder

ADHD is a neurodevelopmental disorder characterized by challenges regulating attention and/or behavior. ADHD has been associated with atypical development of brain networks, particularly those involving the frontal lobes (Friedman & Rapoport, 2015). ADHD is heritable and associated with higher rates of academic difficulty, risky behaviors, and lower levels of employment and financial stability (Faraone et al., 2015, 2021). There is also considerable comorbidity with other neurodevelopmental disorders (e.g., learning disorders, autism spectrum disorder) and psychiatric disorders (e.g., major depression, anxiety, substance abuse) (Tistarelli et al., 2020).

Intervention, through behavioral therapy and/or medication, has been associated with more positive outcomes (Boland et al., 2020; Faraone et al., 2021).

Diagnostic criteria for ADHD have changed over time. With the transition to DSM-5 in 2013, attention-deficit disorder (ADD) was renamed ADHD with three possible subtypes: (1) inattentive, (2) hyperactive-impulsive, and (3) combined inattentive and hyperactive-impulsive. Inattentive signs and symptoms include distractibility, careless mistakes, and missing details but also sometimes a tendency to hyperfocus on areas of interest. Hyperactive-impulsive signs and symptoms include excessive activity or restlessness, as well as a tendency to act without fully thinking through the consequences of one's actions (American Psychiatric Association, 2013).

Diagnostic criteria require that ADHD signs and symptoms are present in early development. ADHD presentation can also change over time; many young children present with inattention, hyperactivity, and impulsivity, but hyperactive and impulsive symptoms may wane over time. Some diagnosed with ADHD in childhood will no longer meet full diagnostic criteria in adulthood, but many will remain affected. At any stage in development, diagnosis of ADHD requires evidence that symptoms significantly interfere with functioning in daily life across multiple environments (American Psychiatric Association, 2013).

In clinical practice, pediatricians frequently diagnose and treat ADHD, given its prevalence and the shortage of mental health clinicians (Wolraich et al., 2019). During 2020, first-time visits to pediatricians for assessment of ADHD symptoms declined significantly. Fewer children were diagnosed with ADHD for the first time, which was associated with fewer first-time medication prescriptions for treatment of ADHD (Bannett et al., 2022), likely reflecting a general trend for children to have had less contact with their pediatrician during the early stages of the COVID-19 pandemic (Schweiberger et al., 2021). Indeed, even among children who had already been diagnosed with ADHD, the frequency of ADHD-related visits to pediatricians dropped by 33% in the first quarter of 2020, although it quickly rebounded. The numbers of prescriptions written by pediatricians for ADHD treatment remained constant (Bannett et al., 2022).

First-time diagnoses of ADHD are most commonly made by analyzing responses to standardized symptom checklists to determine the frequency and severity (number) of symptoms in multiple environments (Wolraich et al., 2019). Typically, parents complete a questionnaire about functioning at home, while teachers complete a questionnaire about functioning at school. If clinically significant numbers of symptoms of ADHD are endorsed in both environments, then a diagnosis is conferred. If there are only significant symptoms in either home or school, then a diagnosis is often deferred.

The combination of delayed visits to pediatricians and changes in the observational data available to teachers and school personnel likely delayed diagnosis and treatment initiation for children and adolescents who have ADHD during the COVID-19 pandemic, as illustrated by the following case:

Marco is a 9-year-old boy whose parents first came to their pediatrician in Fall 2020 with concerns about possible ADHD. At that time, Marco was in first grade and attending school remotely due to the COVID-19 pandemic. His parents had arranged their work schedules so that they could alternate sitting with Marco during remote instruction, as otherwise, he was likely to get up and walk away from the computer to play with his Legos. While many of the other children in his classroom also required parent facilitation, Marco's parents observed that they seemed better able to listen to their teacher and sustain focus on the tasks that they were asked to do.Marco's pediatrician asked his parents to complete a standardized questionnaire assessing symptoms of ADHD. Following standard practice, they also asked Marco's teacher to complete the same questionnaire. Results indicated clinically significant ADHD symptoms at home. However, Marco's teacher, who had only observed him through remote instruction, did not endorse clinically significant symptoms, presumably because Marco was receiving 1:1 parent facilitation during lessons. Marco's pediatrician deferred formal diagnosis of ADHD.

When Marco returned to in-person schooling in Winter 2021, the teacher did observe that he was struggling with attentional regulation and impulsivity, and also that he seemed more restless than many of the other students. However, she noted similar concerns in many other students, and explained to Marco's parents that he may need time to adjust to the demands of a first-grade classroom.

Finally, in spring of second grade, Marco's teacher called a parent conference due to concerns about both behavioral regulation and academic performance. Marco's parents gave permission for the school to complete a psychoeducational evaluation, which included parent and teacher rating questionnaires. Responses were consistent with ADHD symptoms, but as this was not a clinical evaluation, no formal diagnosis was made. However, the school did implement special education services and accommodations as part of an IEP. Accommodations were aimed to improve attention and behavioral regulation, and services were required to address lagging academic skills.

Now in the fall of third grade, Marco's teacher reported that he was benefiting from specialized academic support, but there were ongoing challenges with attentional regulation, impulsivity, and hyperactivity that the teacher felt were interfering with his academic progress. Marco had also started to verbalize feeling "dumb" and that he disliked school because he was "always in trouble." At his well-child visit with his pediatrician, Marco's parents raised these concerns, prompting readministration of the standardized questionnaires that had been first completed 2 years earlier. This time, both parents and teacher endorsed significant ADHD symptoms. Marco's pediatrician prescribed medication to treat ADHD symptoms, and Marco's performance in school finally began to improve.

The cost of delayed diagnosis and intervention for ADHD is potentially high, with increased rates of mental health concerns and risky behaviors. Indeed, treatment of ADHD symptoms may decrease the risk of anxiety (Coughlin et al., 2015) and depression (Boland et al., 2020). Treatment of ADHD is also associated with reduced long-term risk of substance use (Biederman et al., 2008) and decreased risk of motor vehicle accidents, injuries, and traumatic brain injury (Boland et al., 2020).

Diagnosis and treatment of ADHD are also more complicated if secondary emotional concerns emerge. Psychiatric conditions, particularly anxiety and depression, are associated with decreased cognitive efficiency and attention, which can mimic and/or exacerbate ADHD symptoms (American Psychiatric Association, 2013). As will be discussed in greater detail in Chapter 7, the psychosocial stressors associated with the COVID-19 pandemic led to increased rates of emotional distress in children and adolescents, which may have further delayed diagnosis and treatment.

Finally, ADHD treatment in the post-pandemic era has been complicated by limited availability of stimulant medication. Before the COVID-19 pandemic, more adults had started seeking stimulant treatment for ADHD. This trend increased significantly during the COVID-19 pandemic as telehealth facilitated evaluations and, by extension, prescriptions for medication to treat the condition. In contrast, stimulant use in children and adolescents remained largely stable (Danielson et al., 2023). Despite increased demand, there was not a commensurate increase in the amounts of medication that companies are permitted to produce. At the same time, there were supply chain disruptions during the COVID-19 pandemic, especially during lockdown phases when factories were not able to operate as usual (Schmidt, 2023). As a result, treatment options have been limited, even when children have been evaluated and diagnosed. This has likely particularly impacted children with ADHD who have been exposed to multiple psychosocial stressors and/or who have comorbid neurodevelopmental conditions.

Language Disorder

"Language disorder" is a broad term that includes difficulties with one or more aspects of speech, expression, or comprehension. Speech disorders primarily relate to the production of sounds and include difficulties with articulation (e.g., speech sound disorder), fluency (e.g., stuttering), and/or orofacial control (e.g., dysarthria). Expressive language disorders may impact the retrieval and organization of language so that the child can clearly communicate their knowledge, thoughts, and feelings. Receptive language disorders impact comprehension, or understanding of what others are communicating to the child. It is possible to have mixed expressive-receptive language disorders. There may also be difficulties with pragmatic language, or the common use of language in social interactions, which may require resolving ambiguity or multiple meanings to "know what someone is trying to say" (e.g., idioms, metaphors, sarcasm). Finally, those with language disorders are at increased likelihood to have language-based learning disabilities (Pennington et al., 2019).

Language disorders may result from a neurological or medical condition (e.g., perinatal stroke), but most emerge idiopathically, or without a known cause. As with many other idiopathic neurodevelopmental disorders, there is also likely a genetic component, and developmental language disorder (DLD) may co-occur with other neurodevelopmental disorders (e.g., ADHD, autism) (American Psychiatric Association, 2013). DLD is relatively common and heritable; it is estimated to impact one in 14 kindergarten students, and 50%–70% of children with DLD have at least one family member with DLD (NIDCD, 2023). It is important to note that DLD is not caused by decreased auditory acuity and that deaf and hard-of-hearing children may also have DLD (Hardman et al., 2023).

The number of children presenting with language delays has increased dramatically during the COVID-19 pandemic. In a large analysis of first-time diagnosis codes, researchers found that in 2022, the number of children between birth and age 12 years who were diagnosed with a speech disorder more than doubled, to approximately 1.2 million children, compared to the average rate in the 2 years leading up to the COVID-19 pandemic. While all groups under age 13 years showed an increase in speech and language disorder diagnosis, this was most pronounced in infants and toddlers. Children between ages birth to 2 years saw a 136% increase in new diagnoses in 2022, compared to the pre-pandemic rate. Diagnostic rates were stable in teens ages 13 to 17 years, suggesting that the changes during the COVID-19 pandemic had a larger impact on the development of communication skills in young children (Khan et al., 2023).

Consistent with these findings, several large-scale studies of infant development during the COVID-19 pandemic have found circumscribed delays in language and communication skills. A study of more than 300 babies born between March 2020 and May 2020 found that they were more likely to be delayed in demonstrating first spoken words and pointing compared to a pre-pandemic cohort (Byrne et al., 2023). In a meta-analysis of eight studies that included more than 21,000 infants whose parents completed a standardized developmental questionnaire (*Ages and Stages Questionnaire*, 3rd ed.), results indicated significant delays in communication skills, but not in other areas of motor or cognitive development (Hessami et al., 2022). Presumably, these changes are at least partly related to having had decreased opportunities to communicate with individuals with whom the child was not living.

Compounding any effect of changes in the psychosocial environment on the development of language skills, there were likely delays in assessment of and intervention for DLD and hearing loss. Like neuropsychologists, speech and language pathologists continued to provide in-person services using personal protective equipment (PPE) or telehealth (Tohidast et al., 2020). However, in Winter 2022–2023, a national poll of audiologists and speech and language pathologists reported significant backlogs created by deferred care during the COVID-19 pandemic. Audiologists reported delayed diagnosis of hearing loss and seeing more children with persistent ear infections, which can interfere with language development. Speech and language pathologists reported seeing a greater number of children presenting with language delays, including in social communication (American Speech-Language-Hearing Association [ASHA], 2023).

It will be important to follow this cohort of children into childhood and adolescence, to understand whether early language delays as a result of the COVID-19 pandemic persist or whether these children "catch up" over time. Persistent delays may increase the need for future special education services and private speech and language therapy, particularly to decrease the risk of associated learning disorders. In Chapter 8, we will also consider the possibility that the differences in language development may have long-lasting effects.

References

Altarac, M., & Saroha, E. (2007). Lifetime prevalence of learning disability among US children. *Pediatrics, 119* (Suppl. 1), S77–83. https://doi.org/10.1542/peds.2006-2089L

American Psychiatric Association. (2013). *Diagnostic and statistical manual of mental Disorders* (5th ed.). https://doi.org/10.1176/appi.books.9780890425596

American Speech-Language-Hearing Association (ASHA). (2023). Poll shows increases in hearing, speech, and language referrals, more communication challenges in young children. *ASHA.* https://www.asha.org/news/2023/poll-shows-increases-in-hearing-speech-and-language-referrals-more-communication-challenges-in-young-children/

Bannett, Y., Dahlen, A., Huffman, L. C., & Feldman, H. M. (2022). Primary care diagnosis and treatment of attention-deficit/hyperactivity disorder in school-age children: Trends and disparities during the COVID-19 pandemic. *Journal of Developmental and Behavioral Pediatrics, 43*(7), 386–392. https://doi.org/10.1097/dbp.0000000000001087

Biederman, J., Monuteaux, M. C., Spencer, T., Wilens, T. E., Macpherson, H. A., & Faraone, S. V. (2008). Stimulant therapy and risk for subsequent substance use disorders in male adults with ADHD: A naturalistic controlled 10-year follow-up study. *American Journal of Psychiatry, 165*(5), 597–603. https://doi.org/10.1176/appi.ajp.2007.07091486

Boland, H., DiSalvo, M., Fried, R., Woodworth, K. Y., Wilens, T., Faraone, S. V., & Biederman, J. (2020). A literature review and meta-analysis on the effects of ADHD medications on functional outcomes. *Journal of Psychiatric Research, 123,* 21–30. https://doi.org/10.1016/j.jpsychires.2020.01.006

Braaten, E. B., Ward, A. K., Forchelli, G., Vuijk, P. J., Cook, N. E., McGuinness, P., . . . Doyle, A. E. (2020). Characteristics of child psychiatric outpatients with slow processing speed and potential mechanisms of academic impact. *European Child & Adolescent Psychiatry, 29*(10), 1453–1464. https://doi.org/10.1007/s00787-019-01455-w

Byrne, S., Sledge, H., Hurley, S., Hoolahan, S., Franklin, R., Jordan, N., . . . Hourihane, J. (2023). Developmental and behavioural outcomes at 2 years in babies born during the COVID-19 pandemic: Communication concerns in a pandemic birth cohort. *Archives in Diseases of Childhood*. https://doi.org/10.1136/archdischild-2022-325271

Colvin, M. K., Forchelli, G. A., Reese, K. L., Capawana, M. R., Beery, C. S., Murphy, J., . . . Braaten, E. B. (2022). Neuropsychology consultation to identify learning disorders in children and adolescents: A proposal based on lessons learned during the COVID-19 pandemic. *Child Neuropsychology, 28*(5), 671–688. https://doi.org/10.1080/09297049.2021.2005010

Colvin, M. K., Reesman, J., & Glen, T. (2022). Reforming learning disorder diagnosis following COVID-19 educational disruption. *Nature Reviews in Psychology, 1*(5), 251–252. https://doi.org/10.1038/s44159-022-00052-0

Corona, L., Hine, J., Nicholson, A., Stone, C., Swanson, A., Wade, J., . . . Warren, Z. (2020). TELE-ASD-PEDS: A telemedicine-based ASD evaluation tool for toddlers and young children. *Vanderbilt University Medical Center*. https://vkc.vumc.org/vkc/triad/tele-asd-peds

Coughlin, J. M., Wang, Y., Munro, C. A., Ma, S., Yue, C., Chen, S., . . . Pomper, M. G. (2015). Neuroinflammation and brain atrophy in former NFL players: An in vivo multimodal imaging pilot study. *Neurobiological Disease, 74*, 58–65. https://doi.org/10.1016/j.nbd.2014.10.019

Danielson, M. L., Bohm, M. K., Newsome, K., Claussen, A. H., Kaminski, J. W., Grosse, S. D., . . . Robinson, L. R. (2023). Trends in stimulant prescription fills among commercially insured children and adults—United States, 2016–2021. *Morbidity and Mortality Weekly Report, 72*(13), 327–332. https://doi.org/10.15585/mmwr.mm7213a1

Faraone, S. V., Asherson, P., Banaschewski, T., Biederman, J., Buitelaar, J. K., Ramos-Quiroga, J. A., . . . Franke, B. (2015). Attention-deficit/hyperactivity disorder. *Nature Reviews Disease Primers, 1*, 15020. https://doi.org/10.1038/nrdp.2015.20

Faraone, S. V., Banaschewski, T., Coghill, D., Zheng, Y., Biederman, J., Bellgrove, M. A., . . . Wang, Y. (2021). The World Federation of ADHD International Consensus Statement: 208 evidence-based conclusions about the disorder. *Neuroscience Biobehavioral Review, 128*, 789–818. https://doi.org/10.1016/j.neubiorev.2021.01.022

Fletcher, J. M., & Grigorenko, E. L. (2017). Neuropsychology of learning disabilities: The past and the future. *Journal of International Neuropsychology Society, 23*(9–10), 930–940. https://doi.org/10.1017/s1355617717001084

Friedman, L. A., & Rapoport, J. L. (2015). Brain development in ADHD. *Current Opinion in Neurobiology, 30*, 106–111. https://doi.org/10.1016/j.conb.2014.11.007

Fuller, E. A., & Kaiser, A. P. (2020). The effects of early intervention on social communication outcomes for children with autism spectrum disorder: A meta-analysis. *Journal of Autism and Developmental Disorders, 50*(5), 1683–1700. https://doi.org/10.1007/s10803-019-03927-z

Gabrieli, J. D. (2009). Dyslexia: A new synergy between education and cognitive neuroscience. *Science, 325*(5938), 280–283. https://doi.org/10.1126/science.1171999

Grigorenko, E. L., Compton, D. L., Fuchs, L. S., Wagner, R. K., Willcutt, E. G., & Fletcher, J. M. (2020). Understanding, educating, and supporting children with specific learning disabilities: 50 years of science and practice. *American Psychologist, 75*(1), 37–51. https://doi.org/10.1037/amp0000452

Hardman, G., Herman, R., Kyle, F. E., Ebbels, S., & Morgan, G. (2023). Identifying developmental language disorder in deaf children with cochlear implants: A case study of three children. *Journal of Clinical Medicine, 12*(17). https://doi.org/10.3390/jcm12175755

Hessami, K., Norooznezhad, A. H., Monteiro, S., Barrozo, E. R., Abdolmaleki, A. S., Arian, S. E., . . . Shamshirsaz, A. A. (2022). COVID-19 pandemic and infant neurodevelopmental impairment: A systematic review and meta-analysis. *JAMA Network Open, 5*(10), e2238941. https://doi.org/10.1001/jamanetworkopen.2022.38941

Hyman, S. L., Levy, S. E., Myers, S. M., Council on Children with Disabilities, Pediatrics, Kuo, D., . . . Bridgemohan, C. (2020). Executive summary: Identification, evaluation, and management of children with autism spectrum disorder. *Pediatrics, 145*(1). https://doi.org/10.1542/peds.2019-3448

Jang, J., White, S. P., Esler, A. N., Kim, S. H., Klaiman, C., Megerian, J. T., . . . Kanne, S. M. (2022). Diagnostic evaluations of autism spectrum disorder during the COVID-19 pandemic. *Journal of Autism and Developmental Disorders, 52*(2), 962–973. https://doi.org/10.1007/s10803-021-04960-7

Khan, T., Freeman, R., & Druet, A. (2023). Louder than words: Pediatric speech disorders skyrocket throughout pandemic. https://www.komodohealth.com/insights/louder-than-words-pediatric-speech-disorders-skyrocket-throughout-pandemic

Lord, C., Brugha, T. S., Charman, T., Cusack, J., Dumas, G., Frazier, T., . . . Veenstra-VanderWeele, J. (2020). Autism spectrum disorder. *Nature Reviews Disease Primers*, *6*(1), 5. https://doi.org/10.1038/s41572-019-0138-4

Luna Perez v. Sturgis Public Schools. (2023). 143 S.Ct. 859. United States Supreme Court.

Mallett, C. A. (2017). The school-to-prison pipeline: Disproportionate impact on vulnerable children and adolescents. *Education and Urban Society*, *49*(6), 563–592. https://doi.org/10.1177/0013124516644053

Margolis, A. E., Broitman, J., Davis, J. M., Alexander, L., Hamilton, A., Liao, Z., . . . Milham, M. P. (2020). Estimated prevalence of nonverbal learning disability among North American children and adolescents. *JAMA Network Open*, *3*(4), e202551. https://doi.org/10.1001/jamanetworkopen.2020.2551

Miller, A., & Gold, J. (2022). "Heartbreaking" delays in autism diagnosis and treatment got even worse during pandemic. *CNN*. https://www.cnn.com/2022/03/28/health/autism-delays-pandemic-khn-partner/index.html

National Association of School Psychologists. (2020). The pandemic's impact on special education evaluations and SLD identification. https://www.nasponline.org/resources-and-publications/resources-and-podcasts/covid-19-resource-center/return-to-school/the-pandemics-impact-on-special-education-evaluations-and-sld-identification

National Center for Education Statistics. (2023). Enrollment rates of young children. U.S. Department of Education, Institute of Education Sciences. https://nces.ed.gov/programs/coe/indicator/cfa/enrollment-of-young-children

National Center for Learning Disabilities. (2014). The state of learning disabilities: Facts, trends, and emerging issues, 3rd ed. New York, NY: National Center for Learning Disabilities.

NIDCD. (2023). Developmental language disorder. 44th Annual Report to Congress on the Implementation of the Individuals with Disabilities Education Act, 2022. Office of Special Education and Rehabilitative Services U.S. Department of Education, Alexandria VA.

Office of Special Education and Rehabilitative Services. (2023). 44th annual report to Congress on the implementation of the Individuals with Disabilities Education Act, 2022. https://www.nidcd.nih.gov/health/developmental-language-disorder

Pennington, B. F., McGrath, L. M., & Peterson, R. L. (2019). *Diagnosing learning disorders: From science to practice*. New York: Guilford.

Peterson, R. L., & Pennington, B. F. (2015). Developmental dyslexia. *Annual Review of Clinical Psychology*, *11*, 283–307. https://doi.org/10.1146/annurev-clinpsy-032814-112842

Schmidt, H. (2023). The policy problem behind Adderall's pharmaceutical supply chain crisis. https://pharmanewsintel.com/features/the-policy-problem-behind-adderalls-pharmaceutical-supply-chain-crisis

Schweiberger, K., Patel, S. Y., Mehrotra, A., & Ray, K. N. (2021). Trends in pediatric primary care visits during the coronavirus disease of 2019 pandemic. *Academy of Pediatrics*, *21*(8), 1426–1433. https://doi.org/10.1016/j.acap.2021.04.031

Shaw, K., Bilder, D., McArthur, D., Williams, A., Amoakohene, E., Bakian, A., . . . Maenner, M. (2023). Early identification of autism spectrum disorder among children aged 4 years—Autism and Developmental Disabilities Monitoring Network, 11 sites, United States, 2020. *Morbidity and Mortality Weekly Report*, *72*, 1–15. https://doi.org/10.15585/mmwr.ss7201a1

Tistarelli, N., Fagnani, C., Troianiello, M., Stazi, M. A., & Adriani, W. (2020). The nature and nurture of ADHD and its comorbidities: A narrative review on twin studies. *Neuroscience and Biobehavioral Review*, *109*, 63–77. https://doi.org/10.1016/j.neubiorev.2019.12.017

Tohidast, S. A., Mansuri, B., Bagheri, R., & Azimi, H. (2020). Provision of speech-language pathology services for the treatment of speech and language disorders in children during the COVID-19 pandemic: Problems, concerns, and solutions. *International Journal of Pediatric Otorhinolaryngology*, *138*, 110262. https://doi.org/10.1016/j.ijporl.2020.110262

Tsatsanis, K. D., Fuerst, D. R., & Rourke, B. P. (1997). Psychosocial dimensions of learning disabilities: External validation and relationship with age and academic functioning.

Journal of Learning Disabilities, 30(5), 490–502. https://doi.org/10.1177/002221949703000505

U.S. Department of Education. (2019). IDEA: Section 1414. https://sites.ed.gov/idea/statute-chapter-33/subchapter-ii/1414

Wagner, L., Corona, L. L., Weitlauf, A. S., Marsh, K. L., Berman, A. F., Broderick, N. A., . . . Warren, Z. (2021). Use of the TELE-ASD-PEDS for autism evaluations in response to COVID-19: Preliminary outcomes and clinician acceptability. *Journal of Autism and Developmental Disorders, 51*(9), 3063–3072. https://doi.org/10.1007/s10803-020-04767-y

Wallis, K. E., Nekrasova, E., Bennett, A. E., Fiks, A. G., Gerdes, M., Jenssen, B. P., . . . Guthrie, W. (2022). Autism spectrum disorder screening during the COVID-19 pandemic in a large primary care network. *Academy of Pediatrics, 22*(8), 1384–1389. https://doi.org/10.1016/j.acap.2022.04.005

Willcutt, E. G., Betjemann, R. S., McGrath, L. M., Chhabildas, N. A., Olson, R. K., DeFries, J. C., & Pennington, B. F. (2010). Etiology and neuropsychology of comorbidity between RD and ADHD: The case for multiple-deficit models. *Cortex, 46*(10), 1345–1361. https://doi.org/10.1016/j.cortex.2010.06.009

Willcutt, E. G., & Pennington, B. F. (2000). Psychiatric comorbidity in children and adolescents with reading disability. *Journal of Child Psychology and Psychiatry, 41*(8), 1039–1048.

Wolraich, M. L., Hagan, J. F., Jr, Allan, C., Chan, E., Davison, D., Earls, M., . . . Disorder, A. W. A.-D. H. (2019, October). Clinical practice guideline for the diagnosis, evaluation, and treatment of attention-deficit/hyperactivity disorder in children and adolescents. *Pediatrics, 144*(4), e20192528. https://doi.org/10.1542/peds.2019-2528

7
Psychosocial Stressors and Mental Health Concerns

Increased Mental Health Concerns and Reduced Access to Services

Almost immediately after initial widespread school closures, experts in child and adolescent mental health raised concerns about the potential impact of pandemic-related stressors on youth emotional and brain development. Psychological harm would not occur simply due to fear of illness or the deaths of family members, researchers noted, but would also result from prolonged school closures, reduced access to mental health evaluation and treatment, and social isolation. And in fact, the mental health impacts have led to what has been called a "psychiatric epidemic" and a "pandemic within the pandemic" (Bozzola et al., 2022; Hossain et al., 2020; Parker-Pope et al., 2021).

While there was a pre-pandemic trend of increasing rates of mental illness in children and adolescents (Office of the Surgeon General [OSG], 2021), it is now clear there has been an increase in behavioral and mood dysfunction since the onset of the pandemic, with disproportionate impact on children of color (Eboigbe et al., 2023; Fegert et al., 2020), those with preexisting psychiatric or neurodevelopmental disorders, and those with economic instability (Chavira et al., 2022; Williams et al., 2022). For instance, Racine et al. (2021) in a meta-analysis, documented a doubling of rates of depression in youth (12.9% to 25.2%), with rates of anxiety increasing from 11.6% to 20.5%. Hill et al. (2021) documented a 20% increase in suicidal ideation and a 30% increase in youth suicide attempts from 2019 to 2020.

Large-scale trends reveal increasing gaps as demand for behavioral health care outpaces supply of behavioral health providers, and that the COVID-19 pandemic exacerbated the existing behavioral health crisis (Jain, 2023). As a percentage of overall demand, behavioral health care demand grew in 2022 at a rate of 18% compared to 2019 visits (Jain, 2023). In terms of the specific conditions driving some of this increase, they were primarily

Neurodevelopment in the Post-Pandemic World. Molly Colvin, Jennifer Linton Reesman, and Tannahill Glen, Oxford University Press. © Oxford University Press 2024. DOI: 10.1093/9780197762660.003.0007

driven by increases in visits for eating disorders, anxiety disorders, alcohol and substance use disorders, and depressive and bipolar disorders that all increased compared to 2019. This same report found that telehealth utilization increased dramatically, with 32% of behavioral health visits delivered via telehealth in 2022. Behavioral health concerns for adolescents increased at rates higher than the population overall and correlated positively with increased utilization of social media. With this increase in significant mental health concerns has come an increase in mental-health-related prescriptions, with the share of mental health prescriptions for youth 17 years and younger representing 21.8% of overall prescription volume, compared to 16.2% in 2017 (Jain, 2023).

Studies now clearly document increased rates of psychiatric dysfunction in children and adolescents. In a study across 25 countries, the number of emergency department evaluations for self-harm and psychiatric distress doubled from 2019 to 2021 (Wong et al., 2023). Levine et al. (2023) studied pediatric mental health emergencies in New York City from 2016 to 2022 and documented increases in those cases during each of five successive COVID-19 waves, with the highest increases for females, adolescents, and patients of Asian descent. Interestingly, the authors documented increased mental health emergency department visits through June 2022, despite high vaccination uptake and return to in-person classes, which they opine may reflect in part barriers to access to mental health resources for youth. Another intriguing finding from the study was that children and adolescents from zip codes associated with *greater* access to outpatient mental health resources exhibited *higher* emergency room utilization, perhaps, according to the authors, reflecting the relative loss of commonly used resources compared to those from underserved areas.

Vidal, Holland, and Duriseti (2023) acknowledged that published studies cannot dissociate the effects of educational disruption and broader societal lockdowns; the sheer proportion of time children and adolescents spend in school makes their closures a highly likely major factor in the youth mental health crisis. The authors also cite the effects of educational disruption on social determinants of health: because schools were shut, exposure to high-risk events increased, contributing to the increase in gun deaths, domestic violence, and drug overdose.

Vidal, Holland, and Duriseti (2023) summarized the increase in youth suicide and suicidal ideation compared to pre-pandemic data and described the likely contribution of school closures to increased youth mental health problems. The authors suggested that school closures, especially for vulnerable youth, may have exposed children and adolescents to more adverse childhood experiences and unhealthy behaviors, such as decreased exercise and increased screen time. Critically, the authors opined that school closure in and of itself may not have been the sole cause of psychiatric disturbance, but for youth who most require stable routine and structure, school closures may have resulted in a "cascade" of negative effects from the disruption. This viewpoint is echoed across other studies and summary reports, in which educational disruption was a common and exacerbating factor experienced by large numbers of children and is complicated by a simultaneous incapacity of the mental health care system to provide support to all of the children needing care.

Madigan et al. (2023) disagreed with the notion that youth mental health problems post-pandemic simply followed a trajectory noted prior to COVID-19. In their systematic review and meta-analysis of 53 longitudinal studies, they documented a clear and significant increase in symptoms of depression and anxiety. Their findings note that depression symptoms were particularly likely to increase among females and those from higher income backgrounds and that anxiety symptom increase was smaller, but also noteworthy for children from higher income backgrounds.

While pandemic-related stress (e.g., fear of infection or actual loss of a loved one) has likely played a role in the mental health crisis, youth were particularly vulnerable due to pandemic containment measures like quarantines and school closures (Centers for Disease Control and Prevention [CDC], 2022; Loades et al., 2020; Singh et al., 2020). Even pre-pandemic, those infection containment measures and restrictions were shown to negatively impact youth mental health (Magson et al., 2021; Sprang & Silman, 2013); and since the onset of COVID-19, studies have shown that psychological distress for both youth and adults has been worsened by containment measures and societal disruption rather than illness anxiety per se (Magson et al., 2021; Sprang & Silman, 2013; West & Lake, 2021).

Some researchers have specifically cited school closures as a major contributor to increased youth mental health disorders (Bagnall et al., 2022; Chaabane et al., 2021; Hallin et al., 2022). Beyond the core mission of educating youth, schools provide opportunities for development of important social and emotional development, and socialization. School "connectedness" is correlated with positive health and psychological adjustment (Diendorfer et al., 2021; Grapin et al., 2016; Jose et al., 2012), while social isolation increases the risk for mental health problems like mood dysfunction (Loades et al., 2020). COVID-19-related school closures have been associated with increased screen use and decreased physical activity. Negative effects were greatest for the most vulnerable students, for example, those from economically disadvantaged households (Manchia et al., 2022; Viner et al., 2021). Even time on the school playground may play a critical role in psychological and social development. Free play promotes social maturity, group belonging, and well-being (Evaldsson & Corsaro, 1998; McNamara et al., 2017, Murray & Ramstetter, 2013) and children learn cooperation, conflict management, risk-taking, social competence, and independence (Jarvis et al., 2014; Veiga et al., 2017).

School-based health centers (SBHCs) are the front line of programs for psychological, medical, and nutritional support for approximately six million students in the United States (Lear et al., 2008; Richards et al., 2023). Most SBHCs suspended in-person services during the initial pandemic shutdowns, with only about 1 in 10 remaining open during initial closures (Duong et al., 2021). Many children lost access to regular meals (Kenney et al., 2022) and daily visits with the school nurse, who might document vaccinations, make sure that medications were administered, or notice when the child had a health condition that needed to be evaluated by their pediatrician (Rothstein & Olympia, 2020).

School closures also removed a key provider of mental health services at precisely the time when they were needed, exacerbating a national crisis in access to psychiatric treatment, and likely increasing wait times for treatment in community clinics and hospitals. More than 13% of adolescents (3 million students) received mental health services in school prior to the pandemic (Lipari et al., 2013). Of adolescents engaged in psychiatric care, more than half received school-based care, and 35% *only* received school-based care (Ali et al., 2019). Of these students, a disproportionate number are from traditionally under-represented groups: students of color and those from economically disadvantaged households (Richards et al., 2023). As is a common theme of this text, those that were from already marginalized groups faced the greatest challenge and impact from prolonged educational disruption.

In addition to disrupting access to mental health services for those who were receiving it, the closure of SBHCs likely also delayed intervention for students who developed a need during the COVID-19 pandemic. Richards et al. (2023) hypothesized that teachers, lacking in-person casual interactions, were less likely to notice mental health concerns, and students who might normally agree to "drop in" to a SBHC may not have been able or willing to make a formal appointment and access psychological services virtually. The authors analyzed electronic medical records of more than 5,000 public high school students seen in Massachusetts SBHCs from 2018 through 2021. Unsurprisingly, they found a dramatic 77% decline in number of students referred for mental health services, and contrary to expectations, neither number of students referred for treatment nor number of patient visits rebounded in 2021 after SBHCs reopened with virtual care. Those numbers only increased in late 2021, once in-person mental health services were re-established. The authors opined that perhaps students viewed virtual interactions as a major factor in their isolation or distress, and thus were understandably less apt to view virtual therapy as a viable solution.

The psychological burden was not purely due to families and children struggling with virtual instruction and shuttered schools. Some parents of children with disabilities or chronic medical conditions were torn between return to in-person education and worries about risk for severe illness (Vanhalst et al., 2018).

Some researchers have opined that the quality of evidence linking school closures to youth mental health problems is lacking (Black et al., 2023). However, a rejoinder to that argument (Vaillancourt et al., 2023) cites the precautionary principle, the idea that advocates of novel interventions should first prove their proposed actions do no harm (Thierer, 2019). The authors note under that principle, making recommendations to mitigate harms to youth mental health based on imperfect evidence is supported, as the potential benefits far outweigh the risks of delaying urgent advocacy.

Unfortunately, the increase in psychiatric distress has not been transient. Even in the second year of the pandemic, the share of emergency room visits resulting in psychiatric hospitalization increased by more than 8%, suggesting increased severity of clinical presentations. The shortage of inpatient mental health services led to a 76% increase in the percentage of cases involving prolonged "boarding" or waiting for inpatient hospitalization (Overhage et al., 2023).

The effects of prolonged social isolation have been identified as a significant contributor to increases in mental health dysfunction during the pandemic. This is unsurprising, as pre-pandemic research consistently demonstrated negative effects of social isolation on psychological development (Vanhalst et al., 2018). Data from the Centers for Disease Control and Prevention (CDC; 2022) identified "school connectedness" as an important moderator of emotional distress during the period of disruption, but only 47% of students surveyed reported positive school connectedness. Social connectedness with an extended community, including school, is a known protective factor from the negative impacts of trauma, especially in youth who face additional disadvantages. Social connectedness is associated with diminished emotional distress, suicide attempts and violence involvement (Svetaz et al., 2000). Indeed, decline in school connectedness during the COVID-19 pandemic was associated with greater symptoms of anxiety and depression in students, and access to peer and family support has been consistently found to be a protective factor (Cohodes et al., 2021; Rodman et al., 2022). Those with preexisting mental health conditions may have been at particular risk for exacerbation of those concerns (Fegert et al., 2020). Further, Program for International Student Assessment (PISA) test results indicated that in school systems in which student test performance and sense of belonging in school remained stable, longer school closures were less frequently reported (OECD, 2023).

Fortunately, the burgeoning research on pandemic-era mental health has also allowed investigators to elucidate protective factors against psychiatric dysfunction and characteristics associated with psychological resilience. Chavira and colleagues (2022) described studies focused on identification of factors associated with psychological health. They detailed evidence showing less passive screen time, maintenance of routine/structure, and positive relations with family were associated with better mental health functioning.

Reduced Access to Services at a Time of Crisis

The mental health crisis for youth has coincided with a grave national shortage of access to mental health evaluation and treatment for children and adolescents. After a steep decline in appointments for psychiatric evaluation when closures occurred in March 2020, there was a corresponding sharp increase in visits to the emergency room for mental health evaluation (Leeb et al., 2020).

There was a bidirectional impact, in that increasing mental health concerns acted to reduce access to services as demand for services outstripped capacity of the mental health care system. Second, delayed or disrupted access to care (virtual or limited in-person care) exacerbated the mental health of individuals who required access to mental health care. In general, psychologists have faced increased demand for services since March 2020, increased severity of clinical presentations, and increased wait times for evaluation and treatment (American Psychological Association, 2022). Increased demand for mental health services has been widespread and repeatedly documented in large-scale surveys of psychologists in 2020, 2021, and 2022 (American Psychological Association, 2022). These consecutive nationwide surveys of practicing psychologists documented that demand for trauma, stress, and substance use disorders has grown in the years that the survey was conducted.

With increased demand for services has come increased difficulty for many individuals in accessing desired or needed mental health care, with half of psychologists surveyed reporting being unable to meet the demand for increased service and resorting to adding to or starting a waiting list for services. These accessibility difficulties may be most prominent for individuals from marginalized backgrounds, those requiring specialized services, and those who live in areas that were already underserved in mental health professional access and overall health care access (American Psychological Association, 2022).

Once clinics began to reopen, they were quickly met by increased demand, which has resulted in long waiting lists that continue to be problematic even now, despite the implementation of telepsychology. The American Psychological Association and the University of Michigan School of Public Health Behavioral Health Workforce Research Center (2021) measured the number of child and adolescent psychologists at half the number required to meet demand. Interestingly, the survey was performed in April and May 2021, more than a year into the pandemic, and 88% of psychologists were seeing patients either remotely or in hybrid fashion. This is significant, as studies have shown telepsychology may be less appropriate or desirable for younger children and those with severe symptoms (Islam et al., 2023).

This crisis of access to help makes it less likely that pediatric mental health issues are diagnosed as early as possible and treatment is initiated. This, in turn, is important because early intervention is associated with improved functioning, employment, and education and decreased risk for relapse (Read et al., 2018).

Risk Factors for Declines in Physical Health Increased

Physical health factors also influence both mental health status and neurocognitive performance (Jirout et al., 2019), and research has shown children and adolescents have demonstrated more indicators of physical health challenges thought to relate to pandemic disruptions (Chaabane et al., 2021), such as signs of cardiopulmonary deconditioning (Dayton et al., 2021) and altered sleep and eating behaviors (Spitzer, 2021; Storz, 2020). Pediatric ophthalmologists noted decreases in treatment seeking for ocular trauma, and disruption of youth vision screening programs, with potentially delayed ophthalmologic diagnoses and interventions (Kaur et al., 2023). Youth with preexisting or chronic medical conditions experienced numerous disruptions, such as absence of school-based care, closures of outpatient clinics, or stress-related exacerbation of symptoms (Garcia-Prats et al., 2021).

Participation in organized and informal sports and physical recreation activities confers medical, psychological, and cognitive benefits for youth, and greater school connectedness, which is in turn associated with greater resilience. Access to youth sports was severely curtailed during the pandemic, even after schools reopened (Johnson et al., 2023). This was an especially difficult challenge for high-poverty schools, often located in areas with fewer options for non-school physical activities/recreation or green space.

LaForge-MacKenzie et al. (2022) specifically examined the effect of disruption in extracurricular activities (ECAs) and sports for youth during the pandemic. ECAs and sports participation, they wrote, have been consistently associated with lower levels of psychological distress, higher academic performance, and increased physical activity (itself associated with youth mood functioning). ECAs and sports participation prior to and/or during the pandemic were associated with fewer mental health symptoms during the outbreak. Johnson et al. (2023) found that learning mode (virtual or in person/hybrid) was associated with sports participation: those in virtual classes were less likely to be engaged in organized sports. More recent reporting on the inequality gap of sports participation has been documented, with children from marginalized backgrounds and those with economic disadvantage less likely to be engaged in organized sports compared with prior to pandemic (Black et al., 2022). Public schools have (on the whole) reduced access to physical education, gym time, and equipment to promote physical activity, with the 2022 Report Card on Physical Activity for Children and Youth giving an overall grade of D– (reduced from a C– in 2014), for Overall Physical Activity (Kuzik et al., 2023). Of concern, sports may become targets of budget cuts as financially challenged school systems (see the fiscal cliff described in Chapter 6) prioritize academic services and face declining enrollment and increasing demand and need for academic interventions. In Illinois, where educational disruption was prolonged, 2024–2025 proposed budget cuts eliminate junior varsity sports, a trend Richtel (2023) referred to as "the physical divide," a trend exacerbated by the pandemic-era impact on the fiscal crisis in high-poverty schools.

Participation in ECAs and part-time work was also significantly reduced during the COVID-19 pandemic, especially the first year of the pandemic (Ilari et al., 2022). Artistic activities such as music were the least impacted extracurricular activities, followed by participation in scout, religious/spiritual, academic (e.g., science), and athletic activities. Team sports (e.g., soccer, basketball, baseball) were the most impacted, with an almost 90% reduction in access to these sports (Ilari et al., 2022). Combined with ongoing cuts to youth sports access, there may be an ongoing reduction in overall access to organized physical activity for youth in high-poverty areas that were more likely to experience prolonged educational disruption.

Given the substantial evidence of the positive effects of spending time in outdoor spaces on psychological, physical, and cognitive health, there is reason to be concerned that pandemic-related changes and reductions in outdoor activities such as sports and "play dates" could have negative implications for child development (Scott et al., 2022). Chapter 8 addresses how reduced access to certain environmental enrichment can impact brain development.

The Impact of Psychological Distress and Physical Functioning on Neurocognitive Performance and Diagnoses

The measurable increase in rates of psychiatric disorders in youth is a central issue for neuropsychologists, because both psychological and physical conditions have been shown to influence performance on neurocognitive, psychological, and other types of tests (Silver et al., 2022). It is notable that children and adolescents with preexisting neurodevelopmental, neurological, and psychiatric conditions have experienced disproportionate worsening of symptoms such as depression, anxiety, irritability, inattention, and hyperactivity (Colizzi et al., 2020; Conti et al., 2020; Cost et al., 2022; Nonweiler et al., 2020): these symptoms can influence performance on neuropsychological tests (Kavanaugh et al., 2016).

Increased Exposure to Adverse Childhood Experiences

Adverse childhood experiences (ACEs) are defined by the CDC as childhood (age 0–17 years) exposure to trauma from abuse, or neglect, and household dysfunction (Centers for Disease Control Prevention, 2022). The COVID-19 pandemic increased the risk for exposure to ACEs, due to, for instance, increased household economic instability (Sahle et al., 2020; Sonu et al., 2021) and parental stress, especially working mothers, who reported significantly higher rates of anxiety and depression during the pandemic (Panchal et al., 2020). Furthermore, social isolation and economic insecurity predict the risk for domestic violence and child maltreatment (Schneider et al., 2016; Wong et al., 2020) and, of course, those two stressors were present during the pandemic. The risk of experiencing an ACE is higher for racial and ethnic minorities and those with fewer financial resources (Sonu et al., 2021), who are also more likely to be among the estimated 40,000 children who had lost a parent to COVID-19 by April 2021 (Kidman et al., 2021). As a result, nearly a third of U.S. adolescents reported ACE exposure during the pandemic (Hertz et al., 2023).

The risk of ACEs during the COVID-19 pandemic was exacerbated by educational disruption and the attendant loss of school- and community-based services. School officials and home visits from state welfare agencies are common sources of reports of suspected child abuse and domestic violence (Fegert et al., 2020; Sharma et al., 2021). Indeed, there were fewer reports of possible child abuse throughout 2020 (Sharma et al., 2021), but increased reports of domestic violence (Fegert et al., 2020) and more severe abusive injuries in children presenting to emergency departments (Kaiser et al., 2021), suggesting the reduction in child abuse reports was not due to an actual decline in abuse.

Children who experience ACEs have an increased risk for attention problems, poor academic skills, aggression, and social problems (Jimenez et al., 2016). These are common presenting concerns in pediatric neuropsychological evaluations, which may mean that in the near future clinicians will see more youth with recent ACE exposure. Longer term, ACE exposure increases risk of future physical, cognitive, and mental health difficulties that may prompt neuropsychological evaluations in adulthood (Brown et al., 2009, 2010; Chapman et al., 2004; Holman et al., 2016; McLaughlin et al., 2012). As such, the impact of the COVID-19 pandemic on cognitive and mental health functioning can be expected to be long-lasting and will need to be considered in current and future psychological, psychoeducational, and neuropsychological evaluations across the lifespan.

Increased Risk for Youth With Disabilities

Youth with disabilities were not immune to the psychiatric crisis, and access to mental health care for individuals with disabilities may have been even more curtailed. The American Speech-Language-Hearing Association (2023) published a survey of audiologists and speech language pathologists querying rates of referrals for children from birth to 5 years of age during the pandemic. They found that about a third of audiologists reported seeing more children with delayed diagnosis of hearing loss, while more than three quarters of speech language pathologists reported seeing more children with language delays, language disorders, or social communication impairment. In one state, Maryland, an estimated 50% of infants born with hearing loss in 2021 may be delayed in receiving a diagnosis of hearing loss (Jenks et al., 2022). Factoring in backlogs related to clinic closures, clinicians endorsed factors including increases in screen time, reduced daycare and pre-kindergarten social interactions, and reduced peer-to-peer social interactions perceived as contributing to the increases in referrals.

Even with the return to classrooms and more typical instructional patterns in the 2022–2023 academic year, the increased need for psychosocial support has persisted, with most large school systems and health care systems unable to meet the demand for services. To better understand this phenomenon and to place it into context of what may be expected in the future for policymakers, educators, and mental health professionals, this section traces the rates, supports, and empirical evidence available. Indeed, a cohort effect for psychological distress during the pandemic has already been described in adults. Alteration of pre-pandemic psychological distress trajectories in British women across several cohorts was measured by Moreno-Agostino et al (2023): instead of the typical midlife peak and then decline in psychological distress, a new peak in distress was measured in the first year of the pandemic. The implications for longer term disability, mortality, and other outcomes remains unclear. There is concern that this long-term prolonged exposure to a significant risk factor may pose long-term consequences for mental health in the future for this generation that experienced significant educational disruption and represent a unique risk factor for mental health challenges later in life.

An international study of youth with autism spectrum disorder (ASD) and other neurodevelopmental disorders (NDDs) found that severity and extent of increased mental health symptoms were correlated with perception of greater illness risk and, importantly, pandemic-related psychosocial changes, such as restrictions on movement and cancellation of events (Vibert et al., 2023).

Dose–Response Relationship

Researchers have identified a dose–response relationship between virtual learning and mental health symptoms in high school students: more virtual learning was associated with greater mental health symptom reporting. The authors noted these results suggest virtual education was a specific contributor to the increase in youth mental health problems worldwide. Tsujimoto et al. (2022) explored the impact of different learning environments during the pandemic. They surveyed families of school-aged children in Ontario regarding mental health concerns such as depression, anxiety, and attention-deficit disorder symptoms, and they also queried contextual factors related to school settings, such as physical distancing, frequency of group work, one-on-one time with teachers, avoidance of gatherings and physical contact, and mask use. Significant levels of mood symptoms were noted across all groups, consistent with other studies showing increased psychological dysfunction in children and adolescents during the pandemic. Interestingly, they found that children attending in-person instruction at school did not engage in the social learning activities associated with in-person education. The strongest predictor of current mental health concerns was a pre-pandemic mental health condition; however, children with no pre-pandemic psychiatric diagnosis who engaged in virtual education demonstrated about the same level of mental health symptom reporting as those (also in virtual school) with pre-pandemic psychiatric conditions.

Fahle et al. (2023) noted that learning losses were not only due to instruction modality. More restrictive local infection containment policies may have had a subtle impact on psychological adjustment and educational engagement; more severe curtailment of regular activities was correlated with learning losses in their study.

Viner et al. (2022) conducted a systematic review of studies on youth mental health and health-related behaviors, with a specific focus on data collected during the "second wave" of the COVID-19 pandemic in the 2020–2021 school year, when restrictions on movement had been lifted though educational disruption was still common. Evaluating more than 2,800 articles, covering 27,787 students, the authors found a significant association between school closures and mental health problems. Viner and colleagues (2022) caution that social isolation resulting from restrictive measures may confound efforts to measure the mental health effects of prolonged school closures. However, another point can be made: even if mental health problems during the pandemic stemmed from socially isolating policies rather than school closures, per se, in-person education would then theoretically mitigate mental health challenges associated with isolation.

Lessons learned from the 1960s and extended school closures of Prince Edward County, Virginia, are instructive. Looking back to the 1966 study by Green on Virginia's Black students who were denied education for 5 years, there was the recognition that in-person education conveyed importance beyond the aspects of learning: "Many indicated that the resumption of schooling was a very significant aspect of their lives. This finding supported an earlier assumption that the closing of the schools had a traumatic effect" for both Black adults and school-aged children (Green et al., 1966, p. 106). Further, large gaps in achievement for the cohort have been attributed in part to children staying home during the time when they normally would receive instruction: more than half of the Black students who remained in Prince Edward County during massive resistance stayed home, as opposed to working or moving to nearby schools (Heaton, 2008).

Family Life Changes

The COVID-19 pandemic and associated widespread educational disruption had an immediate impact on family life. As children were adjusting to the demands of remote learning, many parents were also adjusting to the demands of remote work and/or limited childcare options. Many daycare and private preschool programs closed due to a combination of factors, including reduced enrollment, compliance with government regulations, and the increased expense associated with trying to maintain health and safety regulations. Reflecting these forces, employment in daycare facilities dropped 35% in April 2020 (Crouse et al., 2023).

For many families, the combination of taking care of children while also working from home proved impossible. The number of women in the workforce with children under age 6 years declined precipitously during the COVID-19 pandemic, from 10.1 million in 2019 to 9.7 million in 2021 (Crouse et al., 2023). Within this group, women in low-wage earning positions were more likely to exit the workforce than those with high-wage earning positions (Lim & Zabek, 2023).

Placing concerns regarding the changes to family life that impacted working parents into context, literature on international surveys conducted prior to the pandemic are informative. Large, international surveys of men and women indicated that daughters of employed mothers were more likely to be employed and earn higher incomes than peers who did not have employed mothers (McGinn et al., 2019). In follow-up to that work, McGinn found that COVID-19 did not wipe out all of the gains in employment that were made. Rather, women and mothers were more likely to take advantage of flexibility in their work and engage in more work from home when able to, and fathers were somewhat less likely to engage in demands for flexibility from their employer (Kray et al., 2022).

Family and lifestyle factors present during the widespread disruption associated with the pandemic impacted adolescents; it decreased access to quality food, reduced physical activity, and increased screen time (de Figueiredo et al., 2021). These authors suggested that possible long-term consequences from these prolonged stressors included underdeveloped brain circuitry, obesity, substance abuse, psychiatric disorders, and an increase in suicidal thoughts (de Figueiredo et al., 2021).

Large-scale outcome studies of mental health of children and adolescents appear to be forthcoming, with some promising international samples still in collection phase at the time of this writing. The Collaborative Outcomes study on Health and Functioning during Infection Times—Children & Adolescents (COH-FIT-C&A) is a large-scale, international survey available in 30 languages that actively examines adolescents and children via self- and parent ratings, including examination of psychopathology, family factors, and quality of life (Solmi et al., 2022).

Substance Use, Misuse, and Abuse

The topic of substance use, misuse, and abuse in children and adolescents during the pandemic and prolonged educational disruption presents the opportunity for a nuanced view of the findings and recognition that across multiple studies youth appear to present with more risk factors that make them vulnerable to future substance use or abuse. Depending on the timing of studies, many researchers found that there may have been decreased access to peers and, for many adolescents, a lack of access and opportunity to access substances (Layman et al., 2022). In the decade before the pandemic, youth substance use was declining in the United States (Hoots et al., 2023), and it continued to decline in the period from 2019 to 2021.

In a large sample of adolescents surveyed and followed from 2018 and through 2020 (N = 1,188), there were noteworthy findings related to both mental health and substance use. COVID-19-related stress and loneliness were associated with depression, and a negative change in family financial situation was related to an increase in alcohol use among adolescents (Temple et al., 2022). These authors concluded that significant and structural resources will be needed for the future to mitigate the negative impact on adolescent psychosocial health and substance use.

In a longitudinal survey of high school students in Los Angeles County, California, researchers found that adolescents who experienced negative daily life changes due to COVID-19 were more likely to initiate cannabis use (Herzig et al., 2023). Odds of initiating cannabis use increased with COVID-19 negative daily life changes. This is broadly consistent with other literature on parent coping and increasing use of alcohol and cannabis reported by parents during a mandatory home-schooling period (Deacon et al., 2021). This also suggests a relationship between parent and child coping strategies such that teens may be more likely to access or turn to substance use if parents are also using substances as a coping strategy.

Surveys of parents in March and April 2020 indicated unique pandemic-related stressors of parents; one survey found 26.5% of parents were reporting problematic alcohol use, and almost half of parents had reported using at least one substance in the past 2 weeks (Lamar et al., 2021). Implications of new or worsened parental substance use or abuse has a wide range of impact on child development, particularly if the parent may develop problematic use or abuse and may have had difficulty in accessing help or treatment for problematic use.

Large-scale review studies of youth well-being indicated mixed findings regarding substance use, mirroring large-scale monitoring studies such as those performed by the CDC (Layman et al., 2022). Findings of this large-scale systematic review were consistent and found an overall decline in youth substance use, with some other drugs or unspecified drugs showing an increase in use in some studies and a decrease in use in others. Despite the empirical positivity, the researchers reviewing the studies provide caution in interpretation, as all of the studies note concerning increase in other factors that are known correlates of later life substance use and abuse. Layman and colleagues (2022) suggest that findings indicate a need for prioritizing community-wide surveillance and prevention of substance use due to the increased risk to this generation of youth.

At the time of this writing, the large-scale dataset on youth substance use from the CDC has several noteworthy limitations. Schools were the primary source of data collection, and data collection for the Youth Risk Behavior Surveillance System (YRBS) was conducted in the spring of 2021, when many students had returned to schools in person for the first time since the spring of 2020. The CDC reported an overall response rate to the national YRBS at 57.5%, which was lower than previous years and thought to be due to the challenge of conducting a school-based survey during the COVID-19 pandemic (Mpofu et al., 2023).

Another important source of longitudinal data is the Adolescent Brain Cognitive Development (ABCD) study, and this prospective, longitudinal, nationwide cohort found generally stable substance use, with some exceptions. The exceptions were an increase in nicotine use and prescription drug misuse and an increase in use associated with pandemic-related uncertainty, when parents used alcohol or drugs, when their family experienced material hardship, or when they experienced increased anxiety and depression (Pelham et al., 2021).

The next decade will determine if the increasing risk factors that youth experienced during the pandemic will relate to increases in substance use and abuse overall, or if this generation will continue to display a continued pre-pandemic trend of overall lowered rates of substance use and abuse. The presence of a challenging psychosocial landscape gives reason for pause about optimism and significant reason to redouble efforts aimed to reduce substance use and abuse among vulnerable youth.

References

Ali, M. M., West, K., Teich, J. L., Lynch, S., Mutter, R., & Dubenitz, J. (2019). Utilization of mental health services in educational setting by adolescents in the United States. *Journal of School Health*, *89*(5), 393–401. https://doi.org/10.1111/josh.12753

American Psychological Association. (2022). 2022 COVID-19 practitioner impact survey. https://www.apa.org/pubs/reports/practitioner/2022-covid-psychologist-workload

American Psychological Association, & University of Michigan School of Public Health Behavioral Health Workforce Research Center. (2021). Estimating supply of child and adolescent psychologists. https://www.behavioralhealthworkforce.org/wp-content/uploads/2022/03/Y6P2_Child-and-Adolescent-Psych_Brief-1.pdf

American Speech-Language-Hearing Association (ASHA). (2023). Poll shows increases in hearing, speech, and language referrals, more communication challenges in young children. https://www.asha.org/news/2023/poll-shows-increases-in-hearing-speech-and-language-referrals-more-communication-challenges-in-young-children/

Bagnall, C. L., Skipper, Y., & Fox, C. L. (2022). Primary-secondary school transition under Covid-19: Exploring the perceptions and experiences of children, parents/guardians, and teachers. *British Journal of Educational Psychology, 92*(3), 1011–1033. https://doi.org/https://doi.org/10.1111/bjep.12485

Black, L. I., Terlizzi, E. P., & Vahratian, A. (2022). *Organized sports participation among children aged 6–17 years: United States, 2020*. Hyattsville, MD: NCHS Data Brief National Center for Health Statistics.

Black, T. R., Virk, P., Woodward, M. L., Stea, J. N., & Doan, Q. (2023). Commentary: School closures, the pandemic, and pediatric mental health: Scrutinizing the evidence. *Journal of the Canadian Academy of Child and Adolescent Psychiatry, 32*(2), 71–78.

Bozzola, E., Spina, G., Agostiniani, R., Barni, S., Russo, R., Scarpato, E., . . . Staiano, A. (2022). The use of social media in children and adolescents: Scoping review on the potential risks. *International Journal of Environmental Research and Public Health, 19*(16), 9960. https://doi.org/10.3390/ijerph19169960

Brown, D. W., Anda, R. F., Felitti, V. J., Edwards, V. J., Malarcher, A. M., Croft, J. B., & Giles, W. H. (2010). Adverse childhood experiences are associated with the risk of lung cancer: a prospective cohort study. *BMC Public Health, 10*, 20. https://doi.org/10.1186/1471-2458-10-20

Brown, D. W., Anda, R. F., Tiemeier, H., Felitti, V. J., Edwards, V. J., Croft, J. B., & Giles, W. H. (2009). Adverse childhood experiences and the risk of premature mortality. *American Journal of Preventive Medicine, 37*(5), 389–396. https://doi.org/10.1016/j.amepre.2009.06.021

Centers for Disease Control and Prevention. (2022). Youth risk behavior survey: Data summary and trends report 2011–2021. https://www.cdc.gov/healthyyouth/data/yrbs/pdf/YRBS_Data-Summary-Trends_Report2023_508.pdf

Centers for Disease Control and Prevention (CDC). (2022). Impact of the COVID-19 pandemic early identification of developmental delays and disabilities and opportunities for improvement: A summary of findings from the Act Early Response to COVID-19 Needs Assessment. https://www.cdc.gov/ncbddd/actearly/pdf/Impact-COVID-DevelopDisabil-508.pdf

Centers for Disease Control Prevention. (2022). Fast facts: Preventing adverse childhood experiences. *National Center for Injury Prevention and Control, Division of Violence Prevention*. https://www.cdc.gov/violenceprevention/aces/fastfact.html

Chaabane, S., Doraiswamy, S., Chaabna, K., Mamtani, R., & Cheema, S. (2021). The impact of COVID-19 school closure on child and adolescent health: A rapid systematic review. *Children (Basel), 8*(5), 415. https://doi.org/10.3390/children8050415

Chapman, D. P., Whitfield, C. L., Felitti, V. J., Dube, S. R., Edwards, V. J., & Anda, R. F. (2004). Adverse childhood experiences and the risk of depressive disorders in adulthood. *Journal of Affective Disorders, 82*(2), 217–225. https://doi.org/https://doi.org/10.1016/j.jad.2003.12.013

Chavira, D. A., Ponting, C., & Ramos, G. (2022). The impact of COVID-19 on child and adolescent mental health and treatment considerations. *Behavioral Research and Therapy, 157*, 104169.

Cohodes, E. M., McCauley, S., & Gee, D. G. (2021). Parental buffering of stress in the time of COVID-19: Family-level factors may moderate the association between pandemic-related stress and youth symptomatology. *Research in Child and Adolescent Psychopathology, 49*(7), 935–948. https://doi.org/10.1007/s10802-020-00732-6

Colizzi, M., Sironi, E., Antonini, F., Ciceri, M. L., Bovo, C., & Zoccante, L. (2020). Psychosocial and behavioral impact of COVID-19 in autism spectrum disorder: An online parent survey. *Brain Sciences, 10*(6), 341. https://doi.org/10.3390/brainsci10060341

Conti, E., Sgandurra, G., De Nicola, G., Biagioni, T., Boldrini, S., Bonaventura, E., . . . Battini, R. (2020). Behavioural and emotional changes during COVID-19 lockdown in an Italian paediatric population with neurologic and psychiatric disorders. *Brain Sciences, 10*(12), 918. https://doi.org/10.3390/brainsci10120918

Cost, K. T., Crosbie, J., Anagnostou, E., Birken, C. S., Charach, A., Monga, S., . . . Korczak, D. J. (2022). Mostly worse, occasionally better: Impact of COVID-19 pandemic on the mental health of Canadian children and adolescents. *European Child & Adolescent Psychiatry, 31*(4), 671–684. https://doi.org/10.1007/s00787-021-01744-3

Crouse,G., Ghertner, R., & Chien, N. (2023). Child care industry trends during the recovery from the COVID-19 pandemic. U. S. Department of Health and Human Services Office of the Assistant Secretary for Planning and Evaluation. https://aspe.hhs.gov/sites/default/files/documents/a6108c6a08b6bc61732f50c2d3220f83/covid-19-child-care-industry.pdf

Dayton, J. D., Ford, K., Carroll, S. J., Flynn, P. A., Kourtidou, S., & Holzer, R. J. (2021). The Deconditioning effect of the COVID-19 pandemic on unaffected healthy children. *Pediatric Cardiology, 42*(3), 554–559. https://doi.org/10.1007/s00246-020-02513-w

de Figueiredo, C. S., Sandre, P. C., Portugal, L. C. L., Mázala-de-Oliveira, T., da Silva Chagas, L., Raony, Í., . . . Bomfim, P. O. (2021). COVID-19 pandemic impact on children and adolescents' mental health: Biological, environmental, and social factors. *Progress in Neuropsychopharmacology and Biological Psychiatry, 106*, 110171.

Deacon, S. H., Rodriguez, L. M., Elgendi, M., King, F. E., Nogueira-Arjona, R., Sherry, S. B., & Stewart, S. H. (2021). Parenting through a pandemic: Mental health and substance use consequences of mandated homeschooling. *Couple and Family Psychology: Research and Practice, 10*(4), 281–293. https://doi.org/10.1037/cfp0000171

Diendorfer, T., Seidl, L., Mitic, M., Mittmann, G., Woodcock, K., & Schrank, B. (2021). Determinants of social connectedness in children and early adolescents with mental disorder: A systematic literature review. *Developmental Review, 60*, 100960. https://doi.org/https://doi.org/10.1016/j.dr.2021.100960

Duong, M. T., Bruns, E. J., Lee, K., Cox, S., Coifman, J., Mayworm, A., & Lyon, A. R. (2021). Rates of mental health service utilization by children and adolescents in schools and other common service settings: A systematic review and meta-analysis. *Administration Policy and Mental Health, 48*(3), 420–439. https://doi.org/10.1007/s10488-020-01080-9

Eboigbe, L. I., Simon, C. B., Wang, Y. S., & Tyrell, F. A. (2023). The compounded effect of the dual pandemic on ethnic-racial minority adolescents' mental health and psychosocial well-being. *Current Opinion in Psychology, 52*, 101626. https://doi.org/10.1016/j.copsyc.2023.101626

Evaldsson, A.-C., & Corsaro, W. A. (1998). Play and games in the peer cultures of preschool and preadolescent children: An interpretative approach. *Childhood, 5*(4), 377–402.

Fahle, E. M., Kane, N. T. J., Patterson, T., Reardon, S. F., Staiger, D. O., & Stuart, E. A. (2023). School district and community factors associated with learning loss during the COVID-19 pandemic. Center for Education Policy Research at Harvard University, Cambridge MA. https://cepr.harvard.edu/sites/hwpi.harvard.edu/files/cepr/files/explaining_covid_losses_5.23.pdf

Fegert, J. M., Vitiello, B., Plener, P. L., & Clemens, V. (2020). Challenges and burden of the Coronavirus 2019 (COVID-19) pandemic for child and adolescent mental health: a narrative review to highlight clinical and research needs in the acute phase and the long return to normality. *Child and Adolescent Psychiatry and Mental Health, 14*(1), 20. https://doi.org/10.1186/s13034-020-00329-3

Garcia-Prats, A. J., McAdams, R. M., Matshaba, M., Thahane, L., Butteris, S. M., Conway, J. H., . . . Haq, H. (2021). Mitigating the impacts of COVID-19 on global child health: A call to action. *Current Tropical Medicine Reports, 8*(3), 183–189. https://doi.org/10.1007/s40475-021-00241-6

Grapin, S. L., Sulkowski, M. L., & Lazarus, P. J. (2016). A multilevel framework for increasing social support in schools. *Contemporary School Psychology, 20*(2), 93–106. https://doi.org/10.1007/s40688-015-0051-0

Green, R., Hofmann, L. J., Morse, R., & Morgan, R. (1966). The educational status of children during the first school year following four years of little or no schooling. https://files.eric.ed.gov/fulltext/ED010118.pdf

Hallin, A. E., Danielsson, H., Nordström, T., & Fälth, L. (2022). No learning loss in Sweden during the pandemic: Evidence from primary school reading assessments. *International Journal of Education Research, 114*, 102011. https://doi.org/10.1016/j.ijer.2022.102011

Heaton, P. (2008). Childhood educational disruption and later life outcomes: Evidence from Prince Edward County. *Journal of Human Capital, 2*, 154–187.

Hertz, M., Heim Viox, M., Massetti, G. M., Anderson, K. N., Bacon, S., Fordyce, E., . . . Verlenden, J. V. (2023). Adverse childhood experiences among US adolescents over the course of the COVID-19 pandemic. *Pediatrics, 151*(6), e2022060799. https://doi.org/10.1542/peds.2022-060799

Herzig, S. E., Albers, L., Sotor, D., Lee, R., Ramirez, C., Rahman, T., & Unger, J. B. (2023, September). Pandemic-related life changes and adolescent initiation of cannabis and tobacco/nicotine use. *Addictive Behaviors, 144*, 107724.https://doi.org/10.1016/j.addbeh.2023.107724. Epub 2023 Apr 14. PMID: 37087769; PMCID: PMC10103764

Hill, R. M., Rufino, K., Kurian, S., Saxena, J., Saxena, K., & Williams, L. (2021). Suicide ideation and attempts in a pediatric emergency department before and during COVID-19. *Pediatrics, 147*(3), e2020029280. https://doi.org/10.1542/peds.2020-029280

Holman, D. M., Ports, K. A., Buchanan, N. D., Hawkins, N. A., Merrick, M. T., Metzler, M., & Trivers, K. F. (2016). The association between adverse childhood experiences and risk of cancer in adulthood: A systematic review of the literature. *Pediatrics, 138*(Suppl. 1), S81–S91. https://doi.org/10.1542/peds.2015-4268L

Hoots, B., Li, J., & Hertz, M. (2023). Alcohol and other substance use before and during the COVID-19 pandemic among high school students—Youth Risk Behavior Survey, United States, 2021. *Morbidity and Mortality Weekly Report, 72*, 84–92.

Hossain, M. M., Tasnim, S., Sultana, A., Faizah, F., Mazumder, H., Zou, L., . . . Ma, P. (2020). Epidemiology of mental health problems in COVID-19: A review. *F1000Res, 9*, 636. https://doi.org/10.12688/f1000research.24457.1

Ilari, B., Cho, E., Li, J., & Bautista, A. (2022). Perceptions of parenting, parent-child activities and children's extracurricular activities in times of COVID-19. *Journal of Child and Family Studies, 31*(2), 409–420. https://doi.org/10.1007/s10826-021-02171-3

Islam, S., Sanchez, A. L., McDermott, C. L., Clapp, D., Worley, J., & Becker-Haimes, E. M. (2023). To proceed via telehealth or not? Considerations for pediatric anxiety and related disorders beyond COVID-19. *Cognitive Behavioral Practice.* https://doi.org/10.1016/j.cbpra.2023.01.004

Jain, S. (2023). *Trends shaping the health economy: Behavioral health.* Trilliant Health. https://www.trillianthealth.com/hubfs/Trends%20Shaping%20the%20Health%20Economy_%20Behavioral%20Health%20(5).pdf?hsCtaTracking=e8c9afaf-cda4-40da-9ac4-3a266069b38b%7C46f82a59-c09c-4431-8203-ad92ac5b8421

Jarvis, P., Newman, S., & Swiniarski, L. (2014). On "becoming social": The importance of collaborative free play in childhood. *International Journal of Play, 3*(1), 53–68. https://doi.org/10.1080/21594937.2013.863440

Jenks, C. M., DeSell, M., & Walsh, J. (2022). Delays in infant hearing detection and intervention during the COVID-19 pandemic: Commentary. *166*(4), 603–604). https://doi.org/10.1177/01945998211067728. Epub 2021 Dec 21. PMID: 34933634

Jimenez, M. E., Wade, R., Jr., Lin, Y., Morrow, L. M., & Reichman, N. E. (2016). Adverse experiences in early childhood and kindergarten outcomes. *Pediatrics, 137*(2), e20151839. https://doi.org/10.1542/peds.2015-1839

Jirout, J., LoCasale-Crouch, J., Turnbull, K., Gu, Y., Cubides, M., Garzione, S., . . . Kranz, S. (2019). How lifestyle factors affect cognitive and executive function and the ability to learn in children. *Nutrients, 11*(8), 1953. https://doi.org/10.3390/nu11081953

Johnson, A. M., Knell, G., Walker, T. J., & Kroshus, E. (2023). Differences in American adolescent sport participation during the COVID-19 pandemic by learning mode: A national survey. *Preventive Medicine Report, 32*, 102151. https://doi.org/10.1016/j.pmedr.2023.102151

Jose, P. E., Ryan, N., & Pryor, J. (2012). Does social connectedness promote a greater sense of well-being in adolescence over time? *Journal of Research on Adolescence, 22*(2), 235–251. https://doi.org/https://doi.org/10.1111/j.1532-7795.2012.00783.x

Kaiser, S. V., Kornblith, A. E., Richardson, T., Pantell, M. S., Fleegler, E. W., Fritz, C. Q., . . . Puls, H. T. (2021). Emergency visits and hospitalizations for child abuse during the COVID-19 pandemic. *Pediatrics, 147*(4) e2020038489. https://doi.org/10.1542/peds.2020-038489

Kaur, K., Muralikrishnan, J., Hussaindeen, J. R., Deori, N., & Gurnani, B. (2023). Impact of Covid-19 on pediatric ophthalmology care: Lessons learned. *Pediatric Health, Medicine and Therapeutics, 14*, 309–321. https://doi.org/10.2147/PHMT.S395349

Kavanaugh, B. C., Gaudet, C. E., Dupont-Frechette, J. A., Tellock, P. P., Maher, I. D., Haisley, L. D., & Holler, K. A. (2016). Verbal memory abilities in severe childhood psychiatric disorders and the influence of attention and executive functions. *Archives in Clinical Neuropsychology, 31*(8), 934–943. https://doi.org/10.1093/arclin/acw020

Kenney, E. L., Walkinshaw, L. P., Shen, Y., Fleischhacker, S. E., Jones-Smith, J., Bleich, S. N., & Krieger, J. W. (2022). Costs, reach, and benefits of COVID-19 pandemic electronic benefit transfer and grab-and-go school meals for ensuring youths' access to food during school closures. *JAMA Network Open, 5*(8), e2229514. https://doi.org/10.1001/jamanetworkopen.2022.29514

Kidman, R., Margolis, R., Smith-Greenaway, E., & Verdery, A. M. (2021). Estimates and projections of COVID-19 and parental death in the US. *JAMA Pediatrics, 175*(7), 745–746. https://doi.org/10.1001/jamapediatrics.2021.0161

Kray, L., Townsend, C., Chan-Ahuja, S., Feldberg, A., Turek, A., Affinito, S. J., . . . Whillans, A. (2022). Work hard parent hard: Gender and work life conflict in the COVID-19 pandemic. *Academy of Management Proceedings, 2022*(1), 12531. https://doi.org/10.5465/AMBPP.2022.12531symposium

Kuzik, N., Cameron, C., Carson, V., Chaput, J. P., Colley, R., Doiron, J., . . . Tremblay, M. S. (2023). The 2022 ParticipACTION Report Card on physical activity for children and youth: Focus on the COVID-19 pandemic impact and equity-deserving groups. *Frontiers in Public Health, 11*, 1172168. https://doi.org/10.3389/fpubh.2023.1172168

LaForge-MacKenzie, K., Tombeau Cost, K., Tsujimoto, K. C., Crosbie, J., Charach, A., Anagnostou, E., . . . Korczak, D. J. (2022). Participating in extracurricular activities and school sports during the COVID-19 pandemic: Associations with child and youth mental health. *Frontiers in Sports and Active Living, 4*, 936041. https://doi.org/10.3389/fspor.2022.936041

Lamar, M. R., Speciale, M., Forbes, L. K., & Donovan, C. (2021). The mental health of U.S. parents during the COVID-19 pandemic. *Journal of Mental Health Counseling, 43*(4), 319–335. https://doi.org/10.17744/mehc.43.4.03

Layman, H. M., Thorisdottir, I. E., Halldorsdottir, T., Sigfusdottir, I. D., Allegrante, J. P., & Kristjansson, A. L. (2022). Substance use among youth during the COVID-19 pandemic: A systematic review. *Current Psychiatry Report, 24*(6), 307–324.

Lear, G. J., Barnwell, A. E., & Behrens, D. (2008). Health-care reform and school-based health care. *Public Health Reports, 123*(6), 704–708. https://doi.org/10.1177/003335490812300606

Leeb, R. T., Bitsko, R. H., Radhakrishnan, L., Martinez, P., Njai, R., & Holland, K. M. (2020). Mental health-related emergency department visits among children aged <18 years during the COVID-19 pandemic—United States, January 1–October 17, 2020. *Morbidity and Mortality Weekly Report, 69*(45), 1675–1680. https://doi.org/10.15585/mmwr.mm6945a3

Levine, D. A., Oh, P. S., Nash, K. A., Simmons, W., Grinspan, Z. M., Abramson, E. L., . . . Green, C. (2023). Pediatric mental health emergencies during 5 COVID-19 waves in New York City. *Pediatrics, 152*(5), e2022060553. https://doi.org/10.1542/peds.2022-060553

Lim, K., & Zabek, M. (2023). Women's labor force exits during Covid-19: Differences by motherhood, race, and ethnicity. *Journal of Family and Economic Issues*, 1–24. Finance and Economics Discussion Series 2021-067r1. Washington: Board of Governors of the Federal Reserve System. https://doi.org/10.17016/FEDS.2021.067r1

Lipari, R. N., Hedden, S., Blau, G., & Rubenstein, L. (2013). Adolescent mental health service use and reasons for using services in specialty, educational, and general medical settings. In *The CBHSQ Report* (pp. 1–16). Washington, DC: Substance Abuse and Mental Health Services Administration.

Loades, M. E., Chatburn, E., Higson-Sweeney, N., Reynolds, S., Shafran, R., Brigden, A., . . . Crawley, E. (2020). Rapid systematic review: The impact of social isolation and loneliness on the mental health of children and adolescents in the context of COVID-19. *Journal of the American Academy of Child and Adolescent Psychiatry, 59*(11), 1218–1239. https://doi.org/10.1016/j.jaac.2020.05.009

Madigan, S., Racine, N., Vaillancourt, T., Korczak, D. J., Hewitt, J. M. A., Pador, P., . . . Neville, R. D. (2023). Changes in depression and anxiety among children and adolescents from before to during the COVID-19 pandemic: A systematic review and meta-analysis. *JAMA Pediatrics, 177*(6), 567–581. https://doi.org/10.1001/jamapediatrics.2023.0846

Magson, N. R., Freeman, J. Y. A., Rapee, R. M., Richardson, C. E., Oar, E. L., & Fardouly, J. (2021). Risk and protective factors for prospective changes in adolescent mental health during the COVID-19 pandemic. *Journal of Youth and Adolescence, 50*(1), 44–57. https://doi.org/10.1007/s10964-020-01332-9

Manchia, M., Gathier, A. W., Yapici-Eser, H., Schmidt, M. V., de Quervain, D., van Amelsvoort, T., . . . Vinkers, C. H. (2022). The impact of the prolonged COVID-19 pandemic on stress resilience and mental health: A critical review across waves. *European Neuropsychopharmacology, 55*, 22–83. https://doi.org/10.1016/j.euroneuro.2021.10.864

McGinn, K. L., Ruiz Castro, M., & Lingo, E. L. (2019). Learning from mum: Cross-national evidence linking maternal employment and adult children's outcomes. *Work, Employment and Society, 33*(3), 374–400. https://doi.org/10.1177/0950017018760167

McLaughlin, K. A., Greif Green, J., Gruber, M. J., Sampson, N. A., Zaslavsky, A. M., & Kessler, R. C. (2012). Childhood adversities and first onset of psychiatric disorders in a national sample of US adolescents. *Archives of General Psychiatry, 69*(11), 1151–1160. https://doi.org/10.1001/archgenpsychiatry.2011.2277

McNamara, L., Colley, P., & Franklin, N. (2017). School recess, social connectedness and health: A Canadian perspective. *Health Promotion International, 32*(2), 392–402. https://doi.org/10.1093/heapro/dav102

Moreno-Agostino, D., Fisher, H. L., Goodman, A., Hatch, S. L., Morgan, C., Richards, M., . . . Ploubidis, G. B. (2023). Long-term psychological distress trajectories and the COVID-19 pandemic in three British birth cohorts: A multi-cohort study. *PLoS Medicine, 20*(4), e1004145. https://doi.org/10.1371/journal.pmed.1004145

Mpofu, J., Underwood, J., & Thornton, J. (2023). Overview and methods for the youth risk behavior surveillance system—United States, 2021. *Morbidity and Mortality Weekly Report, 72*(Suppl. 1), 1–12.

Murray, R., & Ramstetter, C. (2013). The crucial role of recess in school. *Pediatrics, 131*(1), 183–188. https://doi.org/10.1542/peds.2012-2993

Nonweiler, J., Rattray, F., Baulcomb, J., Happé, F., & Absoud, M. (2020). Prevalence and associated factors of emotional and behavioural difficulties during COVID-19 pandemic in children with neurodevelopmental disorders. *Children (Basel), 7*(9), 128. https://doi.org/10.3390/children7090128

OECD. (2023). PISA 2022 results: Factsheets. *OECD*. https://www.oecd.org/publication/pisa-2022-results/country-notes/united-states-a78ba65a/#chapter-d1e11

Office of the Surgeon General (OSG). (2021). Publications and reports of the Surgeon General. In *Protecting youth mental health: The U.S. Surgeon General's advisory*. Washington, DC: US Department of Health and Human Services. https://www.hhs.gov/sites/default/files/surgeon-general-youth-mental-health-advisory.pdf

Overhage, L., Hailu, R., Busch, A. B., Mehrotra, A., Michelson, K. A., & Huskamp, H. A. (2023). Trends in acute care use for mental health conditions among youth during the COVID-19 pandemic. *JAMA Psychiatry, 80*(9), 924–932. https://doi.org/10.1001/jamapsychiatry.2023.2195

Panchal, N., Kamal, R., Orgera, K., Cox, C., Garfield, R., Hamel, L., & Chidambaram, P. (2020). The implications of COVID-19 for mental health and substance use. *Kaiser Family Foundation, 21*, 1–16.

Parker-Pope, T., Caron, C., & Sancho, M. (2021, December 17). U.S. mental health professionals say they can't keep up with demand for therapy. *The New York Times*. https://www.nytimes.com/2021/12/17/us/us-mental-health-professionals-say-they-cant-keep-up-with-demand-for-therapy.html

Pelham, W. E., Tapert, S. F., Gonzalez, M. R., McCabe, C. J., Lisdahl, K. M., Alzueta, E., ... Brown, S. A. (2021). Early adolescent substance use before and during the COVID-19 pandemic: A longitudinal survey in the ABCD study cohort. *Journal of Adolescent Health, 69*(3), 390–397. https://doi.org/https://doi.org/10.1016/j.jadohealth.2021.06.015

Racine, N., McArthur, B. A., Cooke, J. E., Eirich, R., Zhu, J., & Madigan, S. (2021). Global prevalence of depressive and anxiety symptoms in children and adolescents during COVID-19: A meta-analysis. *JAMA Pediatrics, 175*(11), 1142–1150. https://doi.org/10.1001/jamapediatrics.2021.2482

Read, H., Roush, S., & Downing, D. (2018). Early intervention in mental health for adolescents and young adults: A systematic review. *American Journal of Occupational Therapy, 72*(5). https://doi.org/10.5014/ajot.2018.033118

Richards, E. C., Allen, M. R., & Weiss, M. D. (2023). The impact of school closures on service utilization in school-based health centers. *International Journal of Environmental Research and Public Health, 20*(5), 4588. https://doi.org/10.3390/ijerph20054588

Richtel, M. (2023). The income gap is becoming a physical-activity divide. *The New York Times*. https://www.nytimes.com/2023/03/24/health/sports-physical-education-children.html

Rodman, A. M., Rosen, M. L., Kasparek, S. W., Mayes, M., Lengua, L., Meltzoff, A. N., & McLaughlin, K. A. (2024). Social experiences and youth psychopathology during the COVID-19 pandemic: A longitudinal study. *Developmental Psychopathology, 36*(1), 366–378. https://doi.org/10.1017/s0954579422001250

Rothstein, R., & Olympia, R. P. (2020). School nurses on the front lines of healthcare: The approach to maintaining student health and wellness during COVID-19 school closures. *NASN School Nurse, 35*(5), 269–275. https://doi.org/10.1177/1942602x20935612

Sahle, B. W., Ofori-Asenso, R., & Renzaho, A. M. N. (2020). Adverse childhood experiences should be priority in global response to COVID-19. *Journal of Paediatrics and Child Health, 56*(10), 1656–1657. https://doi.org/https://doi.org/10.1111/jpc.15132

Schneider, D., Harknett, K., & McLanahan, S. (2016). Intimate partner violence in the Great Recession. *Demography, 53*(2), 471–505. https://doi.org/10.1007/s13524-016-0462-1

Scott, S., Gray, T., Charlton, J., & Millard, S. (2022). The impact of time spent in natural outdoor spaces on children's language, communication and social skills: A systematic review protocol. *International Journal of Environmental Research and Public Health, 19*(19), 12038. https://doi.org/10.3390/ijerph191912038

Sharma, S., Wong, D., Schomberg, J., Knudsen-Robbins, C., Gibbs, D., Berkowitz, C., & Heyming, T. (2021). COVID-19: Differences in sentinel injury and child abuse reporting during a pandemic. *Child Abuse & Neglect, 116*, 104990. https://doi.org/https://doi.org/10.1016/j.chiabu.2021.104990

Silver, D., Saavedra, A., & Polikoff, M. (2022). Low parent interest in COVID-recovery interventions should worry educators and policymakers alike. *Brookings*.

Singh, S., Roy, D., Sinha, K., Parveen, S., Sharma, G., & Joshi, G. (2020). Impact of COVID-19 and lockdown on mental health of children and adolescents: A narrative review with recommendations. *Psychiatry Research, 293*, 113429. https://doi.org/10.1016/j.psychres.2020.113429

Solmi, M., Estradé, A., Thompson, T., Agorastos, A., Radua, J., Cortese, S., . . . Correll, C. U. (2022). Physical and mental health impact of COVID-19 on children, adolescents, and their families: The Collaborative Outcomes study on Health and Functioning during Infection Times—Children and Adolescents (COH-FIT-C&A). *Journal of Affective Disorders, 299*, 367–376.

Sonu, S., Marvin, D., & Moore, C. (2021). The intersection and dynamics between COVID-19, health disparities, and adverse childhood experiences: "Intersection/dynamics between COVID-19, health disparities, and ACEs." *Journal of Child and Adolescent Trauma, 14*(4), 517–526. https://doi.org/10.1007/s40653-021-00363-z

Spitzer, M. (2021). Open schools! Weighing the effects of viruses and lockdowns on children. *Trends in Neuroscience Education, 22*, 100151. https://doi.org/10.1016/j.tine.2021.100151

Sprang, G., & Silman, M. (2013). Posttraumatic stress disorder in parents and youth after health-related disasters. *Disaster Medicine and Public Health Preparation, 7*(1), 105–110. https://doi.org/10.1017/dmp.2013.22

Storz, M. A. (2020). The COVID-19 pandemic: An unprecedented tragedy in the battle against childhood obesity. *Clinical Experience in Pediatrics, 63*(12), 477–482. https://doi.org/10.3345/cep.2020.01081

Svetaz, M. V., Ireland, M., & Blum, R. (2000). Adolescents with learning disabilities: risk and protective factors associated with emotional well-being: Findings from the National Longitudinal Study of Adolescent Health. *Journal of Adolescent Health, 27*(5), 340–348. https://doi.org/10.1016/s1054-139x(00)00170-1

Temple, J. R., Baumler, E., Wood, L., Guillot-Wright, S., Torres, E., & Thiel, M. (2022). The impact of the COVID-19 pandemic on adolescent mental health and substance use. *Journal of Adolescent Health, 71*(3), 277–284. https://doi.org/10.1016/j.jadohealth.2022.05.025

Thierer, A. (2019). How many lives are lost due to the precautionary principle? *Mercatus Center.* https://www.mercatus.org/economic-insights/expert-commentary/how-many-lives-are-lost-due-precautionary-principle

Tsujimoto, K. C., Cost, K. T., LaForge-MacKenzie, K., Anagnostou, E., Birken, C. S., Charach, A., . . . Korczak, D. J. (2023). School and learning contexts during the COVID-19 pandemic: Implications for child and youth mental health. *Current Psychology, 42*, 29969–29985. https://doi.org/10.1007/s12144-022-03941-y

Vaillancourt, T., Korczak, D. J., Madigan, S., Cost, K. T., Racine, N., & Szatmari, P. (2023). Rejoinder 1: Advocating for children in the presence of imperfect evidence: A reply to Black et al. *Journal of the Canadian Academy of Child and Adolescent Psychiatry, 32*(2), 79–84.

Vanhalst, J., Luyckx, K., Van Petegem, S., & Soenens, B. (2018). The detrimental effects of adolescents' chronic loneliness on motivation and emotion regulation in social situations. *Journal of Youth and Adolescence, 47*(1), 162–176. https://doi.org/10.1007/s10964-017-0686-4

Veiga, G., De Leng, W., Cachucho, R., Ketelaar, L., Kok, J. N., Knobbe, A., . . . Rieffe, C. (2017). Social competence at the playground: Preschoolers during recess. *Infant and Child Development, 26*(1), e1957.

Vibert, B., Segura, P., Gallagher, L., Georgiades, S., Pervanidou, P., Thurm, A., . . . Di Martino, A. (2023). CRISIS AFAR: an international collaborative study of the impact of the COVID-19 pandemic on mental health and service access in youth with autism and neurodevelopmental conditions. *Molecular Autism, 14*(1), 7. https://doi.org/10.1186/s13229-022-00536-z

Vidal, C., Holland, E. T., & Duriseti, R. S. (2023). Rejoinder 3: School closures: The trigger point in the decline in pediatric mental health outcomes during the COVID-19 pandemic. *Journal of the Canadian Academy of Child and Adolescent Psychiatry, 32*(2), 88–92.

Viner, R., Russell, S., Saulle, R., Croker, H., Stansfeld, C., Packer, J., . . . Minozzi, S. (2021). Impacts of school closures on physical and mental health of children and young people: a systematic review. *medRxiv*. https://doi.org/10.1101/2021.02.10.21251526

Viner, R., Russell, S., Saulle, R., Croker, H., Stansfield, C., Packer, J., . . . Minozzi, S. (2022). School closures during social lockdown and mental health, health behaviors, and well-being among children and adolescents during the first COVID-19 wave: A systematic review. *JAMA Pediatrics, 176*(4), 400–409. https://doi.org/10.1001/jamapediatrics.2021.5840

West, M. R., & Lake, R. (2021). How much have students missed academically because of the pandemic? A review of the evidence to date. *Center on Reinventing Public Education*. https://files.eric.ed.gov/fulltext/ED614130.pdf

Williams, T. S., Deotto, A., Roberts, S. D., Ford, M. K., Désiré, N., & Cunningham, S. (2022). COVID-19 mental health impact among children with early brain injury and associated conditions. *Child Neuropsychology, 28*(5), 627–648. https://doi.org/10.1080/09297049.2021.1998407

Wong, B., Cross, S., Zavaleta-Ramírez, P., Bauda, I., Hoffman, P., Ibeziako, P., . . . Ougrin, D. (2023). Self-harm in children and adolescents who presented at emergency units during the COVID-19 pandemic: An international retrospective cohort study. *Journal of the American Academy of Child and Adolescent Psychiatry, 62*(9), 998–1009. https://doi.org/10.1016/j.jaac.2022.11.016

Wong, C. A., Ming, D., Maslow, G., & Gifford, E. J. (2020). Mitigating the impacts of the COVID-19 pandemic response on at-risk children. *Pediatrics, 146*(1), e20200973. https://doi.org/10.1542/peds.2020-0973

8
Altered Neurodevelopmental Trajectories

Brain development over the course of childhood and adolescence is a rapid and complex process that is dynamically shaped by a combination of genetic and environmental influences. While the temporal and spatial dynamics of brain maturation are tightly regulated, they are also highly influenced by the child's environment. The lack of expected input at particular time periods or exposure to unexpected stressors may lead to suboptimal development, which may have lifelong repercussions. There is emerging research suggesting that some environmental influences, particularly traumatic events, may even influence development in subsequent generations.

We are only at the beginning of understanding the full impact of the COVID-19 pandemic on the development of the brain and behavior in children and adolescents. Each generation is shaped by the time period in which they grew up, but the impact of events differs depending on a child's developmental stage. For example, the impact of major world events, such as President Kennedy's assassination or 9/11, may have very different implications for a teenager than for a toddler. The duration of the event also matters: the COVID-19 pandemic spanned several years, representing a significant proportion of most children's lives, particularly compared to adults.

Compounding matters, not all skills develop at the same pace and at the same time. While there is good reason to focus on the acquisition of academic skills following pandemic-related educational disruption, academic exposure also fosters higher order skills like reasoning, planning, and organization. Being in the school environment and within the community promotes the development of social communication skills, as well as emotional and behavioral regulation skills. The development of all these kinds of skills may have been impacted—albeit some more than others—depending on the child's circumstances and developmental stage.

In this chapter, we begin with an overview of brain development to understand the mechanisms that may be influenced by a child's environment and experiences, focusing on normal maturation patterns that regulate the emergence of cognitive, emotional, social, behavioral, and adaptive skills. This

Neurodevelopment in the Post-Pandemic World. Molly Colvin, Jennifer Linton Reesman, and Tannahill Glen, Oxford University Press. © Oxford University Press 2024. DOI: 10.1093/9780197762660.003.0008

work outlines how all children may have been impacted by the period of the COVID-19 pandemic. Not all of these changes will be negative, but there are a few aspects of development that should be closely monitored, particularly for children who already had developmental risk factors.

Fundamentals of Brain Development

The early phase of the prenatal period is characterized by cell proliferation and migration that is tightly controlled by genetics. By the end of the prenatal period, the major architectural elements of the brain are in place. Most neurons will have found their way to their final positions, creating six layers of neocortex in largely an inside-out manner, with the older neurons settling in the deepest layers and the newer neurons traveling the furthest from the central progenitor regions of the brain. Neurons begin to differentiate, or to take on characteristics that will allow them to carry out specific roles. Neurons that are no longer needed, either because their role has become obsolete or they are redundant, will die as the system becomes more streamlined, in a process known as pruning. The major pathways will then emerge as highways for transmission of sensory and motor information to and from the cortex (Stiles & Jernigan, 2010).

During the postnatal period, connectivity becomes increasingly sophisticated. In early childhood, the inhibitory and excitatory interactions between neurons begin to establish feedback and feedforward loops. As pathways emerge, some become permanent, while others are transitory. Myelination increases dramatically; white matter pathways linking cortical and subcortical regions develop quickly within the first 2–3 years of life. By age 6 years, the brain has largely reached adult size by increasing four-fold during the preschool period. For these reasons, early childhood experiences may play an outsized role in literally shaping the brain.

Yet the dynamic processes of brain development extend well into adolescence and early adulthood. Neuronal stabilization occurs first in posterior regions, particularly those involving sensory and motor processing, and last in anterior regions, that are multimodal and involved in higher order cognitive processes (Stiles & Jernigan, 2010). While highly patterned, this process also allows for individual differences in the development of higher order cortical areas. A recent study demonstrated that individual differences in frontoparietal cortical organization at ages 9–10 years were highly correlated with individual differences in cognition (Keller et al., 2023). White matter pathways that connect cortical and subcortical regions to the frontal lobes are now estimated to reach a developmental plateau in the third decade of life (Somerville, 2016). Neuroimaging studies have only recently begun to combine large datasets to identify normal patterns of development across the lifespan (Bethlehem et al., 2022).

Plasticity and Sensitive Periods in Neurodevelopment

Neuroplasticity refers to the brain's malleability or adaptability, and it is fundamental to learning across the lifespan. In the postnatal period, neurons are more likely to survive and to make connections with other neurons if they receive input from the environment. Neurons and pathways that are more frequently activated are also reinforced and gradually become more dominant and influential than those that are used less frequently (Kolb et al., 2017). Those that respond simultaneously to a stimulus also begin to work in concert. This type of plasticity is known as Hebbian plasticity and is now colloquially known as "neurons that fire together, wire together" (Hebb, 2005). Hebbian plasticity occurs throughout the lifespan and plays a critical role in learning and memory.

While the brain continues to change in response to experience and environmental input at all ages, it is most receptive to certain kinds of input at specific times in development. Experience-expectant plasticity refers to the brain's readiness to receive typical or expected input (Kolb et al., 2017). One of the earliest examples of this was the finding that young birds will "imprint" or establish a parental bond immediately after birth, even if the target of their attachment is not their parent (Lorenz, 1935). Later work demonstrated that sensory deprivation in early life could permanently change the cortical organization within sensory systems in ways that are not seen at other points in development. For example, Hubel and Wiesel showed that monocular blindness could change the organization of the visual cortex in young kittens, but similar impacts were not seen in older animals (Hubel & Wiesel, 1970). This work gave rise to the concept of "sensitive periods," or temporal windows during brain development when neurons are more responsive to specific kinds of stimuli than at other points in time.

In human cognitive development, language acquisition occurs during one of the most researched sensitive periods. In infancy, the brain is highly responsive to linguistic input and can process all phonemes, or speech sounds, that comprise words. During language acquisition, neurons gradually respond more strongly to phonemes that are heard most frequently, and the brain begins to efficiently process a child's native language(s). By the end of the first year, an infant's brain exhibits specialization for the smallest units of sound that define the most common languages in the environment. At the same time, it becomes less responsive to unfamiliar languages, which ultimately will limit the ability to develop native proficiency in languages to which it has little exposure (Kuhl & Rivera-Gaxiola, 2008). This is why it is more difficult for most adults to achieve the same level of proficiency with a second language as a native speaker.

The onset and duration of sensitive periods may vary depending on the type of skill. Basic neuroscience research has shown that skills emerge when the brain region linked to the skill has reached peak synaptogenesis (Goldman-Rakic, 1987). Some sensitive periods may be open from birth and gradually close, others may be fully open for a period of time and then suddenly close, while others may open and close at particular points in development (Fuhrmann et al., 2015; Knudsen, 2004). In general, windows for primary or "lower level" skills may close before "higher level" skills (Thomas & Knowland, 2009), which also follows the general pattern of cortical maturation from posterior sensory and motor cortices to more anterior association cortices.

Indeed, later sensitive periods may require certain brain networks or skills to have developed so that a group of skills can be integrated. For example, adolescence may be a sensitive period in the development of social and emotional regulation skills, when language and executive function skills have developed to the degree that they can support the development of perspective-taking and emotion identification (Blakemore, 2008; Choudhury et al., 2006). Similarly, cognitive training may be most effective in older adolescents (Knoll et al., 2016) because the teen has mastered fundamental skills and the frontal lobes can also now support the integration and application of knowledge (e.g., facts, memories) in different ways.

So what happens when some of the building blocks aren't in place, or they aren't as well developed as they normally would be because of pandemic-related educational disruption? In some cases, it may be that the gaps or holes in knowledge can be filled, so that the child "catches up." However, studies of children who have sustained brain damage suggest it may not be quite so simple. Recovery from early childhood brain damage is often greatest in these cases: (1) if the injury occurs while intact brain areas retain plasticity and may assume some of the responsibility of the damaged cortex, and (2) the brain has also had some time to develop some specialization (Dennis et al., 2013). In other words, plasticity can be age-dependent, with very different outcomes depending on developmental stage (Kolb & Gibb, 2011).

Even in the best-case scenarios, "recovery" from brain damage can be associated with persistent difficulties. When even mildly impaired skills become the building blocks for later higher order skills, deficits can compound over time. In these cases, the gap between a child's current developmental state and the normal developmental curve may widen over time (Dennis et al., 2013, 2014), such that functional limitations become more noticeable as the child gets older. Finally, plasticity is not always beneficial; in response to negative events or experiences, plasticity can be maladaptive (e.g., drug use may alter brain connectivity patterns in ways that negatively impact long-term functioning) (Kolb & Gibb, 2011).

Considering these factors, the impact of changes during the COVID-19 pandemic may vary depending on the child's age or developmental stage. For example, language acquisition and play skills may have been more impacted in toddlers than in older children. The basics of reading, writing, and math may have been more impacted in elementary-aged children, which may increase risk for difficulties with higher order academic skills (e.g., reading comprehension). Social skills and functional independence may have been more impacted in adolescents. Children and adolescents may have reduced resilience in the face of stressors in later life, increasing their risk of mental health challenges and/or late-life cognitive decline in adulthood. These examples will be discussed in greater detail later in this chapter.

How the Environment Impacts Brain Development

Neuroplasticity and the long period of brain development allow for growth to be shaped by the child's environment in ways that may enhance risk or resilience, beginning in the prenatal period. For example, normal maternal levels of folate and vitamin B_{12} promote healthy brain development in utero (Black, 2008). In contrast, toxic exposures (e.g., substance use) and illness may interfere with the complex dynamics that drive brain development. Prenatal adversity is associated with atypical brain development, which may manifest as smaller brain size and differences in functional connectivity (Nolvi et al., 2023), as well as increased risk of neurodevelopmental and psychiatric conditions (Lautarescu et al., 2020; Van den Bergh et al., 2020).

Fortunately, in utero transmission of COVID-19 between mother and child appears to be exceedingly rare (Allotey et al., 2020). However, the maternal immune and/or inflammatory response to the presence of the COVID-19 virus may impact factors known to be involved in brain development, with some studies showing a possible connection between maternal COVID-19 infection and neurodevelopmental comorbidity (Shook et al., 2022). The possible mechanism for this is not well understood and may at least in part reflect the broader indirect influence of prenatal stress on brain development.

In the postnatal period, the potential impact of environmental influence expands considerably. The influential "ecological systems" theory was initially developed by Bronfenbrenner (1977, 1979), who conceptualized the direct and indirect influences of the environment on child development. The individual's ecosystem is conceptualized as having multiple concentric layers. The microsystem is the innermost layer of direct influence, consisting of the child's family, peers, school, neighborhood, and access to community resources. The next layer is the mesosystem, built on relationships between the microsystems. The exosystem is the next layer, with indirect influence on the child through connections between the microsystems (e.g., parent's employment, neighborhood characteristics). The macrosystem describes the broader cultural context, including political, legal, economic, and sociological factors (Bronfenbrenner, 1977, 1979). Over time, the influence of biological factors also became integrated within the model (e.g., (Lehman et al., 2017)

The COVID-19 pandemic impacted all levels of a child's ecosystem. As discussed in Chapter 7, there were significant psychosocial changes within the *microsystem*, including family functioning, the school environment, and social connections, and the interactions among them. There were also changes in the *exosystem* and *macrosystem* that indirectly affected child development, including microeconomic and macroeconomic factors, changes in the political and legal landscapes, and of course, an increase in existential threats to health and safety.

As a result, the dramatic psychosocial changes during the COVID-19 pandemic likely impacted the developmental course of every child. However, the magnitude and specific impact of the COVID-19 pandemic on development will vary depending on an individual's characteristics and resources that interact to determine risk and resilience.

For example, a child who has strong attachment to a parent and no direct exposure to ACEs may be more resilient to the impact of high prenatal maternal stress. Similarly, in a group of children who have learning disorders, long-term outcomes are likely to be better in those whose families have more economic resources, as higher socioeconomic status is associated with prolonged brain maturation that allows for greater efficiency in adulthood (Tooley et al., 2021). In this way, the high degree of neuroplasticity during childhood and adolescence allows for developmental compensation and course correction based on environmental input, and it partly explains why much of the pandemic-related research shows worse outcomes for children and adolescents who were already impacted by disparities.

Risk and resiliency may also be partly determined by epigenetic processes, which can determine which genes are expressed during development. Recent work on transgenerational epigenetics has shown that gene expression may sometimes be determined by generational factors, specifically the experiences of a child's parents or ancestors before they were conceived (Babenko et al., 2015; Bale, 2015; Pembrey et al., 2014). For example, lower cortisol levels have been reported in children of Holocaust survivors with posttraumatic stress disorder (PTSD) and in children of mothers who developed PTSD after 9/11, which may alter an individual's long-term risk of anxiety, depression, and PTSD (Yehuda et al., 2005, 2007). Mortality risk has also been linked to whether an individual's paternal grandparents had adequate food during their childhoods (Pembrey et al., 2014). Transgenerational epigenetic factors may also modulate the risk of psychiatric disease, including bipolar disorder, schizophrenia, depression, and alcohol use disorders (Hime et al., 2021). Because transgenerational trauma may be written into our genetic code, the impact of the COVID-19 pandemic may reach far into the future by shifting the way that genes are expressed in future generations, especially in those that faced greater stress and hardships during this period.

Emerging Research on Brain Development During the COVID-19 Pandemic

To date, only a few studies have examined whether there are structural or functional brain changes in children who have been raised during the

COVID-19 pandemic. In a report on emerging evidence, Stix (2023) stated, "Preliminary results for some of these studies are starting to be reported—and they are sobering." Most studies have focused on the impact of COVID-19-related stressors. Van Drunen et al. (2023) examined brain development (cortical thickness) in regions associated with social development and stress response, together with parent-reported empathy and prosocial behavior in early adolescents (ages 9 to 13 years), before and during the COVID-19 pandemic. There were no pandemic-related effects in parent ratings of their children's behaviors. However, in the group of children imaged during the pandemic, there were differences in the architecture of the prefrontal cortex and hippocampus, consistent with accelerated development. There were also initial changes in the temporoparietal junction, but this seemed to return to a typical developmental pattern later in the pandemic, suggesting resilience within this region (van Drunen et al., 2023).

Similarly, Salomon et al. (2021) used structural neuroimaging to compare regional brain volume data for young adults who underwent scanning before the pandemic and again after it began. For those assessed during the pandemic, there were transient volumetric increases in brain regions implicated in stress and anxiety. Interestingly, in the amygdala, a region associated with anxiety and fear processing, these volumetric changes decreased as pandemic restrictions were lifted (Salomon et al., 2021). Taken together, these studies suggest that there may be at least transitory changes in brain structure associated with the psychosocial experience of the COVID-19 pandemic.

It is yet unknown whether these observed changes will be associated with clinical behavior or lead to permanent shifts in brain development and activity. However, there is cause for concern: studies of those who have had prior exposure to trauma suggest that there can be permanent anatomical changes, even after emotional recovery from a traumatic stressor. As described earlier, neuroplasticity can be both adaptive and maladaptive.

For example, a neuroimaging study of healthy adults who were proximal to the 9/11 terrorist attacks on the World Trade Center found smaller volumes in the amygdala, anterior hippocampus, insula, anterior cingulate, and medial prefrontal cortex more than 3 years after the tragedy (Ganzel et al., 2008). Similarly, in a study of adult earthquake survivors, there were changes in functional connectivity involving the frontal-limbic-striatal and default-mode networks 3 weeks after the disaster that were also observed 2 years later, even though participants had completely recovered from high initial levels of anxiety (Du et al., 2015).

Moving forward, there will be a need to extend this work to examine brain development over the long term, focusing not just on the potential impact of psychosocial stress but also on the degree to which maturation patterns have shifted based on the changes in the psychosocial environment. With the recent development of large-scale studies that detail normal brain maturation patterns (Alex et al., 2024; Bethlehem et al., 2022), it will be possible to compare the cohort of children and adolescents who grew up in the time of the COVID-19 pandemic to those who grew up earlier. We expect these results to be heterogeneous, particularly regarding the impact on brain development and observed behavior. For the remainder of this chapter, we discuss particular areas of interest.

Implications for Cognitive Development in Childhood and Adolescence

Knowledge of the interaction between the environment and brain development suggests that there will be an impact of the changes during the COVID-19 pandemic on child cognitive development, at least for certain skills. The magnitude of these impacts may vary depending on a child's age and the type of skill. In some cases, the impact may be entirely benign, or it may have little impact on a child's ability to meet external demands, particularly if the child developed skills that help to meet the needs of the current times. For other skills, there may be more reason for concern, particularly given the extent to which educational experiences were disrupted.

Academic Skills

There is a well-established bidirectional relationship between academic and cognitive skill development; academic skill acquisition fosters the development of cognitive skills and vice versa. Studies have also shown a positive correlation between overall intellectual functioning and schooling that strengthens over time (Peng & Kievit, 2020). On formal testing, academic achievement is correlated to general cognitive ability (i.e., intellectual functioning) (Tikhomirova et al., 2020).

Therefore, there is reason to suspect that estimates of intellectual functioning may be lower in those who experienced prolonged school disruption during the pandemic. In a recent German study, IQ scores of middle school students were assessed in summer 2020 and found to be significantly lower than pre-pandemic cohorts assessed in 2012 and 2002 (Breit et al., 2023). However, recent research from one of our own clinics also suggests stability in overall cognitive functioning in pediatric patients who have psychiatric and neurodevelopmental disorders, with only selective declines in skills that are most closely related to academic skills (Colvin et al., in press). Longitudinal studies will be needed to monitor the development of overall cognitive functioning over time in typically developing children and adolescents to determine whether the cognitive impacts are global or more restrictive.

There is reason to be concerned about the development of specific academic skills. In Chapter 3, we described the significant "learning losses" or attenuated learning gains associated with changes in academic instruction during the COVID-19 pandemic, including early research suggesting that it would take considerable and intensive intervention to close the gap between students' current and typical skill levels. When combined with our knowledge of brain development and plasticity, there are many unanswered questions about the potential impact of COVID-19-related educational disruption on academic skill acquisition. For instance, how much can we expect typically developing children and adolescents to "catch up" in the acquisition of academic skills if their brains are not optimally wired to receive the input, *especially* if adequate remediation services are not provided? Will gains depend on the child's developmental stage? What if the missing or suboptimal academic skills are prerequisites for a more complex academic skill that hasn't yet been learned? Will suboptimal learning compound over the child's entire academic experience?

We really haven't even begun to answer these questions. What we do know is that the development of certain academic skills is tied to known sensitive periods. For example, phonological processing is critical not only for spoken and auditory language processing but also for reading. As a result, children with early language delays are at higher risk for developmental dyslexia (Peterson & Pennington, 2015), and phonics-based reading intervention for developmental dyslexia is more effective prior to third grade (Sanfilippo et al., 2020). Similarly, in children who have brain injuries, earlier lesions have been associated with lower academic abilities than later lesions. However, academic skills usually still develop and often reach levels that are only mildly below age-based expectations (Anderson et al., 2009; Sullivan et al., 2022).

Altogether, this research suggests vulnerability to compounding deficits over time, especially if there are interruptions in skill acquisition in early childhood, but there is continued growth and development over all of childhood and adolescence. Consistent with this, neuroimaging studies have shown that the development of academic skills is associated with prolonged structural and functional brain changes, even in early adulthood (Qiu et al., 2008).

While these studies of academic skill acquisition are somewhat reassuring, the impact of prolonged educational disruption during the COVID-19 pandemic may be different than what we see following childhood injury or illness, as it will be caused by a lack of expected environmental input in a typically developing brain. At the time of this book's writing, only a handful of studies had examined academic skills development during the COVID-19 pandemic. A Finnish study found that a pandemic-period sample of children did not differ from a pre-pandemic sample in reading or math skills in first or second grade. However, the pandemic-period sample exhibited slower progress in reading fluency and reading comprehension gains from second to fourth grade, while math progress remained stable, suggesting that the impact may vary depending on developmental stage (Lerkkanen et al., 2023). In a recent study of children and adolescents who have neurodevelopmental and psychiatric disorders, Colvin et al. (in press) found that in the first year of the pandemic, youth scored lower than a pre-pandemic cohort on math scores and this persisted into the second year of the pandemic. For reading, scores were similar to a pre-pandemic cohort in the first year of the pandemic, but they were lower in the second year of the pandemic (Colvin et al., in press). These findings suggest that the impact on academic skill acquisition may be most notable with longer periods of disruption and/or that the impact of early delays may compound over time.

The risk of compounding deficits is of particular concern. As children get older, academic skill acquisition often involves the integration of multiple cognitive skills. Reading requires language and visual skills. Numeracy requires attention, language, and an ability to understand representational analogues (i.e., that a number corresponds to a particular quantity). These fundamental building blocks may emerge at different points of development, but all may be necessary for higher order academic skills to develop (Thomas & Knowland, 2009).

Indeed, effective teaching requires the right timing (i.e., for skills to be presented to students at appropriate points in development) and the right sequencing. For example, single-word spelling is taught before paragraph writing. Addition is usually taught before subtraction, and students master manipulating single digits before multidigit problems or equations are introduced. When these steps are skipped or a child fails to master one of these basic skills, then a child may encounter greater difficulty when they are presented with more complex skills. Likewise, if skills are introduced too early, then the child may not show optimal learning (Thomas & Knowland, 2009)—hence, the concerns about disrupted "foundational learning" are so critical to future progress (World Bank et al., 2022).

Clinically, in the post-pandemic era, we have seen evidence of selective gaps in academic knowledge. For example, in small group children who were engaged in remote learning when they were first exposed to addition, they had no trouble solving problems presented horizontally, but they did not know how to approach the operation when the problems were presented vertically. We have also seen children who can manipulate fractions but do not understand phrases like "half past 9" because they did not learn to tell time using an analog clock. Left unaddressed, these gaps make it harder for students to "catch up" because they will not be able to master or perhaps even acquire new skills that require others to be in place. Thus, it is critical to minimize lost instruction time and aggressively implement remediation strategies to prevent the gap between typical and atypical developmental trajectories from widening.

Given concerns about missing skills, the numbers of students repeating a grade skyrocketed in the immediate aftermath of pandemic-related educational disruption. Of 26 states that had available data, 22 reported a significant increase in the number of students who repeated a grade. In three states, retention rates doubled (Schultz & Hollingsworth, 2022), despite considerable pre-pandemic evidence showing worse educational outcomes for students who repeated grades (Özek & Mariano, 2023). However, for some children, the unique circumstances of pandemic-related educational disruption may have increased the likelihood for retention to be beneficial. Pre-pandemic research suggested that the negative effects of retention are mitigated when a student's skills are below grade-based expectations, but not because the student needs considerable special education support that has not been provided. In other words, retention may be less harmful for students whose academic skills are lagging due to lack of exposure rather than lack of access to appropriate individualized academic instruction. In these cases, there may also be some psychosocial benefit to retention, especially in the short term (Goos et al., 2021).

Within a grade, older students are less likely to be diagnosed with attention-deficit/hyperactivity disorder (ADHD) and learning disorders than younger students, presumably because the younger students' skills are more likely to seem discrepant from their older peers (Elder & Lubotsky, 2009). Older students may approach tasks in ways that younger students have not yet learned, perhaps in ways that enhance learning or make it more efficient (Thomas & Knowland, 2009). However, much of the evidence about "redshirting," or delaying academic instruction so that a child can be older than most of their classmates, suggests that the short-term benefit may not transfer to long-term advantages (Elder & Lubotsky, 2009). Given the number of children who delayed kindergarten entry during the COVID-19 pandemic, the developmental progress of this cohort will need to be monitored closely.

Altogether, greater plasticity in childhood entails potential risks and benefits in considering remediation strategies and post-pandemic academic instruction. Each child will need to be considered individually, but this can be done systematically. Post-pandemic educational policies and clinical care decisions should weigh the child's current developmental stage, their developmental stage at the time of the COVID-19 educational disruption, and whether there may be neurodevelopmental or psychiatric comorbidities that compound learning challenges. Understanding these factors will help to make decisions about promoting optimal development of academic skills in the post-pandemic era, recognizing that the ripple effects from early learning losses may manifest well into the future.

Executive Functions

"Executive functions" is a term that has been defined in many different ways. Broadly speaking, these are skills that allow us to pursue goal-directed activities or to integrate and apply what we know to appropriately navigate the world. Skills related to cognitive efficiency include cognitive flexibility, inhibitory control, processing speed (i.e., how quickly you can integrate and act upon information), and working memory (i.e., holding new information in mind for brief periods of time). These are closely aligned with attentional regulation (i.e., being able to focus, sustain, and shift attention). Higher order executive functions include planning, organization, problem-solving, reasoning, and allocation of resources (e.g., time management, setting priorities and goals). While traditionally conceptualized as cognitive skills, executive functions are also critically involved in social and emotional processing (Cristofori et al., 2019; Diamond, 2020).

The relationship between executive functions and everyday life has been studied since the famous case of Phineas Gage first sparked an interest in the role of the frontal lobes in meeting the demands of the external environment. As the story goes, Gage was a young man working on a railroad construction project in 1848 when a large iron rod penetrated his left frontal lobe. He survived the injury, but there were significant changes in his personality, social functioning, and behavior due to diminished impulse control, insight, and reasoning skills, detailed by his neurologist (Ratiu et al., 2004).

Executive functions typically develop gradually over the course of childhood and adolescence, reflecting the protracted development of the frontal lobes and their connections throughout the brain (Diamond, 2020). As discussed earlier in this chapter, the frontal lobes have the longest maturation period; the frontal cortex likely stabilizes in our 20s, while connectivity may continue to develop into our 30s (Somerville, 2016). As first appreciated with Gage, difficulties with executive functions are associated with mental health challenges, poor physical health, lower quality of life, lower levels of educational and occupational achievement, and increased association with crime or violence (Cristofori et al., 2019).

Educational disruption during the COVID-19 pandemic may have had a significant impact on the development of executive function skills. Executive functions are necessary to successfully meet the behavioral and social demands of the educational setting. At the transition to elementary school, executive function skills such as inhibitory control and attentional regulation promote the development of self-regulation (van Lier & Deater-Deckard, 2016). Executive functions are also important in making for a successful transition to middle school (Jacobson et al., 2011), where they may foster both learning and positive social interactions with peers and teachers (van Lier & Deater-Deckard, 2016).

Indeed, executive functions become increasingly important as students' progress academically. In late elementary school, the curriculum often shifts from basic skill acquisition to the application of those skills. For example, in reading, there is a move from learning to decode fluently to developing reading comprehension skills; understanding written material becomes more important than the mechanics of reading and involves skills like working memory and abstract reasoning. Similarly, in math, there is a move from learning basic operations to knowing how to apply those skills to solve problems. This requires multiple executive functions, including abstract reasoning (e.g., understanding that quantity can be symbolically represented), sequencing, and monitoring for accuracy (Bull et al., 2008; Bull & Lee, 2014; Männamaa et al., 2012; Ribner et al., 2018). The same skills are reinforced as students begin to do projects and write essays, which require them to plan and execute a series of steps.

Furthermore, it can be argued that some academic skills are executive function skills. In education, there is often discussion of the development of metacognitive skills that support "learning to learn"; the terms "metacognitive skills" and "executive functions" are often used interchangeably. As children go further in school, metacognitive skills become increasingly important. How well students study, take notes, see connections between bodies of knowledge, or anticipate what will be on a test based on prior experience is sometimes even more important than how well they know the material.

For these reasons, the attenuated academic gains that students have made, particularly in math, are concerning for delayed development of executive function skills. Because executive function skills facilitate academic skill acquisition, the combination of delays in academic and executive function skills may make it harder for students to "catch up" over time, especially without remediation. In other words, developmental delays may compound over time to increase the gap between current students and pre-pandemic learning trajectories.

Given this relationship between academic and executive function skills, it is reasonable to consider targeting the executive function development to support remediation of attenuated learning gains. Indeed, in many areas of the United States, it is common for affluent families to enlist the assistance of executive function coaches to support academic success. Anecdotally, this intervention can be highly effective and many students report a benefit. However, there is limited rigorous empirical evidence supporting the efficacy of executive function coaching. Studies are often small, vary in intervention strategies, and do not implement rigorous methodologies needed to isolate effects (e.g., randomized control trials).

Beyond the possible impact of academic disruption on the development of executive functions, there is reason for concern that pandemic-related psychosocial stress may shift the development of these skills. Psychosocial stress in children has been associated with a decline in executive function skills, including processing speed and working memory (Andrews et al., 2021; Diamond, 2013). In some cases, the impact of acute stress on executive functions may resolve over time (Liston et al., 2009; Schoofs et al., 2008). However, chronic stress and/or trauma experiences may selectively impact the development of executive functions (Hawkins et al., 2021; Pechtel & Pizzagalli, 2011; Sheridan & McLaughlin, 2014).

Altogether, as has been discussed repeatedly throughout this book, some children will likely be at increased risk for disruptions in executive function development. Those who experienced prolonged educational disruption and psychosocial stressors may be especially vulnerable. Similarly, children who had preexisting weaknesses in executive functions may have had less ability to compensate for attenuations in executive function development; this likely includes children who have learning disorders (Willcutt et al., 2005), ADHD (Willcutt et al., 2005), autism (Demetriou et al., 2019), trauma exposure (e.g., Malarbi et al., 2017), and mental health disorders (Doyle et al., 2018). This idea is supported by early research evaluating the relationship between executive functions and impact of virtual learning in children and adolescents across seven European countries. Thorell et al. (2022) found lower executive functioning was associated with more negative experiences with virtual learning, most notably for older students.

Language and Communication Skills

Earlier in the chapter, we discussed how language develops rapidly during a sensitive period that extends from infancy and early childhood. During this developmental window, the brain is uniquely attuned to linguistic input. This allows for a rapid and patterned progression from babbling and responding preferentially to a few words in infancy, to using simple sentences and following simple multistep commands by preschool.

Research has shown that the amount and quality of linguistic input from the external environment are critical in language acquisition. Decreased linguistic input in early childhood negatively affects cortical development within the language networks (Cheng et al., 2023) and the efficacy of language development (Cheng et al., 2019). Likewise, higher levels of in-home language exposure and maternal education have been strongly associated with greater myelination of white matter pathways involved in language processing, even as early as age 30 months (Fibla et al., 2023). The amount and quality of linguistic input determine how well the brain's language networks are wired.

There is strong evidence that language development is also facilitated by social communication, which was less available during the COVID-19 pandemic. Infants learn best when linguistic input is received through direct social interactions (Goldstein et al., 2003; Kuhl & Rivera-Gaxiola, 2008). For example, monolingual English-speaking babies developed sensitivity to Mandarin Chinese phonemes when they were engaged with a live tutor, but not when they were only exposed through television or audio alone (Kuhl & Rivera-Gaxiola, 2008). However, if a peer was involved, then infants did show some second-language learning through video (Lytle et al., 2018). Further evidence for the interaction between social interactions and language acquisition comes from studies of autism. Infants who have autism show decreased interest in social interactions and speech, which is likely related to greater rates of language impairment in the disorder (Kuhl & Rivera-Gaxiola, 2008).

Parent facilitation is particularly important in language development. Parents often speak to their infants and toddlers with slower and exaggerated speech that facilitates word discrimination and recognition. The frequency and quality of parent–child interactions also influences language acquisition; when parents learn to increase turn-taking with their babies, their children have improved language outcomes (Ramírez et al., 2020). Indeed, parent–child turn-taking correlates with myelination of language-related white matter pathways through age 2 years, regardless of total speech exposure and infant-initiated vocalizations (Huber et al., 2023).

Changes in the frequency and type of social interactions during the COVID-19 pandemic may have influenced language development. Greater interactions with primary caregivers and their family's primary language(s) may have been beneficial for some children. For example, one study found that compared to a pre-pandemic cohort, bilingual (Mandarin/English) children who attended English-speaking schools had greater proficiency in Mandarin, while the pre- and post-pandemic groups were equivalent in English (Sheng et al., 2021). Similarly, another study found that monolingual and bilingual children were equivalent in vocabulary acquisition during the pandemic. However, the bilingual children showed attenuated reading comprehension gains in English, suggesting that the impact of the pandemic on language development may vary depending on the type of skill and exposure to different environments (Sun et al., 2023).

Indeed, declines in exposure to speech and social interactions may have been harmful, especially for those who were younger, who lived in areas with longer periods of lockdown and social distancing, whose families had lower levels of socioeconomic resources and parental education levels, and/or who did not attend daycare or preschool. The CORAL study was designed to examine behavioral and developmental outcomes in children born in Ireland during the first 3 months of the COVID-19 pandemic. Due to lockdowns, quarantines, and social distancing, these babies had limited social interaction outside of the home for the first year. At age 24 months, they demonstrated lower communication scores compared to babies from a pre-pandemic longitudinal study. Critically, there were no other significant developmental or behavioral differences (Byrne, Sledge, et al., 2023).

Reduced language proficiency in infants born during the early phase of the pandemic may in part relate to decreased exposure to speech input. In a study of children who have cochlear implants, the device logs showed significant reductions in the percentage of speech exposure during the early part of the COVID-19 pandemic, most notably for school-aged children and those with smaller families (Gordon et al., 2021). This effect was likely greater for children whose families have fewer socioeconomic resources, a known moderator for language skill development even beyond early childhood (Brito et al., 2017). For example, among kindergarteners who are from lower socioeconomic backgrounds, certain language skills were lower during the COVID-19 pandemic compared to a similar pre-pandemic cohort (Nevo, 2023).

Although widespread and prolonged use of facemasks was instituted in many areas to control the spread of the COVID-19 virus, especially before the availability of effective vaccines, there is emerging research suggesting a possible impact on language and communication skill development. The pairing of speech with visual cues is well known to improve spoken language comprehension. Speechreading (which involves using the visual clues of the speaker's lip and facial movements) also helps those with typical hearing in situations where there is considerable background noise or the acoustic signal is degraded. So it is perhaps not surprising that even in those with normal hearing, face masks have been shown to reduce speech intelligibility by degrading the sound signal, reducing access to facial cues, and preventing speechreading (Sönnichsen et al., 2022; Yi et al., 2021). For children with hearing loss, the prolonged use of face masks may have been particularly challenging, especially if they exclusively rely on cochlear implants (Charney et al., 2021; Sönnichsen et al., 2022).

Combined audiovisual input (e.g., watching mouth movements while listening) may be particularly important at certain stages of language development; infants and toddlers who are rapidly acquiring words are more likely to spend time looking at the mouth of someone who is talking (de Boisferon et al., 2018; Tenenbaum et al., 2013). Watching mouth movements may help to parse words from a continuous stream of speech; masking invariably makes this a harder task. Recent studies of infants have shown that they have a decreased ability to segment words in speech compared to a pre-pandemic cohort (Frota et al., 2022) and may be less interested in masked faces. In an eye-tracking study of some in the CORAL cohort at age 18 months, babies spent less time exploring masked than unmasked faces (Byrne, O'Flaherty, et al., 2023). These findings are highly concerning for younger children given that masks were used daily, in some cases for 1–2 years, by peers, teachers, and/or caregivers. This may have had less of an impact in older children, who may be able to more effectively use compensatory communication techniques (Mitsven et al., 2022; Schwarz et al., 2022).

The importance of seeing others' faces in language processing demonstrates that not all communication is verbal. Nonverbal communication cues, including facial expressions, significantly augment spoken language. The ability to accurately identify facial expressions also develops over the course of childhood and adolescence (Guarnera et al., 2018; Herba & Phillips, 2004) and involves seeing the mouth, as well as the eyes (Blais et al., 2012). For typically developing children who have already reached middle childhood, access to the eyes may be sufficient for them to recognize facial expressions (Ruba & Pollak, 2020). However, in a study of younger children (ages 4–8 years), they were considerably less accurate in identifying emotions from masked faces, especially happy and sad faces (Bourke et al., 2023), which raises questions about whether prolonged mask wearing may have negatively impacted the development of affect recognition.

For children with autism, mask wearing may have compounded preexisting challenges with language and social communication. Due to sensory sensitivities and behavioral rigidity, many children with autism found it difficult to tolerate masking (Tamon et al., 2022), which may have limited their social exposure to public settings where masks were required. In addition, studies have found that compared to typically developing individuals, those with autism often spend more time studying mouths than eyes, which may mean that masks cause greater interference with communication skill acquisition in this population (Pazhoohi et al., 2021).

Beyond the issue of communication development, masking may have interfered with auditory verbal learning/recall, especially in classrooms where students and teachers were masked for long periods of time. There is a correlation between auditory acuity and verbal learning. Even mild hearing impairment is associated with lower scores on a verbal memory task (van Boxtel et al., 2000; Willis et al., 2014). Masking attenuates the speech signal, which may limit the amount of information that enters auditory memory (Truong & Weber, 2021). This would potentially interfere with auditory verbal learning/recall and/or measures of phonological processing, such that prolonged mask use may be associated with increased risk of language-based learning difficulties, particularly in children who may have had other developmental risk factors (e.g., family history of learning disorders, prematurity). Children who have hearing loss may have been especially vulnerable because they tend to rely more on speechreading.

Given that masking was such a point of contention in the United States at later stages in the pandemic, we want to reiterate that we understand the critical role that masking played in mitigating the risk of COVID-19 transmission, and that we defer to our colleagues in public health and infectious disease for their expertise in this area. However, we also want to acknowledge that the potential lasting impact of masking on the development of language and communication skills is an open and important question, especially if some children require remediation.

As with academic skill acquisition, the impact of masking may vary depending on individual characteristics, including the child's age, duration of masking, and other risk factors for lower language skills. Research on the impact of hearing loss in children and adolescents may provide some clues about the possible range of outcomes. In children who have mild to severe hearing loss, speech and spoken language acquisition may be delayed. Treatment of hearing loss with hearing aids is associated with better language outcomes, especially in children who began to use them at younger ages (Tomblin et al., 2015). Children who receive cochlear implants prior to age 12 months also have significantly better spoken language outcomes than children who receive cochlear implants after 1 year (Sharma et al., 2020).

Thus, we might expect masking to have had the greatest impact on younger children (babies and toddlers), especially if they had lower levels of language and communication exposure at home. Older children may be less affected, particularly those whose speech and language skills were well-established when the pandemic began. Finally, those who have autism and who are deaf or hard of hearing were also more likely to struggle with masking.

Implications for Emotional and Social Development in Childhood and Adolescence

In the last two decades, there has been a dramatic increase in research into the neural bases of emotional and social development. These skills are critically tied to cognitive skills, in that there is a continuous interaction among thoughts, feelings, and actions. During childhood and adolescence, there may be a series of overlapping sensitive periods that determine how the brain perceives and responds to threats, responds to rewards or pleasure, and understands social cues and relationships. As with cognition, optimal learning of these skills critically depends on interaction with the environment, and disruption at any of these stages may interfere with subsequent development and increase risk for serious mental health concerns. In this section, we consider the impact of the psychosocial environment during the COVID-19 pandemic on the development of emotional and social development.

School Readiness and Behavioral Regulation

A successful school experience involves more than learning academic skills. In school, children learn about group dynamics and meeting external expectations. Behavioral routines, such as sitting at desks, walking in lines, keeping track of belongings, following directions, and maintaining appropriate social boundaries are all reinforced in the school environment. These expectations often shift over time, such that older students have greater independence than younger students, but older students are also held at higher standards of personal responsibility, requiring self-monitoring skills and the ability to modify one's behavior with feedback.

In Fall 2021, when many students began to return to consistent in-person instruction, there was a marked increase in behavioral disruptions in schools (Lonas, 2023). In the popular media, there were frequent reports of vandalism in middle schools, fueled by social media "challenges" (McCarthy et al., 2021). While pandemic-related stress may have contributed to behavioral dysregulation, there were also concerns that students had not made expected gains in social and behavioral regulation due to educational disruption during the early pandemic years.

Teachers reported that students seemed to be younger than their same-aged peers from earlier cohorts. In one news report, students were described as being "two years behind, socially" (Belsha, 2021). This is not necessarily surprising since a child who was in fifth grade at an elementary school in March 2020 might have entered seventh grade in a middle school in Fall 2021, without time to acclimate to the different expectations of the middle school environment. Similar challenges were also reported for younger students; in one 2021 study, nearly 80% of pre-kindergarten and kindergarten teachers rated students as lower on domains related to "readiness to learn" (Murphy et al., 2023), consistent with lower rates of daycare and preschool attendance and delayed kindergarten entry.

In a U.S. Department of Education survey of public schools about the 2021–2022 school year, 87% reported that the COVID-19 pandemic negatively impacted socioemotional development and 84% reported that students' behavioral development was negatively impacted. There were specific challenges with student misconduct inside and outside of classrooms, more acts of disrespect toward teachers and staff, and more prohibited use of electronic devices. Seventy percent of public schools reported needing more training in socioemotional development, and 51% reported needing more training in classroom management strategies (National Center for Education Statistics, 2022). These numbers are consistent with student and teacher ratings of perceived declines in socioemotional skills. For instance, Bates and Harrell (2023) found nearly half of students perceived a decline in their own socioemotional skills once schools reopened, with those who had previously received school-based supportive resources being most likely to report decline.

Many hoped that the spike in disciplinary problems would resolve once students had time to adjust to their post-pandemic school environments. Unfortunately, recent data suggest there were still high rates of behavioral challenges during the 2022–2023 school year. A 2023 study found that 70% of teachers reported more disruptions compared to 2019, representing a slight increase from the 66% of teachers who reported this in December 2021 (Prothero, 2023).

There are likely multiple factors contributing to residual behavioral challenges in youth, including ongoing pandemic-related aftershocks. However, the possibility of a connection between attenuated learning gains and behavioral dysregulation should not be overlooked. Poor academic performance is associated with increased school-related stress (Pascoe et al., 2020), which may contribute to low school engagement, a known contributing factor for disruptive behavior in schools (Granero-Gallegos et al., 2019). In other words, disruptive behavior in schools may be an indirect marker of the degree to which students are struggling to meet academic expectations, or a mismatch between expectations and ability. Efforts to increase youth engagement with school and academic self-efficacy may be more successful than punitive measures in extinguishing post-pandemic disruptive behaviors.

Addressing the root causes of disruptive behavior in schools is particularly important in adolescents, whose brains are exquisitely sensitive to peer feedback. While many teens dislike when their peers exhibit disruptive behaviors, interactions with disruptive peers are more likely to be perceived as exciting and attractive, which gives power and status to those exhibiting problematic behaviors (Powers & Bierman, 2013). Aggressive or disruptive behaviors may then become rewarding and reinforcing, and they are more likely to become ingrained given heightened neuroplasticity. As discussed earlier in this chapter, plasticity can be just as powerful for maladaptive behaviors as it is for adaptive ones.

Social Skills

In the time period before vaccines, social distancing was the primary means for controlling the spread of COVID-19. This led to dramatic and prolonged changes in social connectivity. Even after schools began to return to in-person instruction, students were often grouped into "pods," and interactions were limited with peers in other classrooms or grades. As discussed in Chapter 7, youth participated in fewer extracurricular activities, including team sports. In the early days of the pandemic, playgrounds and public recreation spaces were shuttered and surrounded with tape reading "Caution."

These measures, although initially necessary to protect medically vulnerable populations, were not without unwanted effects: they also limited the range of experiences that children had at a critical point in the development of social skills. Navigating relationships in childhood and adolescence provides opportunities to integrate a number of basic skills that are important in social cognition, including face processing, joint attention, and language, so that more complex social cognition skills like perspective-taking, conflict resolution, and interpreting emotional states may emerge (Blakemore & Mills, 2014).

So what might be the consequences of pandemic-related social isolation on the developing brain? Youth reported high levels of loneliness during the COVID-19 pandemic. Loneliness is associated with increased risk for mental health problems, including depression and anxiety (Loades et al., 2020). The increased risk is not short term—in a recent meta-analysis of the impact of loneliness, youth showed an increase in risk for up to 9 years (Loades et al., 2020).

Existing research on the changes in behavior and neural development due to social isolation is often confounded by the presence of additional stressors, such as the absence of primary caregivers, environmental stimulation, and food deprivation, making them less than optimal comparisons to the type of social isolation experienced by most youth during the COVID-19 pandemic. Likewise, studies of child brain structure and function during the COVID-19 pandemic also have potentially confounding factors, including parental stress/welfare, educational disruption, household stressors (e.g., physical space), and economic adversity.

With these limitations in mind, neuroimaging studies of those who experienced profound social isolation in early life (e.g., from living within institutions) have shown differences in brain networks important for social cognition, learning and memory, and processing emotions, including regions of the prefrontal cortex, hippocampus, and amygdala, as well as the networks that connect these regions (Bzdok & Dunbar, 2022; Xiong et al., 2023). This is consistent with more controlled studies of social isolation in juvenile mice, finding alterations in neuronal transmission and myelination (Yamamuro et al., 2020). Similarly, in monkeys who were socially isolated for 1.5 years, social rehabilitation was associated with atypical dopaminergic reactivity. For some monkeys, these changes within pathways associated with reward processing increased the likelihood for substance (cocaine) use, presumably as a substitute for the positive feelings that would normally follow from social interactions (Morgan et al., 2002).

Social connectivity through digital technology may have provided some protection during periods of relative isolation. Especially in the beginning of the pandemic, many maintained connections to family and friends, as well as religious and social organizations, through video-conferencing. Parties, weddings, and funerals were all streamed over the Internet, along with regular game nights and book clubs. In 2021, a large poll of Americans found that 81% had used video-conferencing during the pandemic, with more than half of Americans reporting that the Internet had been essential. Usage was particularly high among those who were highly educated and younger (less than 50 years old) (McClain et al., 2021).

Yet most reported that digital interactions were not an adequate replacement for in-person interactions. Some studies found a negative relationship between social media use and mental health in adolescents, but use of technology to facilitate individual communication may have been positive (Marciano et al., 2021). This seemingly paradoxical finding may relate to the unique way that primates, including humans, establish social bonds. Close friendships require a significant time investment, as well as high frequencies of contact to maintain closeness (Bzdok & Dunbar, 2022). Without in-person interactions, media technologies provided a proxy for personalized social exchanges.

There is more limited research on reduced physical contact during the pandemic. Social touching (e.g., hugging, stroking, caressing) is common in social interactions across cultures and often reinforced in groups through dancing, religious rituals, and storytelling (Bzdok & Dunbar, 2022). Social touch is linked to the release of endorphins, which bind to opiate receptors (Bzdok & Dunbar, 2022; Dunbar, 2012), and plays a role in regulating the brain networks involved in metabolism, responding to stress, and maintaining homeostasis (Pilozzi et al., 2020). Behaviorally, social touch plays an important role across childhood and adolescence in defining relationship bonds. In infancy and toddlerhood, social touch fosters attachment between parents and their children and may reduce risk for sensory processing challenges in later life. In childhood, social touch is related to the development of social boundaries (e.g., when navigating physical play), learning behavioral regulation skills (e.g., a touch from a caregiver to signal the need to change behavior), and is associated with positive affect. In adolescence, social touch helps with sexual and gender identity development, as teens learn to differentiate between romantic and nonromantic relationships (Cascio et al., 2019). Given the significant role of physical touch in the development of social skills and relationship bonds across childhood and adolescence, it seems reasonable to anticipate that social distancing had some impact on the brain networks involved in processing these environmental cues.

The impact of social isolation measures may have been particularly negative for teens. Social skills develop over the entire course of childhood and adolescence, but the adolescent brain is particularly sensitive to input from peers and the broader culture, leading some researchers to propose that adolescence is a sensitive period for social skill development. Compared to other age groups, teens are much more attuned to feedback from their peers and their behavior is more likely to be influenced by those outside of their immediate family (Blakemore & Mills, 2014). A reduction in available feedback may have caused shifts in identity development and deprived adolescents of much-needed social feedback. This may be especially true for adolescents who have neurodevelopmental disorders that impact social skill development, including those with autism spectrum disorders and ADHD.

Altogether, the extent to which social skill development was negatively impacted by social isolation during the COVID-19 pandemic remains a largely open area for research. The existing research, which has largely relied on paradigms that are not fully analogous to pandemic circumstances, suggests that social isolation can change functioning within networks that are involved in social cognition, potentially in ways that may increase vulnerability to finding alternative sources of reward stimulation, such as substance abuse or other risky behaviors.

Mental Health

In Chapter 6, we reviewed the overwhelming evidence for a decline in youth mental health during the COVID-19 pandemic that is arguably still ongoing and may have a profound impact on neurodevelopment. Even prior to the pandemic, there was an increasing awareness that the majority of mental health conditions begin prior to age 25 (Kessler et al., 2005; Solmi et al., 2022), which has spurred research into earlier identification and intervention during adolescence, including for serious mental health conditions (Insel & Fenton, 2005).

In a recent perspective piece on the emergence of psychopathology in youth, Uhlhaas et al. (2023) describe five overlapping sensitive periods for skills that are critical in determining mental health outcomes. In order from the earliest to the latest, the associated neural systems are involved in

(1) appropriately responding to threats and stress; (2) regulating the stress response; (3) higher order cognitive functions, regulating excitatory and inhibitory responses, and making long-range connections; (4) responding appropriately to rewards; and (5) social cognition (Uhlhaas et al., 2023).

Stressors or psychosocial disruption during each of these periods may be associated with specific mental health conditions. For example, anxiety disorders tend to have an earlier age of onset and relate to the perception and response to threats or stressors. In contrast, substance use disorders emerge later and are related to reward processing. Furthermore, developmental challenges at any stage may "cascade" downstream to increase risk over time. This accounts for the association between earlier age of onset and longer duration of symptoms, comorbidity (i.e., developing multiple mental health conditions), and poorer outcomes (Uhlhaas et al., 2023).

Applying this framework to understanding the mental health challenges arising from the COVID-19 pandemic, there is a clear need for urgent and ongoing intervention. Left untreated, youth mental health conditions may interfere with the development of later skills that are needed for healthy emotional functioning in adulthood and/or increase the risk of developing more severe or multiple mental health conditions, as the neural systems involved in emotional and social functioning will continue to develop even when there is ongoing dysregulation or the underlying skills are suboptimal.

Within this context, there are several groups of youth who may be at particularly high risk for lasting pandemic-related mental health challenges with associated disruption to neurodevelopment. Children born to mothers who experienced high levels of stress during pregnancy are one of those vulnerable groups. It is well established that prenatal maternal stress is related to poorer mental health outcomes in children. There are likely multiple mechanisms mediating this relationship, including direct disruption to fetal brain development, but there may also be indirect disruption to gene expression that increases risk of mental health disorders in later life (Azar & Booij, 2022).

Several studies have examined the relationship between maternal pandemic-related stress during pregnancy and infant development. Gotlib et al. (2022) found that high maternal pandemic-related stress at baseline was associated with maternal depressive symptoms and infant negative affect 1 year later (Buthmann et al., 2022). High levels of maternal postnatal anxiety were linked to lower regulatory capacity in infancy, although the effect was mediated by parenting stress and infant bonding (Provenzi et al., 2023).

Increased maternal stress and COVID-19 infection during pregnancy also jointly predicted lower infant attention at age 6 months, and infant attention predicted socioemotional function and risk for a neurodevelopmental disorder at 12 months (Werchan et al., 2023). There was also a negative correlation between prenatal depression and motor skills in infancy (Papadopoulos et al., 2022). Altogether, this research suggests that for babies born after the COVID-19 pandemic, there is a relationship between prenatal anxiety and depression and an infant's cognitive, motor, and emotional processing.

Children who experienced pandemic-related trauma or adverse childhood experiences (ACEs) are likely another high-risk group. Trauma and ACEs may alter brain maturation patterns and increase risk for early puberty, biological aging, and changes to the epigenome that may increase susceptibility to mental disorders (Colich et al., 2020; Dunn et al., 2019; McLaughlin et al., 2020). Childhood adversity may specifically impact brain mechanisms involved in threat processing, emotional regulation, and reward processing, thereby increasing the risk of psychopathology (McLaughlin et al., 2019). For example, adverse experiences that involve harm or threat of harm have been associated with altered development of brain networks involved in fear conditioning and detecting threat salience, including smaller amygdala volume (Peverill et al., 2023). Protective effects from trauma include strong caregiver relationships, heightened sensitivity to positive and rewarding stimuli, and mature connections between the amygdala and frontal lobes (McLaughlin & Lambert, 2017).

With this background, Machlin and McLaughlin (2023) recently reviewed the neuroimaging studies examining whether pre-pandemic brain structure and function predicted psychopathology during the COVID-19 pandemic. Studies showed positive relationships between internalizing problems and amygdala reactivity or connectivity, as well as reduced structural integrity within regions involved in cognitive control. Two studies showed that changes in the dorsal striatum in response to social reward predicted depression during the pandemic.

While these studies may help to identify youth who may be at increased risk of psychopathology following the COVID-19 pandemic, there are even fewer studies examining the direct or indirect impact of pandemic-related stressors on neurodevelopment. Gotlib et al. (2022) compared two matched samples of youth before and after the COVID-19 pandemic, finding that the pandemic-era group had more severe internalizing symptoms, reduced cortical thickness, larger hippocampal and amygdala volume, and more advanced brain age. It will be important to examine whether these changes are transient or permanent and whether they have a functional impact. This will require establishing pandemic-era neurodevelopmental trajectories to compare with normative trajectories of earlier cohorts (Gotlib et al., 2022).

Altogether, the emerging research suggests that infants whose mothers experienced anxiety and depression while pregnant during the COVID-19 pandemic may have conferred greater risk of cognitive, motor, and developmental delays. For children who experienced significant trauma or ACEs related to the COVID-19 pandemic, they may be especially vulnerable to changes in brain development and epigenetic factors that may increase the risk of psychopathology to the child and/or other family members.

References

Alex, A. M., Aguate, F., Botteron, K., Buss, C., Chong, Y.-S., Dager, S. R., . . . the, E. O. g. (2024). A global multicohort study to map subcortical brain development and cognition in infancy and early childhood. *Nature Neuroscience, 27*, 176–186. https://doi.org/10.1038/s41593-023-01501-6

Allotey, J., Stallings, E., Bonet, M., Yap, M., Chatterjee, S., Kew, T., . . . Thangaratinam, S. (2020). Clinical manifestations, risk factors, and maternal and perinatal outcomes of coronavirus disease 2019 in pregnancy: Living systematic review and meta-analysis. *British Medical Journal, 370*, m3320. https://doi.org/10.1136/bmj.m3320

Anderson, V., Spencer-Smith, M., Leventer, R., Coleman, L., Anderson, P., Williams, J., . . . Jacobs, R. (2009). Childhood brain insult: Can age at insult help us predict outcome? *Brain, 132*(Pt 1), 45–56. https://doi.org/10.1093/brain/awn293

Andrews, K., Dunn, J. R., Prime, H., Duku, E., Atkinson, L., Tiwari, A., & Gonzalez, A. (2021). Effects of household chaos and parental responsiveness on child executive functions: a novel, multi-method approach. *BMC Psychology, 9*(1), 147. https://doi.org/10.1186/s40359-021-00651-1

Azar, N., & Booij, L. (2022). DNA methylation as a mediator in the association between prenatal maternal stress and child mental health outcomes: Current state of knowledge. *Journal of Affective Disorders, 319*, 142–163. https://doi.org/10.1016/j.jad.2022.09.008

Babenko, O., Kovalchuk, I., & Metz, G. A. (2015). Stress-induced perinatal and transgenerational epigenetic programming of brain development and mental health. *Neuroscience and Biobehavioral Review, 48*, 70–91. https://doi.org/10.1016/j.neubiorev.2014.11.013

Bale, T. L. (2015). Epigenetic and transgenerational reprogramming of brain development. *Nature Reviews Neuroscience, 16*(6), 332–344. https://doi.org/10.1038/nrn3818

Bates, S., & Harrell, D. R. (2024). COVID-19 school closures: Disruptions in school-based support services and socioemotional loss among middle school students. *Journal of School Health, 94*, 209–218. https://doi.org/10.1111/josh.13421

Belsha, K. (2021). Stress and short tempers: Schools struggle with behavior as students return. *KQED*. https://www.kqed.org/mindshift/58572/stress-and-short-tempers-schools-struggle-with-behavior-as-students-return

Bethlehem, R. A. I., Seidlitz, J., White, S. R., Vogel, J. W., Anderson, K. M., Adamson, C., . . . Alexander-Bloch, A. F. (2022). Brain charts for the human lifespan. *Nature, 604*(7906), 525–533. https://doi.org/10.1038/s41586-022-04554-y

Black, M. M. (2008). Effects of vitamin B12 and folate deficiency on brain development in children. *Food Nutrition Bulletin, 29*(2 Suppl.), S126–S131. https://doi.org/10.1177/15648265080292s117

Blais, C., Roy, C., Fiset, D., Arguin, M., & Gosselin, F. (2012). The eyes are not the window to basic emotions. *Neuropsychologia, 50*(12), 2830–2838. https://doi.org/10.1016/j.neuropsychologia.2012.08.010

Blakemore, S. J. (2008). The social brain in adolescence. *Nature Reviews Neuroscience, 9*(4), 267–277. https://doi.org/10.1038/nrn2353

Blakemore, S. J., & Mills, K. L. (2014). Is adolescence a sensitive period for sociocultural processing? *Annual Review of Psychology, 65*, 187–207. https://doi.org/10.1146/annurev-psych-010213-115202

Bourke, L., Lingwood, J., Gallagher-Mitchell, T., & López-Pérez, B. (2023). The effect of face mask wearing on language processing and emotion recognition in young children. *Journal of Experimental Child Psychology, 226*, 105580. https://doi.org/10.1016/j.jecp.2022.105580

Breit, M., Scherrer, V., Blickle, J., & Preckel, F. (2023). Students' intelligence test results after six and sixteen months of irregular schooling due to the COVID-19 pandemic. *PLoS One, 18*(3), e0281779. https://doi.org/10.1371/journal.pone.0281779

Brito, N. H., Piccolo, L. R., & Noble, K. G. (2017). Associations between cortical thickness and neurocognitive skills during childhood vary by family socioeconomic factors. *Brain Cognition, 116*, 54–62. https://doi.org/10.1016/j.bandc.2017.03.007

Bronfenbrenner, U. (1977). Toward an experimental ecology of human development. *American Psychologist, 32*(7), 513–531. https://doi.org/10.1037/0003-066X.32.7.513

Bronfenbrenner, U. (1979). *The ecology of human development: Experiments by nature and design*. Cambridge, MA: Harvard University Press.

Bull, R., Espy, K. A., & Wiebe, S. A. (2008). Short-term memory, working memory, and executive functioning in preschoolers: Longitudinal predictors of mathematical achievement at age 7 years. *Developmental Neuropsychology, 33*(3), 205–228. https://doi.org/10.1080/87565640801982312

Bull, R., & Lee, K. (2014). Executive functioning and mathematics achievement. *Child Development Perspectives, 8*, 36–41. https://doi.org/10.1111/cdep.12059

Buthmann, J. L., Miller, J. G., & Gotlib, I. H. (2024). Maternal-prenatal stress and depression predict infant temperament during the COVID-19 pandemic. *Developmental Psychopathology, 36*(1), 161–169. https://doi.org/10.1017/s0954579422001055

Byrne, S., O'Flaherty, E., Sledge, H., Lenehan, S., Jordan, N., Boland, F., . . . Hourihane, J. (2023, October). Infants born during the COVID-19 pandemic have less interest in masked faces than unmasked faces. *Archives for Disease in Childhood, 108*(10). https://doi.org/10.1136/archdischild-2022-325272

Byrne, S., Sledge, H., Hurley, S., Hoolahan, S., Franklin, R., Jordan, N., . . . Hourihane, J. (2023, October). Developmental and behavioural outcomes at 2 years in babies born during the COVID-19 pandemic: Communication concerns in a pandemic birth cohort. *Archives for Disease in Childhood, 108*(10), 846–851. https://doi.org/10.1136/archdischild-2022-325271

Bzdok, D., & Dunbar, R. I. M. (2022). Social isolation and the brain in the pandemic era. *Nature Human Behavior, 6*(10), 1333–1343. https://doi.org/10.1038/s41562-022-01453-0

Cascio, C. J., Moore, D., & McGlone, F. (2019). Social touch and human development. *Developmental Cognitive Neuroscience, 35*, 5–11. https://doi.org/10.1016/j.dcn.2018.04.009

Charney, S. A., Camarata, S. M., & Chern, A. (2021). Potential impact of the COVID-19 pandemic on communication and language skills in children. *Otolaryngology: Head and Neck Surgery, 165*(1), 1–2. https://doi.org/10.1177/0194599820978247

Cheng, Q., Roth, A., Halgren, E., Klein, D., Chen, J. K., & Mayberry, R. I. (2023). Restricted language access during childhood affects adult brain structure in selective language regions. *Proceedings of the National Academy of Sciences USA, 120*(7), e2215423120. https://doi.org/10.1073/pnas.2215423120

Cheng, Q., Roth, A., Halgren, E., & Mayberry, R. I. (2019, September 19). Effects of early language deprivation on brain connectivity: Language pathways in deaf native and late first-language learners of American Sign Language. *Frontiers in Human Neuroscience, 13*, 320. https://doi.org/10.3389/fnhum.2019.00320

Choudhury, S., Blakemore, S. J., & Charman, T. (2006). Social cognitive development during adolescence. *Social Cognitive and Affective Neuroscience, 1*(3), 165–174. https://doi.org/10.1093/scan/nsl024

Colich, N. L., Rosen, M. L., Williams, E. S., & McLaughlin, K. A. (2020). Biological aging in childhood and adolescence following experiences of threat and deprivation: A systematic review and meta-analysis. *Psychological Bulletin, 146*(9), 721–764. https://doi.org/10.1037/bul0000270

Colvin, M., Koven, M., Vuijk, P., Fleming, L., Reese, K., Cassill, C., . . . Doyle, A. (In press). Differences in cognitive and academic performance during the COVID-19 pandemic in Child Psychiatric Outpatients. *Psychological Assessment.*

Cristofori, I., Cohen-Zimerman, S., & Grafman, J. (2019). Executive functions. In M. D'Esposito & J. H. Grafman (Eds.), *Handbook of clinical neurology* (Vol. 163, pp. 197–219). Elsevier. https://doi.org/https://doi.org/10.1016/B978-0-12-804281-6.00011-2

de Boisferon, A., Tift, A. H., Minar, N. J., & Lewkowicz, D. J. (2018). The redeployment of attention to the mouth of a talking face during the second year of life. *Journal of Experimental Child Psychology, 172*, 189–200. https://doi.org/https://doi.org/10.1016/j.jecp.2018.03.009

Demetriou, E. A., DeMayo, M. M., & Guastella, A. J. (2019). Executive function in autism spectrum disorder: History, theoretical models, empirical findings, and potential as an endophenotype. *Frontiers in Psychiatry, 10*, 753. https://doi.org/10.3389/fpsyt.2019.00753

Dennis, M., Spiegler, B. J., Juranek, J. J., Bigler, E. D., Snead, O. C., & Fletcher, J. M. (2013). Age, plasticity, and homeostasis in childhood brain disorders. *Neuroscience and Biobehavioral Reviews, 37*(10 Pt 2), 2760–2773. https://doi.org/10.1016/j.neubiorev.2013.09.010

Dennis, M., Spiegler, B. J., Simic, N., Sinopoli, K. J., Wilkinson, A., Yeates, K. O., . . . Fletcher, J. M. (2014). Functional plasticity in childhood brain disorders: When, what, how, and whom to assess. *Neuropsychology Review, 24*(4), 389–408. https://doi.org/10.1007/s11065-014-9261-x

Diamond, A. (2013). Executive functions. *Annual Review in Psychology, 64*, 135–168. https://doi.org/10.1146/annurev-psych-113011-143750

Diamond, A. (2020). Executive functions. *Handbook of Clinical Neurology, 173*, 225–240. https://doi.org/10.1016/b978-0-444-64150-2.00020-4

Doyle, A. E., Vuijk, P. J., Doty, N. D., McGrath, L. M., Willoughby, B. L., O'Donnell, E. H., . . . Braaten, E. B. (2018). Cross-disorder cognitive impairments in youth referred for neuropsychiatric evaluation. *Journal of International Neuropsychology Society, 24*(1), 91–103. https://doi.org/10.1017/s1355617717000601

Du, M. Y., Liao, W., Lui, S., Huang, X. Q., Li, F., Kuang, W. H., . . . Gong, Q. Y. (2015). Altered functional connectivity in the brain default-mode network of earthquake survivors persists after 2 years despite recovery from anxiety symptoms. *Social Cognitive and Affective Neuroscience, 10*(11), 1497–1505. https://doi.org/10.1093/scan/nsv040

Dunbar, R. I. (2012). Bridging the bonding gap: The transition from primates to humans. *Philosophical Transactions of the Royal Society of London B Biological Science, 367*(1597), 1837–1846. https://doi.org/10.1098/rstb.2011.0217

Dunn, E. C., Soare, T. W., Zhu, Y., Simpkin, A. J., Suderman, M. J., Klengel, T., . . . Relton, C. L. (2019). Sensitive periods for the effect of childhood adversity on DNA methylation: Results from a prospective, longitudinal study. *Biological Psychiatry, 85*(10), 838–849. https://doi.org/10.1016/j.biopsych.2018.12.023

Elder, T. E., & Lubotsky, D. H. (2009). Kindergarten entrance age and children's achievement: Impacts of state policies, family background, and peers. *Journal of Human Resources, 44*(3), 641–683.

Fibla, L., Forbes, S. H., McCarthy, J., Mee, K., Magnotta, V., Deoni, S., . . . Spencer, J. P. (2023). Language exposure and brain myelination in early development. *Journal of Neuroscience, 43*(23), 4279–4290. https://doi.org/10.1523/jneurosci.1034-22.2023

Frota, S., Pejovic, J., Cruz, M., Severino, C., & Vigário, M. (2022). Early word segmentation behind the mask. *Frontiers in Psychology, 13*, 879123. https://doi.org/10.3389/fpsyg.2022.879123

Fuhrmann, D., Knoll, L. J., & Blakemore, S. J. (2015). Adolescence as a sensitive period of brain development. *Trends in Cognitive Science, 19*(10), 558–566. https://doi.org/10.1016/j.tics.2015.07.008

Ganzel, B. L., Kim, P., Glover, G. H., & Temple, E. (2008). Resilience after 9/11: Multimodal neuroimaging evidence for stress-related change in the healthy adult brain. *Neuroimage, 40*(2), 788–795. https://doi.org/10.1016/j.neuroimage.2007.12.010

Goldman-Rakic, P. S. (1987). Development of cortical circuitry and cognitive function. *Child Development, 58*(3), 601–622.

Goldstein, M. H., King, A. P., & West, M. J. (2003). Social interaction shapes babbling: Testing parallels between birdsong and speech. *Proceedings of the National Academy of Sciences, 100*(13), 8030–8035.

Goos, M., Pipa, J., & Peixoto, F. (2021). Effectiveness of grade retention: A systematic review and meta-analysis. *Educational Research Review, 34*, 100401. https://doi.org/https://doi.org/10.1016/j.edurev.2021.100401

Gordon, K. A., Daien, M. F., Negandhi, J., Blakeman, A., Ganek, H., Papsin, B., & Cushing, S. L. (2021). Exposure to spoken communication in children with cochlear implants during the COVID-19 lockdown. *JAMA Otolaryngology Head and Neck Surgery, 147*(4), 368–376. https://doi.org/10.1001/jamaoto.2020.5496

Gotlib, I. H., Miller, J. G., Borchers, L. R., Coury, S. M., Costello, L. A., Garcia, J. M., & Ho, T. C. (2022). Effects of the COVID-19 pandemic on mental health and brain maturation in adolescents: Implications for analyzing longitudinal data. *Biological Psychiatry Global Open Science, 3*(4), 912–918. https://doi.org/10.1016/j.bpsgos.2022.11.002

Granero-Gallegos, A., Gómez-López, M., Baena-Extremera, A., & Martínez-Molina, M. (2019). Interaction effects of disruptive behaviour and motivation profiles with teacher competence and school satisfaction in secondary school physical education. *International Journal of Environmental Research and Public Health, 17*(1), 114. https://doi.org/10.3390/ijerph17010114

Guarnera, M., Magnano, P., Pellerone, M., Cascio, M. I., Squatrito, V., & Buccheri, S. L. (2018). Facial expressions and the ability to recognize emotions from the eyes or mouth: A comparison among old adults, young adults, and children. *Journal of Genetic Psychology, 179*(5), 297–310. https://doi.org/10.1080/00221325.2018.1509200

Hawkins, M. A. W., Layman, H. M., Ganson, K. T., Tabler, J., Ciciolla, L., Tsotsoros, C. E., & Nagata, J. M. (2021). Adverse childhood events and cognitive function among young adults: Prospective results from the national longitudinal study of adolescent to adult health. *Child Abuse and Neglect, 115*, 105008. https://doi.org/10.1016/j.chiabu.2021.105008

Hebb, D. O. (2005). *The organization of behavior: A neuropsychological theory*. New York: Psychology Press. https://www.taylorfrancis.com/books/mono/10.4324/9781410612403/organization-behavior-hebb

Herba, C., & Phillips, M. (2004). Annotation: Development of facial expression recognition from childhood to adolescence: Behavioural and neurological perspectives. *Journal of Child Psychology and Psychiatry, 45*(7), 1185–1198. https://doi.org/10.1111/j.1469-7610.2004.00316.x

Hime, G. R., Stonehouse, S., & Pang, T. Y. (2021). Alternative models for transgenerational epigenetic inheritance: Molecular psychiatry beyond mice and man. *World Journal of Psychiatry, 11*(10), 711–735. https://doi.org/10.5498/wjp.v11.i10.711

Hubel, D. H., & Wiesel, T. N. (1970). The period of susceptibility to the physiological effects of unilateral eye closure in kittens. *Journal of Physiology, 206*(2), 419–436. https://doi.org/10.1113/jphysiol.1970.sp009022

Huber, E., Corrigan, N. M., Yarnykh, V. L., Ferjan Ramírez, N., & Kuhl, P. K. (2023). Language experience during infancy predicts white matter myelination at age 2 years. *Journal of Neuroscience, 43*(9), 1590–1599. https://doi.org/10.1523/jneurosci.1043-22.2023

Insel, T. R., & Fenton, W. S. (2005). Psychiatric epidemiology: It's not just about counting anymore. *Archives in General Psychiatry, 62*(6), 590–592. https://doi.org/10.1001/archpsyc.62.6.590

Jacobson, L. A., Williford, A. P., & Pianta, R. C. (2011). The role of executive function in children's competent adjustment to middle school. *Child Neuropsychology, 17*(3), 255–280. https://doi.org/10.1080/09297049.2010.535654

Keller, A. S., Pines, A. R., Shanmugan, S., Sydnor, V. J., Cui, Z., Bertolero, M. A., ... Satterthwaite, T. D. (2023). Personalized functional brain network topography is associated with individual differences in youth cognition. *Nature Communications, 14*(1), 8411. https://doi.org/10.1038/s41467-023-44087-0

Kessler, R. C., Berglund, P., Demler, O., Jin, R., Merikangas, K. R., & Walters, E. E. (2005). Lifetime prevalence and age-of-onset distributions of DSM-IV disorders in the National Comorbidity Survey Replication. *Archives in General Psychiatry, 62*(6), 593–602. https://doi.org/10.1001/archpsyc.62.6.593

Knoll, L. J., Fuhrmann, D., Sakhardande, A. L., Stamp, F., Speekenbrink, M., & Blakemore, S. J. (2016). A window of opportunity for cognitive training in adolescence. *Psychological Science, 27*(12), 1620–1631. https://doi.org/10.1177/0956797616671327

Knudsen, E. I. (2004). Sensitive periods in the development of the brain and behavior. *Journal of Cognitive Neuroscience, 16*(8), 1412–1425. https://doi.org/10.1162/0898929042304796

Kolb, B., & Gibb, R. (2011). Brain plasticity and behaviour in the developing brain. *Journal of the Canadian Academy of Child and Adolescent Psychiatry, 20*(4), 265–276.

Kolb, B., Harker, A., & Gibb, R. (2017). Principles of plasticity in the developing brain. *Developmental Medicine and Child Neurology, 59*(12), 1218–1223. https://doi.org/10.1111/dmcn.13546

Kuhl, P., & Rivera-Gaxiola, M. (2008). Neural substrates of language acquisition. *Annual Review in Neuroscience, 31*, 511–534. https://doi.org/10.1146/annurev.neuro.30.051606.094321

Lautarescu, A., Craig, M. C., & Glover, V. (2020). Prenatal stress: Effects on fetal and child brain development. In A. Clow & N. Smyth (Eds.), *International review of neurobiology* (Vol. 150, pp. 17–40). New York: Academic Press. https://doi.org/https://doi.org/10.1016/bs.irn.2019.11.002

Lehman, B. J., David, D. M., & Gruber, J. A. (2017). Rethinking the biopsychosocial model of health: Understanding health as a dynamic system. *Social and Personality Psychology Compass, 11*(8), e12328. https://doi.org/https://doi.org/10.1111/spc3.12328

Lerkkanen, M. K., Pakarinen, E., Salminen, J., & Torppa, M. (2023). Reading and math skills development among Finnish primary school children before and after COVID-19 school closure. *Reading and Writing, 36*(2), 263–288. https://doi.org/10.1007/s11145-022-10358-3

Liston, C., McEwen, B. S., & Casey, B. J. (2009). Psychosocial stress reversibly disrupts prefrontal processing and attentional control. *Proceedings of the National Academy of Sciences, 106*(3), 912–917. https://doi.org/doi:10.1073/pnas.0807041106

Loades, M. E., Chatburn, E., Higson-Sweeney, N., Reynolds, S., Shafran, R., Brigden, A., ... Crawley, E. (2020). Rapid systematic review: The impact of social isolation and loneliness on the mental health of children and adolescents in the context of COVID-19. *Journal of the American Academy of Child and Adolescent Psychiatry, 59*(11), 1218–1239. https://doi.org/10.1016/j.jaac.2020.05.009

Lonas, L. (2023). From bad to worse: Student misbehavior rises further since return of in-person classes. *The Hill.* https://thehill.com/homenews/education/3975

216-from-bad-to-worse-student-misbehavior-rises-further-since-return-of-in-person-classes/#:~:text = Seventy%20percent%20of%20teachers%2C%20principals,misbehaving%20%E2%80%9Ca%20lot%20more.%E2%80%9D

Lorenz, K. (1935). Der Kumpan in der Umwelt des Vogels. *Journal für Ornithologie, 83*(3), 289–413. https://doi.org/10.1007/BF01905572

Lytle, S. R., Garcia-Sierra, A., & Kuhl, P. K. (2018). Two are better than one: Infant language learning from video improves in the presence of peers. *Proceedings of the National Academy of Sciences USA, 115*(40), 9859–9866. https://doi.org/10.1073/pnas.1611621115

Machlin, L., & McLaughlin, K. A. (2023). Pre-pandemic brain structure and function and adolescent psychopathology during the COVID-19 pandemic. *Current Opinion in Psychology, 52*, 101647. https://doi.org/10.1016/j.copsyc.2023.101647

Malarbi, S., Abu-Rayya, H. M., Muscara, F., & Stargatt, R. (2017). Neuropsychological functioning of childhood trauma and post-traumatic stress disorder: A meta-analysis. *Neuroscience and Biobehavioral Review, 72*, 68–86. https://doi.org/10.1016/j.neubiorev.2016.11.004

Männamaa, M., Kikas, E., Peets, K., & Palu, A. (2012). Cognitive correlates of math skills in third-grade students. *Educational Psychology, 32*(1), 21–44. https://doi.org/10.1080/01443410.2011.621713

Marciano, L., Ostroumova, M., Schulz, P. J., & Camerini, A. L. (2021). Digital media use and adolescents' mental health during the Covid-19 pandemic: A systematic review and meta-analysis. *Frontier in Public Health, 9*, 793868. https://doi.org/10.3389/fpubh.2021.793868

McCarthy, C., Algar, S., & Fonrouge, G. (2021, December 17). TikTok threat 'challenge' sends NY school districts scrambling. *New York Post.* https://nypost.com/2021/12/17/tiktok-threat-challenge-sends-ny-schools-scrambling/

McClain, C., Vogels, E. A., Perrin, A., Sechopoulos, S., & Rainie, L. (2021). The internet and the pandemic. Pew Research Center. https://www.pewresearch.org/internet/2021/09/01/the-internet-and-the-pandemic/

McLaughlin, K. A., Colich, N. L., Rodman, A. M., & Weissman, D. G. (2020). Mechanisms linking childhood trauma exposure and psychopathology: A transdiagnostic model of risk and resilience. *BMC Medicine, 18*(1), 96. https://doi.org/10.1186/s12916-020-01561-6

McLaughlin, K. A., DeCross, S. N., Jovanovic, T., & Tottenham, N. (2019). Mechanisms linking childhood adversity with psychopathology: Learning as an intervention target. *Behavior Research and Therapy, 118*, 101–109. https://doi.org/10.1016/j.brat.2019.04.008

McLaughlin, K. A., & Lambert, H. K. (2017). Child trauma exposure and psychopathology: Mechanisms of risk and resilience. *Current Opinion in Psychology, 14*, 29–34. https://doi.org/10.1016/j.copsyc.2016.10.004

Mitsven, S. G., Perry, L. K., Jerry, C. M., & Messinger, D. S. (2022). Classroom language during COVID-19: Associations between mask-wearing and objectively measured teacher and preschooler vocalizations. *Frontiers in Psychology, 13*, 874293. https://doi.org/10.3389/fpsyg.2022.874293

Morgan, D., Grant, K. A., Gage, H. D., Mach, R. H., Kaplan, J. R., Prioleau, O., . . . Nader, M. A. (2002). Social dominance in monkeys: Dopamine D2 receptors and cocaine self-administration. *Nature Neuroscience, 5*(2), 169–174. https://doi.org/10.1038/nn798

Murphy, K., Giordano, K., & Deloach, T. (2024). Pre-K and kindergarten teacher perception of school readiness during the COVID-19 pandemic. *Early Childhood Education Journal, 52*, 551–561. https://doi.org/10.1007/s10643-023-01462-2

National Center for Education Statistics. (2022). More than 80 percent of U.S. public schools report pandemic has negatively impacted student behavior and socio-emotional development. *U.S. Department of Education, Institute of Education Sciences.* https://nces.ed.gov/whatsnew/press_releases/07_06_2022.asp

Nevo, E. (2024). The effect of the COVID-19 pandemic on low SES kindergarteners' language abilities. *Early Childhood Education Journal, 52*, 459–469. https://doi.org/10.1007/s10643-023-01444-4

Nolvi, S., Merz, E. C., Kataja, E. L., & Parsons, C. E. (2023). Prenatal stress and the developing brain: Postnatal environments promoting resilience. *Biological Psychiatry*, *93*(10), 942–952. https://doi.org/10.1016/j.biopsych.2022.11.023

Özek, U., & Mariano, L. T. (2023). Can grade retention help with COVID-19 learning recovery in schools? Brookings Institution. United States of America. https://policycommons.net/artifacts/4140342/can-grade-retention-help-with-covid-19-learning-recovery-in-schools/4949056/ on 12 May 2024. CID: 20.500.12592/zj8d93

Papadopoulos, A., Nichols, E. S., Mohsenzadeh, Y., Giroux, I., Mottola, M. F., Van Lieshout, R. J., & Duerden, E. G. (2022). Prenatal and postpartum maternal mental health and neonatal motor outcomes during the COVID-19 pandemic. *Journal of Affective Disorders Report*, *10*, 100387. https://doi.org/10.1016/j.jadr.2022.100387

Pascoe, M. C., Hetrick, S. E., & Parker, A. G. (2020). The impact of stress on students in secondary school and higher education. *International Journal of Adolescence and Youth*, *25*(1), 104–112. https://doi.org/10.1080/02673843.2019.1596823

Pazhoohi, F., Forby, L., & Kingstone, A. (2021). Facial masks affect emotion recognition in the general population and individuals with autistic traits. *PLoS One*, *16*(9), e0257740. https://doi.org/10.1371/journal.pone.0257740

Pechtel, P., & Pizzagalli, D. A. (2011). Effects of early life stress on cognitive and affective function: an integrated review of human literature. *Psychopharmacology (Berlin)*, *214*(1), 55–70. https://doi.org/10.1007/s00213-010-2009-2

Pembrey, M., Saffery, R., & Bygren, L. O. (2014). Human transgenerational responses to early-life experience: potential impact on development, health and biomedical research. *Journal of Medical Genetics*, *51*(9), 563–572. https://doi.org/10.1136/jmedgenet-2014-102577

Peng, P., & Kievit, R. A. (2020). The development of academic achievement and cognitive abilities: A bidirectional perspective. *Child Development Perspectives*, *14*(1), 15–20. https://doi.org/10.1111/cdep.12352

Peterson, R. L., & Pennington, B. F. (2015). Developmental dyslexia. *Annual Review Clinical Psychology*, *11*, 283–307. https://doi.org/10.1146/annurev-clinpsy-032814-112842

Peverill, M., Rosen, M. L., Lurie, L. A., Sambrook, K. A., Sheridan, M. A., & McLaughlin, K. A. (2023). Childhood trauma and brain structure in children and adolescents. *Developmental Cognitive Neuroscience*, *59*, 101180. https://doi.org/10.1016/j.dcn.2022.101180

Pilozzi, A., Carro, C., & Huang, X. (2020). Roles of β-endorphin in stress, behavior, neuroinflammation, and brain energy metabolism. *International Journal of Molecular Science*, *22*(1), 338. https://doi.org/10.3390/ijms22010338

Powers, C. J., & Bierman, K. L. (2013). The multifaceted impact of peer relations on aggressive-disruptive behavior in early elementary school. *Developmental Psychology*, *49*(6), 1174–1186. https://doi.org/10.1037/a0028400

Prothero, A. (2023). Student behavior isn't getting any better, survey shows. *Education Week*. https://edweek.org/leadership/student-behavior-isnt-getting-any-better-survey-shows/2023/04

Provenzi, L., Grumi, S., Altieri, L., Bensi, G., Bertazzoli, E., Biasucci, G., . . . Borgatti, R. (2023). Prenatal maternal stress during the COVID-19 pandemic and infant regulatory capacity at 3 months: A longitudinal study. *Development and Psychopathology*, *35*(1), 35–43. https://doi.org/10.1017/S0954579421000766

Qiu, D., Tan, L. H., Zhou, K., & Khong, P. L. (2008). Diffusion tensor imaging of normal white matter maturation from late childhood to young adulthood: Voxel-wise evaluation of mean diffusivity, fractional anisotropy, radial and axial diffusivities, and correlation with reading development. *Neuroimage*, *41*(2), 223–232. https://doi.org/10.1016/j.neuroimage.2008.02.023

Ramírez, F. N., Lytle, S. R., & Kuhl, P. K. (2020). Parent coaching increases conversational turns and advances infant language development. *Proceedings of the National Academy of Sciences USA*, *117*(7), 3484–3491. https://doi.org/10.1073/pnas.1921653117

Ratiu, P., Talos, I. F., Haker, S., Lieberman, D., & Everett, P. (2004). The tale of Phineas Gage, digitally remastered. *Journal of Neurotrauma, 21*(5), 637–643. https://doi.org/10.1089/089771504774129964

Ribner, A., Moeller, K., Willougby, M., & Blair, C. (2018). Cognitive abilities and mathematical competencies at school entry. *Mind Brain Education, 12*(4), 175–185. https://doi.org/10.1111/mbe.12160

Ruba, A. L., & Pollak, S. D. (2020). Children's emotion inferences from masked faces: Implications for social interactions during COVID-19. *PLoS One, 15*(12), e0243708. https://doi.org/10.1371/journal.pone.0243708

Salomon, T., Cohen, A., Barazany, D., Ben-Zvi, G., Botvinik-Nezer, R., Gera, R., . . . Assaf, Y. (2021). Brain volumetric changes in the general population following the COVID-19 outbreak and lockdown. *Neuroimage, 239*, 118311. https://doi.org/10.1016/j.neuroimage.2021.118311

Sanfilippo, J., Ness, M., Petscher, Y., Rappaport, L., Zuckerman, B., & Gaab, N. (2020). Reintroducing dyslexia: Early identification and implications for pediatric practice. *Pediatrics, 146*(1), e20193046. https://doi.org/10.1542/peds.2019-3046

Schoofs, D., Preuss, D., & Wolf, O. T. (2008). Psychosocial stress induces working memory impairments in an n-back paradigm. *Psychoneuroendocrinology, 33*(5), 643–653. https://doi.org/10.1016/j.psyneuen.2008.02.004

Schultz, B., & Hollingsworth, H. (2022). More kids are repeating a grade. Is it good for them? *Associated Press*. https://phys.org/news/2022-09-kids-grade-good.html

Schwarz, J., Li, K. K., Sim, J. H., Zhang, Y., Buchanan-Worster, E., Post, B., . . . McDougall, K. (2022). Semantic cues modulate children's and adults' processing of audio-visual face mask speech. *Frontiers in Psychology, 13*, 879156. https://doi.org/10.3389/fpsyg.2022.879156

Sharma, S. D., Cushing, S. L., Papsin, B. C., & Gordon, K. A. (2020). Hearing and speech benefits of cochlear implantation in children: A review of the literature. *International Journal of Pediatric Otorhinolaryngology, 133*, 109984. https://doi.org/10.1016/j.ijporl.2020.109984

Sheng, L., Wang, D., Walsh, C., Heisler, L., Li, X., & Su, P. L. (2021). The bilingual home language boost through the lens of the COVID-19 pandemic. *Frontiers in Psychology, 12*, 667836. https://doi.org/10.3389/fpsyg.2021.667836

Sheridan, M. A., & McLaughlin, K. A. (2014). Dimensions of early experience and neural development: Deprivation and threat. *Trends in Cognitive Science, 18*(11), 580–585. https://doi.org/10.1016/j.tics.2014.09.001

Shook, L. L., Sullivan, E. L., Lo, J. O., Perlis, R. H., & Edlow, A. G. (2022). COVID-19 in pregnancy: Implications for fetal brain development. *Trends in Molecular Medicine, 28*(4), 319–330. https://doi.org/10.1016/j.molmed.2022.02.004

Solmi, M., Radua, J., Olivola, M., Croce, E., Soardo, L., Salazar de Pablo, G., . . . Fusar-Poli, P. (2022). Age at onset of mental disorders worldwide: Large-scale meta-analysis of 192 epidemiological studies. *Molecular Psychiatry, 27*(1), 281–295. https://doi.org/10.1038/s41380-021-01161-7

Somerville, L. H. (2016). Searching for signatures of brain maturity: What are we searching for? *Neuron, 92*(6), 1164–1167. https://doi.org/10.1016/j.neuron.2016.10.059

Sönnichsen, R., Llorach Tó, G., Hochmuth, S., Hohmann, V., & Radeloff, A. (2022). How face masks interfere with speech understanding of normal-hearing individuals: Vision makes the difference. *Otology and Neurotology, 43*(3), 282–288. https://doi.org/10.1097/mao.0000000000003458

Stiles, J., & Jernigan, T. L. (2010). The basics of brain development. *Neuropsychology Review, 20*(4), 327–348. https://doi.org/10.1007/s11065-010-9148-4

Stix, G. (2023, November 17). The pandemic disrupted adolescent brain development. *Scientific American*. https://www.scientificamerican.com/article/the-pandemic-disrupted-adolescent-brain-development/

Sullivan, A. W., Bowren, M. D., Bruss, J., Tranel, D., & Demir-Lira Ö, E. (2022). Academic skills after brain injury: A lifespan perspective. *Neuropsychology, 36*(5), 419–432. https://doi.org/10.1037/neu0000806

Sun, X., Marks, R. A., Eggleston, R. L., Zhang, K., Lau, C., Yu, C. L., . . . Kovelman, I. (2023). Impacts of the COVID-19 disruption on the language and literacy development of monolingual and heritage bilingual children in the United States. *Reading and Writing, 36*(2), 347–375. https://doi.org/10.1007/s11145-022-10388-x

Tamon, H., Itahashi, T., Yamaguchi, S., Tachibana, Y., Fujino, J., Igarashi, M., . . . Aoki, Y. (2022). Autistic children and adolescents with frequent restricted interest and repetitive behavior showed more difficulty in social cognition during mask-wearing during the COVID-19 pandemic: A multisite survey. *BMC Psychiatry, 22*, 608. https://doi.org/10.1186/s12888-022-04249-8

Tenenbaum, E. J., Shah, R. J., Sobel, D. M., Malle, B. F., & Morgan, J. L. (2013). Increased focus on the mouth among infants in the first year of life: A longitudinal eye-tracking study. *Infancy, 18*(4), 534–553. https://doi.org/10.1111/j.1532-7078.2012.00135.x

Thomas, M., & Knowland, V. C. P. (2009). Sensitive periods in brain development: Implications for education policy. *European Psychiatric Review, 2*, 17–20.

Thorell, L. B., Skoglund, C., de la Peña, A. G., Baeyens, D., Fuermaier, A. B. M., Groom, M. J., . . . Christiansen, H. (2022). Parental experiences of homeschooling during the COVID-19 pandemic: Differences between seven European countries and between children with and without mental health conditions. *European Child & Adolescent Psychiatry, 31*(4), 649–661. https://doi.org/10.1007/s00787-020-01706-1

Tikhomirova, T., Malykh, A., & Malykh, S. (2020). Predicting academic achievement with cognitive abilities: Cross-sectional study across school education. *Behavioral Science (Basel), 10*(10), 158. https://doi.org/10.3390/bs10100158

Tomblin, J. B., Harrison, M., Ambrose, S. E., Walker, E. A., Oleson, J. J., & Moeller, M. P. (2015). Language outcomes in young children with mild to severe hearing loss. *Ear and Hearing, 36* (Suppl. 1), 76s–91s. https://doi.org/10.1097/aud.0000000000000219

Tooley, U. A., Bassett, D. S., & Mackey, A. P. (2021). Environmental influences on the pace of brain development. *Nature Reviews Neuroscience, 22*(6), 372–384. https://doi.org/10.1038/s41583-021-00457-5

Truong, T. L., & Weber, A. (2021). Intelligibility and recall of sentences spoken by adult and child talkers wearing face masks. *Journal of the Acoustic Society of America, 150*(3), 1674. https://doi.org/10.1121/10.0006098

Uhlhaas, P. J., Davey, C. G., Mehta, U. M., Shah, J., Torous, J., Allen, N. B., . . . Wood, S. J. (2023). Towards a youth mental health paradigm: A perspective and roadmap. *Molecular Psychiatry, 28*, 3171–3181. https://doi.org/10.1038/s41380-023-02202-z

van Boxtel, M. P., van Beijsterveldt, C. E., Houx, P. J., Anteunis, L. J., Metsemakers, J. F., & Jolles, J. (2000). Mild hearing impairment can reduce verbal memory performance in a healthy adult population. *Journal of Clinical Experimental Neuropsychology, 22*(1), 147–154. https://doi.org/10.1076/1380-3395(200002)22:1;1-8;ft147

Van den Bergh, B. R. H., van den Heuvel, M. I., Lahti, M., Braeken, M., de Rooij, S. R., Entringer, S., . . . Schwab, M. (2020). Prenatal developmental origins of behavior and mental health: The influence of maternal stress in pregnancy. *Neuroscience & Biobehavioral Reviews, 117*, 26–64. https://doi.org/https://doi.org/10.1016/j.neubiorev.2017.07.003

van Drunen, L., Toenders, Y. J., Wierenga, L. M., & Crone, E. A. (2023). Effects of COVID-19 pandemic on structural brain development in early adolescence. *Scientific Reports, 13*(1), 5600. https://doi.org/10.1038/s41598-023-32754-7

van Lier, P. A., & Deater-Deckard, K. (2016). Children's elementary school social experience and executive functions development: Introduction to a special section. *Journal of Abnormal Child Psychology, 44*(1), 1–6. https://doi.org/10.1007/s10802-015-0113-9

Werchan, D. M., Hendrix, C. L., Hume, A. M., Zhang, M., Thomason, M. E., & Brito, N. H. (2024). Effects of prenatal psychosocial stress and COVID-19 infection on infant attention and socioemotional development. *Pediatric Research, 95*, 1279–1287. https://doi.org/10.1038/s41390-023-02807-8

Willcutt, E. G., Pennington, B. F., Olson, R. K., Chhabildas, N., & Hulslander, J. (2005). Neuropsychological analyses of comorbidity between reading disability and attention deficit hyperactivity disorder: In search of the common deficit. *Developmental Neuropsychology, 27*(1), 35–78. https://doi.org/10.1207/s15326942dn2701_3

Willis, S., Goldbart, J., & Stansfield, J. (2014). The strengths and weaknesses in verbal short-term memory and visual working memory in children with hearing impairment and additional language learning difficulties. *International Journal of Pediatric Otorhinolaryngology, 78*(7), 1107–1114. https://doi.org/10.1016/j.ijporl.2014.04.025

World Bank, The Bill & Melinda Gates Foundation, FCDO, UNESCO, UNICEF, & USAID. (2022). Guide for learning recovery and acceleration: Using the RAPID framework to address COVID-19 learning losses and build forward better. Washington, DC: World Bank. https://www.worldbank.org/en/topic/education/publication/the-rapid-framework-and-a-guide-for-learning-recovery-and-acceleration

Xiong, Y., Hong, H., Liu, C., & Zhang, Y. Q. (2023). Social isolation and the brain: effects and mechanisms. *Molecular Psychiatry, 28*(1), 191–201. https://doi.org/10.1038/s41380-022-01835-w

Yamamuro, K., Bicks, L. K., Leventhal, M. B., Kato, D., Im, S., Flanigan, M. E., . . . Morishita, H. (2020). A prefrontal-paraventricular thalamus circuit requires juvenile social experience to regulate adult sociability in mice. *Nature Neuroscience, 23*(10), 1240–1252. https://doi.org/10.1038/s41593-020-0695-6

Yehuda, R., Engel, S. M., Brand, S. R., Seckl, J., Marcus, S. M., & Berkowitz, G. S. (2005). Transgenerational effects of posttraumatic stress disorder in babies of mothers exposed to the World Trade Center attacks during pregnancy. *Journal of Clinical Endocrinology and Metabolism, 90*(7), 4115–4118. https://doi.org/10.1210/jc.2005-0550

Yehuda, R., Teicher, M. H., Seckl, J. R., Grossman, R. A., Morris, A., & Bierer, L. M. (2007). Parental posttraumatic stress disorder as a vulnerability factor for low cortisol trait in offspring of holocaust survivors. *Archives in General Psychiatry, 64*(9), 1040–1048. https://doi.org/10.1001/archpsyc.64.9.1040

Yi, H., Pingsterhaus, A., & Song, W. (2021). Effects of wearing face masks while using different speaking styles in noise on speech intelligibility during the COVID-19 pandemic. *Frontiers in Psychology, 12*, 682677. https://doi.org/10.3389/fpsyg.2021.682677

9

Clinical Practice in a Post-COVID Era

There are four main considerations for clinical practice in the post-COVID era and beyond: (1) the implications for current and future adult development, (2) the utility of pre-pandemic normative data in clinical evaluations, (3) the potential underestimate of learning loss in standardized test results as it relates to remediation and funding needs, and (4) implications for forensic and medicolegal evaluations. In this chapter, we discuss these clinical considerations and offer specific suggestions to help clinicians navigate the post-pandemic clinical environment.

Implications for Current and Future Adult Development

Educational disruption and high levels of psychosocial distress and mental health conditions in youth may impact their functioning as adults. The period between puberty and the mid-20s is often marked by finishing school and establishing independence in social relationships and living arrangements (McGorry, 2019). Anecdotally, we have seen an increase in older teens and college students who rely more heavily on their parents for making plans and daily living skills.

There are some data consistent with these observations. During the COVID-19 pandemic, fewer teens reached critical milestones for functional independence. In Spring 2020, many transitional-aged youth (ages 18 to 24 years) returned to living with their parents. There was a significant increase in the percent of those ages 16 to 24 years who were neither enrolled in school nor working; this number jumped from 11% in February 2020 to 28% in June 2020 (Fry et al., 2020). In 2021, 71% of parents reported a delay in drivers' education for their teens, at least in part because they had fewer external social commitments (Campoamor, 2022). With fewer opportunities to practice developing independence during the COVID-19 pandemic, more young people may have a prolonged transition to adulthood.

Neurodevelopment in the Post-Pandemic World. Molly Colvin, Jennifer Linton Reesman, and Tannahill Glen, Oxford University Press. © Oxford University Press 2024. DOI: 10.1093/9780197762660.003.0009

While we have focused on neurodevelopment in youth, there is also a potential for altered developmental trajectories in adult neurodevelopment. Pre-pandemic research has shown stress levels peak in middle age (30–45 years of age) and then decline throughout the lifespan. By Fall 2020, adult psychosocial stress levels had increased, reaching or exceeding peaks previously associated with middle age. For example, a British study assessed adults in three birth cohorts (persons born in 1946, 1958, and 1970) during the COVID-19 pandemic, finding that all three cohorts reported high levels of psychological distress which may increase future risk of morbidity, disability, and mortality (Moreno-Agostino et al., 2023).

In the current generation of youth, there is also a need to consider the late-life implications of early-life experiences during the COVID-19 pandemic. Changes in brain structure and function due to early exposure to risk factors may continue to impact individuals into old age. For instance, there is growing evidence that higher levels of educational achievement confer a protective effect, known as "cognitive reserve," for late-life cognitive decline due to neurodegenerative disease. Cognitive reserve has been shown to delay the age at which individuals reach critical thresholds for a diagnosis of dementia, or significant functional interference from a neurodegenerative process (Stern et al., 2023). Consistent with this, a recent study showed that high educational achievement can delay the onset of dementia, even in individuals who are genetically predetermined to develop Alzheimer's disease, suggesting that education has an important protective effect against late-life cognitive decline (Langella et al., 2023).

Similarly, there is some evidence linking specific neurodevelopmental disorders to the onset of neurodegenerative disorders later in life. While the specific mechanisms underlying this mechanism are unknown, the logopenic subtype of primary progressive aphasia (PPA) has been associated with higher rates of language-based learning disorders, including dyslexia (Rogalski et al., 2008). Posterior cortical atrophy (PCA) has been linked to mathematical and visuospatial learning disorders (Miller et al., 2018), and Lewy body dementia (LBD) has been linked to attention-deficit/hyperactivity disorder (ADHD; Golimstok et al., 2011). Clinically, the lifelong weaknesses in cognitive skills associated with neurodevelopmental disorders need to be considered before low scores in older adults are interpreted as indicators of cognitive decline. Unfortunately, consideration of learning disorders in the assessment of neurodegenerative disease is not common (Colvin & Sherman, 2020). Combined with evidence for a generalized protective effect from academic instruction, this work raises concerns about increased risk of neurodegenerative disease when the current generation of youth reach old age.

Utility and Sensitivity of Pre-Pandemic Normative Data

The use of normative data to score and interpret standardized test performance is standard practice in neuropsychological evaluations (Merritt et al., 2016). Critically, normative data are most useful when there are minimal differences between the patient and the normative sample in age, education, and culture (Strauss et al., 2006). As we previously described (Colvin et al., 2022), this is especially true for children and adolescents because neurodevelopment and learning occur at such a rapid rate, which is reflected in tighter age bands for child normative data (e.g., 6 months is common for the Wechsler Intelligence Scale for Children–Fifth Edition; Wechsler, 2014).

The following statement is straightforward but carries a potentially profound impact: Normative data collected prior to the COVID-19 pandemic do not account for the impact of prolonged education disruption, slower learning gains, or the psychosocial and mental health challenges most prevalent during the pandemic (Colvin et al., 2022). This concern is not limited to the use of pre-pandemic normative data in interpreting academic achievement scores. As discussed in the previous chapter, there is a bidirectional relationship between academic skill acquisition and cognitive skill development (e.g., math skills have been associated with executive functions, including reasoning and working memory; Clark et al., 2021; Welsh et al., 2010). Even psychological assessment results may be different for the pandemic-era cohort. A recent study showed college students obtained higher scores (suggesting higher anxiety, depression, and somatization) on the Personality Assessment Inventory (PAI) compared to the pre-pandemic cohort (Nails et al., 2023). As a result, compared to pre-pandemic normative data, current neuropsychological scores in otherwise typically developing youth may spuriously appear lower than expected. Thus, if a child is evaluated for concerns related to ADHD, learning disorder, autism spectrum disorder (ASD), or medical conditions like concussion or epilepsy (all very common referral questions), scores that are subtly below average may reflect one or more of those conditions, the effects of educational disruption, or the mental health challenges associated with social isolation (and, of course, these factors are not mutually exclusive). Conversely, if there is a question of whether a child is eligible for an accelerated learning program, scores may fail to meet cutoffs due to modest lowering related to prolonged educational disruption, curriculum changes, or omission of learning objectives.

Furthermore, neuropsychologists use estimated years of formal education to select normative data and estimate premorbid cognitive functioning. Based on declines in academic proficiency scores, continued use of this practice when the current generation of youth reach adulthood is likely to be problematic, given the wide range of academic experiences during the COVID-19 pandemic. There is already evidence that prolonged distance learning is not comparable to an equivalent period of in-person education, which was also potentially affected by infection control measures (e.g., social distancing and face masks).

Neuropsychologists currently face an analogous challenge when accounting for differences in educational experiences between White and Black patients before school desegregation. Research has shown that total years of formal education may inaccurately estimate abilities in Black patient groups who had lower educational quality (Byrd et al., 2005; Manly et al., 2002; Tombaugh & McIntyre, 1992), so perhaps this will prove applicable to other groups disproportionately affected by school closures, students in areas with longer durations of remote learning, or students who did not have access to reliable digital technology or an environment conducive to remote learning. Yet it will be potentially challenging to quantify academic quality. As Fuller, Swiderski, Mikkelsen, and Bastian (2023) remarked:

> In addition, outcomes that rely on specific measurement practices, such as grades and attendance, may not have the same meaning in 2020–21 as pre-pandemic. For example, teachers may have employed more lenient grading practices, while "logging on" to online learning may have been a different kind of attendance than being in school in-person pre-pandemic. However, to the extent that these measures continue to be used by parents, teachers, administrators, and policymakers in interpreting individual- and population-level education outcomes, it is important to understand how they have changed over time. (p. 11)

Neuropsychologists often use academic testing records to determine premorbid levels of functioning. For the foreseeable future, when reviewing standardized academic achievement records from the pandemic era, neuropsychologists will need to consider whether there were changes in test administration. In February 2021, the DOE announced states would still be required to administer annual standardized academic achievement testing for grades three to twelve, a policy that was temporarily waived in March 2020. However, flexible options for testing were allowed, such as extended test period times, abbreviated testing, and remote test-taking (Johnson, 2021), and some states requested waivers allowing them to delay testing or test a smaller group of students (Barnum, 2021). The validity of altered or remote or in-home assessment has not been demonstrated, so comparison of those scores to future evaluations will be tenuous.

Similarly, in the near future, as patients and families present with pandemic-era psychological and neuropsychological assessments for review, it will be important to be alert to limitations of those data. Pre-pandemic normative data may be less reliable for those most impacted by educational disruption, such as very young children; youth with behavioral, social, or emotional challenges; and those who were assessed under nonstandardized conditions (e.g., in-person assessments under safety guidelines—with masks, shields, physical distance, etc.—and remote assessments). As described in Chapter 8, mask use by examiner and examinee may impact phonological processing and/or auditory memory, which may disproportionately impact those with language delays, ADHD, and/or ASD, and this should be considered in clinical review of scores. This is not a concern specific to youth and presents an issue for all neuropsychologists, who must be aware of nonstandardized test administration in reviewing previous findings. For example, Thomas and Tranel (2023) compared pre-pandemic and pandemic groups and demonstrated that geriatric patients wearing masks achieved lower scores on verbally mediated tests; no difference between the two groups was noted for visually mediated tasks.

At the time that many clinicians rapidly transitioned to remote assessment protocols to maintain patient services while adhering to infection control policies, there were few studies investigating whether remote evaluations were comparable to in-person evaluations. The early equivalency studies were largely promising but had primarily examined older adult populations (e.g., Cullum et al., 2014; Kirkwood et al., 2000; Temple et al., 2010; reviewed in Brearly et al., 2017 and Marra et al., 2020). There was more limited data from pediatric populations (e.g., Harder et al., 2020; reviewed in Stifel et al., 2020).

Yet there are still open questions about remote assessment and situations warranting caution. Kronenberger et al. (2021) evaluated verbal memory in children with cochlear implants and found that non-words and context-free verbal material were more affected by remote presentation, to the degree that the authors cautioned against using remote testing for such abilities in this population (Kronenberger et al., 2021). Other studies indicated processing speed, visuospatial, and attention scores may differ in digital platforms (Pearson Corporation, 2021; Raimo et al., 2023; see Walker et al., 2023 for review).

Many studies comparing remote and in-person administration have used a between-subjects design, meaning that remote and in-person scores in the same participant were not directly compared. The direct transfer of visually mediated and motor-dependent tasks to the remote environment warrants scrutiny. One unpublished study in children reported higher scores on processing speed measures when they were administered remotely (cited in Stifel et al., 2020). This is especially notable given that in July 2020, Pearson recalled the WISC-V Coding subtest from its digital (Q-Interactive) platform, noting that it resulted in higher scores than those obtained from the paper version meant for in-person assessment (Pearson Corporation, 2021). Otherwise, Gilbert et al. (2021) found moderate correlations between in-person and digital administration of the WISC-V.

The validity of remote assessment for different ages and populations should also be considered. Applying normative data to interpret test scores from adolescents who completed a remote assessment may be more straightforward than doing the same for an early elementary-aged child. Similarly, validity threats may be more likely in youth with behavioral, social, or emotional challenges.

Remote assessment has contributed to reducing delayed diagnoses and interventions during the COVID-19 pandemic (Pritchard et al., 2020; Ransom et al., 2020). There is also an opportunity to continue to integrate telehealth and teleneuropsychology into clinical practice, especially for underserved communities (Salinas et al., 2020; Sherwood & MacDonald, 2020). However, more research is needed to establish the validity of existing normative data for remote administration across a range of child and adolescent populations. New measures may be needed to assess visual, spatial, and visual-motor skills to replace those that emphasize motor skills or require manipulatives. In the meantime, neuropsychologists will need to carefully interpret future changes in test scores from data collected during remote assessments, especially if reevaluations are performed in-person. Similarly, interpretation of psychoeducational evaluations that were completed remotely will warrant scrutiny for limitations that may impact a child's eligibility for special education services.

Clinical Implications of Underestimating Learning Loss

As described in previous chapters, learning losses may be *underestimated*; standardized test data may not include students who are lost to the system, had inadequate access to technology, or whose exam scores were delayed. This selection bias may then result in inadequate funding and support for vulnerable youth (Kuhfeld et al., 2020), and it may impact clinical case conceptualization, as follows:

> *Dr. X is asked to evaluate a 26-year-old female patient who underwent surgery and radiation for a brain tumor 2 years prior and is now referred by her primary care physician regarding persistent difficulty passing certification courses in her field of work. The patient states that she had "average" grades in an urban, high-poverty school, in a state known to have experienced prolonged school closures. She received no form of remediation after being in remote school for at least 1 year. The clinician, upon seeing low neurocognitive scores compared to a pre-pandemic normative group with the same level of education, may have difficulty determining whether the scores reflect educational disruption 20 years prior, a missed neurodevelopmental disorder, or the effects of the tumor treatment. Differential diagnosis can be complicated by learning disability diagnosis criteria, which require there to have been no resolution with remedial efforts nor can symptoms be attributable to "lack of appropriate instruction" (U.S. Department of Education, 2019).*

There are not only funding and diagnostic risks associated with underestimating losses, but an obvious neurocognitive one: if learning loss is not adequately identified, remediation efforts are likely to be insufficient. An example would be the new proficiency cut scores in some locales: students who otherwise might have been identified as requiring an intensive high-dosage tutoring may now only be referred for a time-limited after-school program. There is an inherent competing interest present, unfortunately, for state and local education agencies (LEAs) who are responsible for documenting severity of need: identification of wide swaths of students who require expensive intervention in a time of instructor shortages and budgetary crises is not compatible with solvency.

Potential Clinical Scenarios

For the foreseeable future, clinicians from all fields with pediatric and mental health expertise can anticipate encountering cases with complexity associated with pandemic-era psychosocial stressors and school closures. Speech-language pathologists, occupational therapists, school teachers, clinical psychologists, pediatric psychiatrists, and pediatricians will be required to assess clinical cases with very specific pandemic-related factors in mind. For clinicians, these cases and questions will be common and may not be readily apparent when reviewing medical records or intake questionnaires commonly completed by families, requiring additional time and consideration during an already overscheduled clinical evaluation setting. A potential scenario for a pediatrician is as follows:

> *Dr. X is seeing a female patient, Matilda, age 12, with significant weight loss, to a level below 85% of expected weight for height. Matilda's parents are concerned that she has metabolic disorder like her maternal grandmother. Matilda, upon examination, reports weakness, headaches, lethargy, and hair loss. During the interview, Dr. X inquires about pandemic-related educational and psychosocial stressors. It is revealed that Matilda developed significant anxiety when her school reopened and she was required to adhere to a rigorous set of infection control procedures, such as walking in one direction in hallways, and masking except to each lunch outside, with social distancing enforced. She also began to fall behind in school, which increased her anxiety, because her learning progress stalled during virtual classes; she attributed this to being unable to pay attention in the same room as her three siblings who were also in virtual classes. Prior to the pandemic Matilda was involved in youth sports and never returned to these when outdoor activities resumed in her area. Behaviorally she presented to her pediatrician wearing a mask and reported that she did in most situations, making it challenging for her parents, friends, and loved ones to gauge her emotional state and expression at times. Matilda admitted that she began to restrict eating in January*

2022, and further questioning and evaluation revealed she met criteria for anorexia nervosa.

As indicated earlier in this text, eating disorder diagnoses increased within the context of the pandemic, and youth experienced increased stressors and reduced supports that may place them at greater risk of an eating disorder. For pediatricians, many youth lost access to physical activities that may have served as a protective factor and finding ways to reengage with healthful behaviors (including physical activity) may be more challenging when youth have been out of their activities for a prolonged time and may find that their peers have moved on in terms of athletic skill and ability, making it more challenging to rejoin later in adolescence.

Implications for Forensic and Medicolegal Evaluations

Neuropsychological evaluations in the medicolegal and forensic arena are performed for several reasons: to help triers of fact determine whether a defendant has the cognitive capacity to commit a crime or to help determine whether a plaintiff has permanent disability related to an injury. They may also be ordered to help the court decide parental custody or testamentary capacity. Any of these evaluations may be impacted, now or in the future, by the effects of prolonged educational disruption.

It is not uncommon to receive requests for remote compulsory neuropsychological examinations (CNEs). This practice is discouraged because of potential threats to test content security and potential for third-party observer effects (Glen et al., 2021) and threats to validity and limitations on the scope of evaluation and observation necessary in a complex CNE (Marra et al., 2020). Further, the American Psychological Association (APA) Specialty Guidelines for Forensic Practice (2011), 10.02, indicates examiners should use assessment techniques and tools in the manner most supported by empirical evidence. Examiners should also pay special attention to any alteration in standardized administration, both in test administration and interpretation. There has been evidence of some alteration in scores on measures under masked conditions (Walker et al., 2023), which can impact reliability of scores and interpretation of cognitive performance.

For neuropsychologists, the most challenging medicolegal and forensic questions are those involving subtle brain dysfunction and differential diagnosis of conditions that may have similar patterns of neurocognitive performance (e.g., depression and recent concussion) (Re, 2023). It is the essential demand for the neuropsychological expert to elucidate and differentiate contributory conditions. The importance of selecting the most appropriate normative data based on case-specific factors and careful consideration of error rates has been discussed in detail (American Academy of Clinical Neuropsychology [AACN], 2021). Use of appropriate normative datasets allows the forensic examiner to compare the examinee's test scores to the most similar reference group. The AACN position statement highlights the risks associated with the use of unrepresentative norms: "Use of unrepresentative norms can result in diagnostic error, as well as stigmatization of minority populations based on supposed disparities in neuropsychological ability" (p. 2).

A recent real-life example is illustrative of the diagnostic risks of unrepresentative norms and broader societal implications. In 2020, Senior U.S. District Judge Anita B. Brody approved a plan to address the use of race-based normative data in evaluations related to the National Football League (NFL) concussion settlement ("National Football League Players' Concussion Injury Litigation," 2014). The plaintiff in the case, a former NFL player, was evaluated by a qualified clinician who performed neuropsychological evaluation and determined the player did qualify for financial award due to neurocognitive impairment. The doctor purposefully used White normative data, resulting in lower performance levels. NFL parties appealed this determination, arguing in part that the examiner did not apply demographic adjustments for race, which would have assigned the player's scores a higher level, one not qualifying for impairment. Judge Brody's order detailed examples of common uses of normative data adjustments, such as those for education. She quoted Heaton, Miller, Taylor, and Grant (2004), who wrote that demographic adjustments such as for education allow clinicians to determine what percentage of healthy test takers with similar demographic characteristics score above, or below, the examinee. Race-based adjustments were developed to decrease the risk of misclassification of cognitive impairment, in effect adjusting scores higher to correct for factors such as tests designed around mostly White samples. Judge Brody described the practice as "enormously consequential" (p. 7), often determining whether a performance reflects brain damage or normal cognitive functioning. Manly and Echemendia (2007) were also cited in the decision, specifically, their warning that using normative data stratified by race may result in examinees of color not receiving needed services, as scores may appear higher, thus above a cutoff for diagnosis or services.

As to why this is so relevant to pandemic-related educational disruption, the same scenario can be envisioned in the near future as examinees in the forensic or medicolegal arena are assessed, and their scores are adjusted, as is so common, for education. If, as we posit, years of education are no longer strongly predictive of expected cognitive and academic achievement, the examinee's scores may appear spuriously low, increasing the risk for diagnostic error or misclassification.

In fact, given there are currently no "pandemic norms," it would also be impossible to estimate the error rate for one's diagnostic classification, which goes directly to the issue of the *Daubert* challenge. The criteria for admissibility of scientific evidence in *Daubert v. Merrell Dow Pharmaceuticals, Inc.*, 509 U.S. 579 (1993) include being able to demonstrate the known or potential rate of error of the technique or theory when applied. While scientific evidence does not need to meet all *Daubert* criteria, being able to identify an error rate (e.g., false-positive rates, sensitivity, and specificity of measures) is very important in a court of law; indeed, some have written that error rate is the most important of the *Daubert* criteria (Jabbar, 2010; Meixner & Diamond, 2014).

Furthermore, the *Daubert* criteria have been elaborated upon more recently, with one of the supplemental factors being the expert's obligation to demonstrate differential diagnosis, or consideration of alternative explanations for findings (Claar v. Burlington N.R.R., 1994). Thus, in the following scenario, the vulnerability of the expert's opinion to a *Daubert* challenge is clear:

> *A forensic expert is asked by the plaintiff's attorney to evaluate a 9-year-old Hispanic child who lived in a state with high duration of remote schooling and experienced psychosocial stressors related to his community sports league shutting down, and a prolonged period of social isolation during lockdowns. His preexisting diagnosis of diabetes mellitus was significant for disrupted routine management in 2020, and he was absent from virtual classes for about 20% of the 2020–2021 school year. No pre-pandemic assessment data were available, but 2022 Department of Education reports for the state indicated his district had low performance in achievement testing compared to other areas, with declines in math achievement of 9 points, and reading declines of 2 points. Examination for complaints of cognitive changes*

related to a motor vehicle accident reveals low average to low scores almost across the board, and teacher ratings of behavioral and attention challenges. The expert, referencing medical records showing a 4-hour loss of consciousness, Glasgow Coma Scale scores of 12, and posttraumatic amnesia of 2 days, diagnosed moderate traumatic brain injury and attributed reported changes and test scores to the traumatic brain injury (TBI).

The defense attorneys for the trucking company involved in the crash quickly mounted a Daubert challenge to the expert's admissibility, hiring two experts of their own to rebut the doctor's opinion and methodology on the basis that (a) pre-COVID normative data adjusted for education did not account for major academic and psychosocial impacts of school closures and thus there was simply no known error rate, and (b) the doctor failed to consider alternative explanations for the test scores and clinical concerns, including disruption of medical care, prolonged virtual instruction with unreliable Internet access, and a reduced curriculum.

Another example is as follows:

In 2029, a 19-year-old Black male on trial for a capital offense is referred for evaluation to determine whether the mitigating factor of intellectual disability diagnosis is present. In Atkins v. Virginia ("Atkins v. Virginia," 2002), the Supreme Court of the United States ruled that execution of persons with intellectual disability is a constitutional violation. This is a critical question, as it relates to sentence recommendations and possibilities for the prosecution. The expert neuropsychologist for the defense evaluated the defendant and diagnosed intellectual disability, as well as ADHD. The defense expert reviewed a prior evaluation that was conducted during the immediate period of returning to classrooms in which the then fifth grader earned an overall Full Scale IQ of 71 on an individually administered cognitive assessment conducted by the school and adaptive functioning assessment was deferred by the school. A later assessment related to this case demonstrated consistent scores of <70 on intellectual assessment measures with adaptive functioning similarly impaired.

The forensic expert for the prosecution testified that the defendant's scores reflected prolonged educational disruption that was associated with a 15-point decline in math proficiency and 7-point decline in reading for Black students in his district. The prosecution expert also testified the defendant's symptoms of ADHD were related to chronic absenteeism and having had virtual and hybrid learning pod arrangements through the schooling he did attend. Finally, it was argued that since he never received an individualized education plan (IEP) or was held back in school, there was no evidence of the presence of a lifelong intellectual disability. The defendant was sentenced to death after the jury rejected the intellectual disability as a mitigating factor.

Jury rejection of a mitigating mental health diagnosis may double the chance for a capital sentence recommendation (Miley et al., 2020). Without clinical practice recommendations or professional society position statements on how to handle the issue of test norm drift addressed in this volume, the issue of test performance and educational experience (or deprivation) will become a life-or-death question for those facing capital offense trials, and where the individual missed out on key opportunities for evaluation, identification and intervention related to their disability.

As a final consideration, forensic experts will need to be aware of the effects of prolonged educational disruption on the pandemic cohort as triers of fact. Jurors are not blank slates. Some may have experienced more than a year of virtual learning and distancing restrictions, now finding it difficult to manage the intimate, sustained interpersonal and cognitive exercise of serving on a jury. Some may have parented and educated a child with sensory disability who had no special education services during the first year of the pandemic, while trying to maintain productivity while working from home. The forensic expert will need to be aware of jurors' personal experiences related to the pandemic and use that information to craft a communication style and analogies relevant to jurors' lived experiences.

Recommendations for Clinical Practice

Colvin, Reesman, and Glen (2022) detailed several suggestions for clinical practice in response to concerns that evaluations of an entirely new cohort of youth and, eventually, adults, would require special considerations.

Experience Matters

- Home learning experiences during COVID-19 may predict academic development and trajectories (Gennetian & Hirsh-Pasek, 2020; Hirsh-Pasek et al., 2020), so clinicians may wish to develop strategic interview formats to collect detailed information on the examinee's psychoeducational experience before, during, and after the COVID-19 pandemic. It is also important to query psychosocial stressors during that period, and, conversely, participation in activities with protective benefits such as organized sports, physical activity, and socialization. Inquiring specifically about exposure to adverse childhood experiences or other risk factors (e.g., excessive unsupervised screen time, lack of access to reliable digital technology) is recommended.

- Because of the disproportionate negative impact on learning for marginalized students, students of color, those with disabilities, emerging English speakers, and students from lower income households, clinicians are encouraged to consider *disparate* impacts of prolonged virtual learning, curriculum changes, altered proficiency and grading policies, and school closures for students in marginalized groups. Early evidence suggests clinicians may need to assertively advocate for educational and clinical services—especially those designed and validated for marginalized groups.

Chronic Absenteeism and Lost Instruction Time

- When there is report or evidence of pandemic-related reduced instruction time, curriculum changes, and/or lack of exposure to expected material, examinees may achieve lower scores on tests if pre-pandemic normative data are applied. Clinicians should consider duration and quality of remote learning when estimating years of education, comparing scores to grade-based normative data, or analyzing standardized achievement test scores.
- Clinicians should be aware that school attendance records may not reflect participation in learning or hours of instruction. Clinicians can inquire about the examinee's definition of attendance as these may vary widely (e.g., was one simply logged on, on-camera, muted, etc.). It may be possible to clarify attendance data and definitions provided with teachers or school staff.
- Chronic absenteeism and precise attendance patterns should be queried whenever possible. Students who return to the educational system should

be identified and prioritized for evaluation, as chronic absenteeism is correlated with negative impact on academic skills and cognitive development. Clinicians are encouraged to describe any impact of chronic absenteeism in reports and include in diagnosis and recommendations whether diagnosis and/or symptoms reflect insufficient technology access, family economic strain, inadequate support of learning, and so on.

- In the future, students who were lost in the system during and after the pandemic will present later in life for evaluation. These individuals may not have crucial observational and performance records typically used in evaluation and diagnosis. Similarly, delayed entry to early education should be identified and weighed as a clinical factor as it may impact learning trajectories. Students with delayed school entry may require proactive progress monitoring and/or early evaluation/intervention. Clinicians may obtain historical information on development and functioning from other sources when possible, for example, parents, employers, relatives, and primary care physician.

Estimating Level of Education

- Clinicians should understand that traditional means of estimating education, for example, using reading level or grades completed, may be less reliable than prior to the pandemic.
- Clinicians are encouraged to review details of closures and virtual education in their area and maintain awareness of changes to curriculum, alterations in pass-fail guidelines, and other changes that may impact academic achievement or exposure to specific content.

Disrupted Disability Services and Diagnosis of Learning Disability

- Implementation of Section 504 plans and individualized education programs was disrupted, remote, or delayed. There may be a prolonged period of disruption of services related to variable interpretation of guidelines (e.g., whether lack of instruction is a disqualifying criterion). Clinicians will need to assess the consistency and intensity of special education services, whether performed by schools or privately, and consider those factors in evaluation of IEP progress and needs.

- Students who have not received appropriate services and accommodations may be eligible for compensatory services so clinicians may monitor federal, state, and local educational guidelines related to compensatory services and consider providing advocacy for patients as needed.
- As on-the-ground experts in impact of policy and mitigation efforts, clinicians should consider offering professional specialist input to policymakers and educators on relevant challenges.
- Delayed evaluation and diagnosis have created exceptionally long wait lists for services which may impact early intervention.
- Current exclusionary criteria for diagnosis of learning disorders (such as psychosocial adversity and lack of instruction) may limit diagnosis and thus eligibility for treatment or special education services. School closures have restricted the sensitivity of DSM-5 diagnostic criteria for learning disorders. Thus, there are several suggestions for clinical practice. Diagnostic criteria for learning disorders should include these considerations, and criteria should permit provisional diagnoses for youth with low academic achievement scores. It is important to keep in mind that although academic achievement scores are important indicators of a learning disorder, these scores should be weighed with clinical symptoms and history. For example, low reading scores in the context of pervasive delays in language acquisition and family history of dyslexia are compelling indicators of learning disability. It will be important to review data for a pattern of strengths and weaknesses consistent with specific learning disabilities (e.g., poor performance across measures of phonological processing in a child suspected of having dyslexia), noting there are arguments against exclusive use of a discrepancy model in the diagnosis of learning disabilities (Fletcher et al., 1998; Fletcher & Miciak, 2019; Francis et al., 2005). Finally, provisional diagnoses should waive the requirement for 6 months of prior intervention.
- Children in groups exhibiting disproportionate negative impact of school closures should be prioritized for school-based evaluation. It is suggested that Individuals with Disabilities Education Act (IDEA) criteria should remain in place, so that children with academic achievement scores below pre-pandemic expectations are eligible for remediation, regardless of whether there are precise clinical criteria met for learning disorder.

Clinicians should endeavor to avoid failure to identify children who have learning disorders during crucial intervention windows of opportunity, errors that would compound the disparate effects of the COVID-19 pandemic on the most vulnerable children.

- Practitioners may consider implementation of systems for prioritizing evaluation for students who demonstrated learning difficulties prior to pandemic-related school closures as candidates for early intervention (National Association of School Psychologists, 2020) and remediation.
- Non-test indicators of functioning should be considered, such as pre-pandemic test scores, learning trajectory, and clinical history.
- Clinicians may choose to review test score reports by grade and subject (e.g., math or ELA) for relevant school districts to determine whether and at what level learning attenuation occurred, keeping in mind normative data characteristics (i.e., whether scores are being compared to cohort or a pre-pandemic normative sample).

Disparities in Educational Technology

- Students from households with economic disadvantage were at greater risk for both inadequate access to educational technology and enrollment in remote instruction. Students with sensory disabilities may have had difficulty obtaining specialized educational technology (e.g., sign language interpretation) and/or difficulty during in-person instruction when the speaker and/or student wore masks. These potential challenges should be queried and clinicians are encouraged to advocate for improved access to reliable educational technology and services to improve digital fluency and parity at the local, state, and federal levels. It is also suggested that clinicians inquire about educational technology disparities, for example, "How many classes per week did you miss because your laptop/Internet was not working?" and "What was your study space like at home?" to provide information about the consistency and quality of instruction time. It is important to keep in mind that access to adequate educational technology and sensory disability assistance may be very relevant to diagnostic opinion and eligibility for remediation services.

Variability in Remediation Plans Across Districts

- Grade retention, grading system policies, and proficiency thresholds vary across states and may affect traditional estimates of achievement. Clinicians should be aware of local policies as they relate to critical interpretation of academic history. It may be necessary to advocate for patients requiring tutoring, extended day instruction, or other intensive remediation.
- It is recommended that clinicians review the body of research on mental health, physical, cognitive, and academic outcomes following Hurricane Katrina in Louisiana (Davis et al., 2020) and effects of post-disaster remediation programs and major educational system restructuring (Pan & Sass, 2020). It has been suggested that interested parties reference existing literature on post-disaster mental health when developing crisis recovery programs such as learning loss remediation plans (Hanover Research, 2020).

Psychological, Physical, and Psychosocial Changes Impact Neuropsychology Practice

- Mental and physical health challenges in youth have increased during the pandemic, resulting in a mental health crisis. Youth with pre-pandemic neurological, neurodevelopmental, and/or psychiatric conditions are disproportionately at risk for worsening of emotional functioning. Notably, psychological and/or physical challenges may impact neuropsychological test scores, so clinicians should carefully inquire about pandemic-related psychosocial stressors, such as domestic discord, social isolation, parental job loss, grief, and economic insecurity.
- It will be particularly important to inquire about and consider potential impact of prolonged social isolation on development (e.g., Did a patient experience greatly reduced exposure to peers? Did the impact of prolonged bidirectional mask wearing impact social communication milestones?).
- It is also important to inquire about physical/medical factors associated with decreased neurocognitive performance, to assess for any changes during the pandemic (e.g., glycemic control, physical activity, severe COVID-19 illness, diet, sleep disturbance).

- It will be important to assess for pandemic-related psychosocial stressors (domestic discord, social isolation, parental job loss, grief, and economic insecurity).
- Special attention should be given to the potential impact of psychological dysfunction on cognitive test scores as it relates to differential diagnosis, mitigating factors, and recommendations for treatments. It may be feasible to adopt mood questionnaires, parent ratings and teacher observations for more comprehensive data on pandemic-era psychosocial functioning.
- The pandemic has increased adverse childhood experience (ACE) exposure risk, and those experiencing COVID-related educational disruption may be more vulnerable to ACE risk, with potential long-term impact on physical, cognitive, and psychological functioning. Clinicians are advised to be alert to the ways in which ACEs have increased during the COVID-19 pandemic. It may be possible to incorporate ACE screening to rapidly identify youth at higher risk for long-term challenges and potentially refer for specialty ACE prevention services and/or case management.
- It is suggested that "COVID-19 pandemic-related stressors" be added as a "V code" in the *Diagnostic and Statistical Manual of Mental Disorders.*
- Validity of remote evaluations for children has not been well established for certain patient populations (e.g., young children and those with sensory disabilities), so practitioners should carefully consider data from evaluations performed remotely and review diagnoses and recommendations accordingly.
- More critically, use of existing normative data for remote evaluations may need to be reviewed for certain patient populations. As stated by Anderson, Blanch, and Suhr (2023, 899), it is unclear whether already-demonstrated deviations from existing normative groups "define a new normal . . . future research should continue evaluating changes from normative reference groups over time with additional instruments, and should these changes prove long lasting, updates to clinical norms may be necessary."
- Likewise, as validity for in-person evaluation performed under various COVID-19 precautions has not been well established for those with hearing difficulty or with phonological processing impairments, among others), clinicians should carefully interpret *future changes* in test scores from data collected during remote assessments, especially if reevaluation is performed face to face.

- Any limitations to data interpretation or assessment (such as reliance on pre-pandemic norms or lack of availability of 2020 grades or test scores) should be clearly described in clinical reports along with potential implications. Clinicians should endeavor to interpret test results in the context of the individual's specific experience (e.g., prolonged school disruption, psychosocial dysfunction, limited access to technology, unsupervised remote instruction) (National Center for Learning Disabilities [NCLD] and National Association of School Psychologists, 2020).
- Practitioners will want to stay apprised of newly published collections of normative data specific to children in the COVID-19 era, such as those experiencing prolonged school closures or extreme isolation. When possible, normative data relevant to local (e.g., state or regional) policies will be particularly useful.
- In the absence of updated normative data, clinicians may wish to interpret test results with caution, reporting measurement error, percentiles, and confidence intervals as approximations rather than absolutes and acknowledgment of any limitations to the evaluation (Allen, 2020).

It is our hope that neuropsychologists take the lead in recognizing profound changes for the pandemic-era youth cohort and act to establish formal recommendations for practice considerations based on empirical evidence as studies continue to emerge. A position paper regarding the complications of reliance on pre-pandemic normative data in youth neuropsychological evaluation would be a welcome addition to the field, and it would drive public awareness of the issue and advocacy for patient needs.

References

Allen, T. (2020). New Jersey Association of School Psychologists (NJASP) guidance: In-person administration, scoring, and interpretation of standardized assessments during COVID-19. https://njasp.org/resources/Committees/GPR/COVID-19%20Eval%20Guidance/In-person%20evaluation%20guidance%20during%20COVID-19.pdf

American Academy of Clinical Neuropsychology (AACN). (2021). Position statement on use of race as a factor in neuropsychological test norming and performance prediction. https://theaacn.org/wp-content/uploads/2021/11/AACN-Position-Statement-on-Race-Norms.pdf

American Psychological Association. (2013, January). Specialty guidelines for forensic psychology. *American Psychologist*, *68*(1):7–19 https://www.apa.org/practice/guidelines/forensic-psychology

Anderson, J. L., Blanch, A., & Suhr, J. A. (2023). Clinical assessment in the time of COVID-19: Introduction to the special issue. *Psychological Assessment, 35*(11), 895–900. https://doi.org/10.1037/pas000128135, 895–900.

Atkins v. Virginia, (Supreme Court of the United States. (2002). https://www.loc.gov/item/usrep536304/

Barnum, M. (2021). After feds say tests still required, critics mobilize and states look for loopholes. *Chalkbeat.* https://www.chalkbeat.org/2021/3/3/22311564/standardized-testing-schools-states-covid-pushback-backlash-critics

Brearly, T. W., Shura, R. D., Martindale, S. L., Lazowski, R. A., Luxton, D. D., Shenal, B. V., & Rowland, J. A. (2017). Neuropsychological test administration by videoconference: A systematic review and meta-analysis. *Neuropsychology Review, 27*(2), 174–186. https://doi.org/10.1007/s11065-017-9349-1

Byrd, D. A., Jacobs, D. M., Hilton, H. J., Stern, Y., & Manly, J. J. (2005). Sources of errors on visuoperceptual tasks: Role of education, literacy, and search strategy. *Brain Cognition, 58*(3), 251–257. https://doi.org/10.1016/j.bandc.2004.12.003

Campoamor, D. (2022). Stuck in neutral: Why more teens are choosing to not get a driver's license. *Today.* https://www.today.com/parents/teens/covid-anxiety-teens-drivers-license-rcna43477

Claar v. Burlington N.R.R. (1994). 9th Circuit. https://case-law.vlex.com/vid/claar-v-burlington-northern-888474469

Clark, E., Tullo, D., & Bertone, A. (2021). Perceptual reasoning skills mediate the relationship between attention and math proficiency in individuals with a neurodevelopmental condition. *Research in Developmental Disability, 111*, 103880. https://doi.org/10.1016/j.ridd.2021.103880

Colvin, M. K., & Sherman, J. C. (2020). Considering learning disabilities and attention-deficit hyperactivity disorder when assessing for neurodegenerative disease. *Neurology in Clinical Practice, 10*(6), 520–526. https://doi.org/10.1212/cpj.0000000000000799

Colvin, M. K. M., Reesman, J., & Glen, T. (2022). The impact of COVID-19 related educational disruption on children and adolescents: An interim data summary and commentary on ten considerations for neuropsychological practice. *Clinical Neuropsychology, 36*(1), 45–71. https://doi.org/10.1080/13854046.2021.1970230

Cullum, C. M., Hynan, L. S., Grosch, M., Parikh, M., & Weiner, M. F. (2014). Teleneuropsychology: Evidence for video teleconference-based neuropsychological assessment. *Journal for International Neuropsychology Society, 20*(10), 1028–1033. https://doi.org/10.1017/s1355617714000873

Daubert v Merrell Dow Pharmaceuticals Inc. (1993). https://www.loc.gov/item/usrep509579/

Davis, S., Rose-Davison, K., & Smith, D. G. (2020). Hurricane Katrina at 15: Introduction to the special section. *American Journal of Public Health, 110*(10), 1461–1462. https://doi.org/10.2105/ajph.2020.305885

Fletcher, J. M., Francis, D. J., Shaywitz, S. E., Lyon, G. R., Foorman, B. R., Stuebing, K. K., & Shaywitz, B. A. (1998). Intelligent testing and the discrepancy model for children with learning disabilities. *Learning Disabilities Research & Practice, 13*(4), 186–203.

Fletcher, J. M., & Miciak, J. (2019). *The identification of specific learning disabilities: A summary of research on best practices.* Austin, TX: Meadows Center for Preventing Educational Risk.

Francis, D. J., Fletcher, J. M., Stuebing, K. K., Lyon, G. R., Shaywitz, B. A., & Shaywitz, S. E. (2005). Psychometric approaches to the identification of LD:IQ and achievement scores are not sufficient. *Journal of Learning Disabilities, 38*(2), 98–108. https://doi.org/10.1177/00222194050380020101

Fry, R., Passel, J. S., & Cohn, D. V. (2020). A majority of young adults in the US live with their parents for the first time since the Great Depression. Pew Research Center. https://www.pewresearch.org/short-reads/2020/09/04/a-majority-of-young-adults-in-the-u-s-live-with-their-parents-for-the-first-time-since-the-great-depression/

Fuller, S., Swiderski, T., Mikkelsen, C., & Bastian, K. (2023). In school, engaged, on-track? The effect of the pandemic on student attendance, course grades, and grade retention in North Carolina. EdWorkingPaper: 23-747. Annenberg Institute at Brown University. https://doi.org/10.26300/58h9-3r54

Gennetian, L., & Hirsh-Pasek, K. (2020). Where's the rallying cry? America's children are unequally prepared to absorb the impacts of COVID-19. Brookings. https://www.brookings.edu/articles/wheres-the-rallying-cry-americas-children-are-unequally-prepared-to-absorb-the-impacts-of-covid-19/

Gilbert, K., Kranzler, J. H., & Benson, N. (2021). An independent examination of the equivalence of the standard and digital administration formats of the Wechsler Intelligence Scale for Children–5th Edition. *Journal of School Psychology*, *85*, 113–124. https://doi.org/10.1016/j.jsp.2021.01.002

Glen, T., Barisa, M., Ready, R., Peck, E., & Spencer, T. R. (2021). Update on third party observers in neuropsychological evaluation: An interorganizational position paper. *Clinical Neuropsychology*, *35*(6), 1107–1116. https://doi.org/10.1080/13854046.2021.1901992

Golimstok, A., Rojas, J. I., Romano, M., Zurru, M. C., Doctorovich, D., & Cristiano, E. (2011). Previous adult attention-deficit and hyperactivity disorder symptoms and risk of dementia with Lewy bodies: A case-control study. *European Journal of Neurology*, *18*(1), 78–84. https://doi.org/10.1111/j.1468-1331.2010.03064.x

Hanover Research. (2020). Best practices in returning to learning. https://wasa-oly.org/WASA/images/WASA/6.0%20Resources/Hanover/BEST%20PRACTICES%20IN%20RETURNING%20TO%20LEARNING%20.pdf

Harder, L., Hernandez, A., Hague, C., Neumann, J., McCreary, M., Cullum, C. M., & Greenberg, B. (2020). Home-based pediatric teleneuropsychology: A validation study. *Archives in Clinical Neuropsychology*, *35*(8), 1266–1275. https://doi.org/10.1093/arclin/acaa070

Heaton, R. K., Miller, S. W., Taylor, M., & Grant, I. (2004). Revised comprehensive norms for an expanded Halstead-Reitan battery: Demographically adjusted neuropsychological norms for African American and Caucasian adults. Psychological Assessment Resources: Lutz.

Hirsh-Pasek, K., Yogman, M., & Golinkoff, R. M. (2020). Should schools reopen? Balancing COVID-10 and learning loss for young children. *Brookings*. https://www.brookings.edu/articles/should-schools-reopen-balancing-covid-19-and-learning-loss-for-young-children/

Jabbar, M. (2010). Overcoming Daubert's shortcomings in criminal trials: Making error rate the primary factor in Daubert's validity inquiry. *New York University Law Review*, *85*, 2034–2064.

Johnson, S. (2021). Schools must give standardized tests this year, Biden administration says. *EdSource*. https://edsource.org/2021/schools-must-give-standardized-tests-this-spring/649751#:~:text = States%20must%20resume%20their%20annual,Biden%20administration%20confirmed%20on%20Monday.&text = States%20are%20required%20to%20administer,federal%20Every%20Student%20Succeeds%20Act

Kirkwood, K. T., Peck, D. F., & Bennie, L. (2000). The consistency of neuropsychological assessments performed via telecommunication and face to face. *Journal of Telemedical Telecare*, *6*(3), 147–151. https://doi.org/10.1258/1357633001935239

Kronenberger, W. G., Montgomery, C. J., Henning, S. C., Ditmars, A., Johnson, C. A., Herbert, C. J., & Pisoni, D. B. (2021). Remote assessment of verbal memory in youth with cochlear implants during the COVID-19 pandemic. *American Journal of Speech Language Pathology*, *30*(2), 740–747. https://doi.org/10.1044/2021_ajslp-20-00276

Kuhfeld, M., Tarasawa, B., Johnson, A., Ruzek, E., & Lewis, K. (2020). Learning during COVID-19: Initial findings on students' reading and math achievement and growth. NWEA. https://www.nwea.org/uploads/2020/11/Collaborative-brief-Learning-during-COVID-19.NOV2020.pdf

Langella, S., Barksdale, N. G., Vasquez, D., Aguillon, D., Chen, Y., Su, Y., . . . Quiroz, Y. T. (2023). Effect of apolipoprotein genotype and educational attainment on cognitive function in autosomal dominant Alzheimer's disease. *Nature Communications, 14*(1), 5120. https://doi.org/10.1038/s41467-023-40775-z

Manly, J. J., & Echemendia, R. J. (2007). Race-specific norms: Using the model of hypertension to understand issues of race, culture, and education in neuropsychology. *Archives in Clinical Neuropsychology, 22*(3), 319–325. https://doi.org/10.1016/j.acn.2007.01.006

Manly, J. J., Jacobs, D. M., Touradji, P., Small, S. A., & Stern, Y. (2002). Reading level attenuates differences in neuropsychological test performance between African American and White elders. *Journal of the International Neuropsychology Society, 8*(3), 341–348. https://doi.org/10.1017/s1355617702813157

Marra, D. E., Hamlet, K. M., Bauer, R. M., & Bowers, D. (2020). Validity of teleneuropsychology for older adults in response to COVID-19: A systematic and critical review. *Clinical Neuropsychology, 34*(7-8), 1411–1452. https://doi.org/10.1080/13854046.2020.1769192

McGorry, P. (2019). Building the momentum and blueprint for reform in youth mental health. *Lancet Psychiatry, 6*(6), 459–461. https://doi.org/10.1016/s2215-0366(19)30050-1

Meixner, J. B., & Diamond, S. S. (2014, December). The hidden Daubert factor: How judges use error rates in assessing scientific evidence. *Wisconsin Law Review*, 1063. https://papers.ssrn.com/sol3/papers.cfm?abstract_id=2406073

Merritt, V. C., Meyer, J. E., Cadden, M. H., Roman, C. A. F., Ukueberuwa, D. M., Shapiro, M. D., & Arnett, P. A. (2016). Normative data for a comprehensive neuropsychological test battery used in the assessment of sports-related concussion. *Archives of Clinical Neuropsychology, 32*(2), 168–183. https://doi.org/10.1093/arclin/acw090

Miley, L. N., Heiss-Moses, E., Cochran, J. K., Heide, K. M., Fogel, S. J., Smith, M. D., & Bejerregaard, B. J. (2020). An examination of the effects of mental disorders as mitigating factors on capital sentencing outcomes. *Behavioral Science Law, 38*(4), 381–405. https://doi.org/10.1002/bsl.2477

Miller, Z. A., Rosenberg, L., Santos-Santos, M. A., Stephens, M., Allen, I. E., Hubbard, H. I., . . . Gorno-Tempini, M. L. (2018). Prevalence of mathematical and visuospatial learning disabilities in patients with posterior cortical atrophy. *JAMA Neurology, 75*(6), 728–737. https://doi.org/10.1001/jamaneurol.2018.0395

Moreno-Agostino, D., Fisher, H. L., Goodman, A., Hatch, S. L., Morgan, C., Richards, M., . . . Ploubidis, G. B. (2023). Long-term psychological distress trajectories and the COVID-19 pandemic in three British birth cohorts: A multi-cohort study. *PLoS Medicine, 20*(4), e1004145. https://doi.org/10.1371/journal.pmed.1004145

Nails, J. G., Maffly-Kipp, J., DeShong, H. L., Lowmaster, S. E., & Kurtz, J. E. (2023). A crisis in college student mental health? Self-ratings of psychopathology before and after the COVID-19 pandemic. *Psychological Assessment, 35*(11), 1010–1018. https://doi.org/10.1037/pas0001241

National Association of School Psychologists. (2020). The pandemic's impact on special education evaluations and SLD identification. NASP. https://www.nasponline.org/resources-and-publications/resources-and-podcasts/covid-19-resource-center/return-to-school/the-pandemics-impact-on-special-education-evaluations-and-sld-identification

National Football League Players' Concussion Injury Litigation. (2014). https://www.nflconcussionsettlement.com/Docs/Amended%20Class%20Action.pdf

Pan, W., & Sass, T. (2020). Potential remediation strategies in the wake of COVID-19 school closures: A review of the literature. *Georgia Policy Labs Reports.*

Pearson Corporation. (2021). Important Q-interactive and WISC-V information. https://email.pearsoned.com/clina/clina15779-23110-q-i-wisc-coding-transactional-cloud-20200203/index.html

Pritchard, A. E., Sweeney, K., Salorio, C. F., & Jacobson, L. A. (2020). Pediatric neuropsychological evaluation via telehealth: Novel models of care. *Clinical Neuropsychology, 34*(7–8), 1367–1379. https://doi.org/10.1080/13854046.2020.1806359

Raimo, S., Santangelo, G., Cropano, M., Gaita, M., Ammendola, L., Malangone, D., . . . Signoriello, E. (2023). Comparing face-to-face and videoconference assessment of the Brief Repeatable Battery of Neuropsychological Tests in people with multiple sclerosis. *Multiple Sclerosis, 29*(10), 1337–1339. https://doi.org/10.1177/13524585231192469

Ransom, D. M., Butt, S. M., DiVirgilio, E. K., Cederberg, C. D., Srnka, K. D., Hess, C. T., . . . Katzenstein, J. M. (2020). Pediatric teleneuropsychology: Feasibility and recommendations. *Archives in Clinical Neuropsychology, 35*(8), 1204–1214. https://doi.org/10.1093/arclin/acaa103

Re, S. (2023). A-50: A review of the dangers of misdiagnosing concussions as depression. *Archives of Clinical Neuropsychology, 38*(5), 852–852. https://doi.org/10.1093/arclin/acad042.50

Rogalski, E., Johnson, N., Weintraub, S., & Mesulam, M. (2008). Increased frequency of learning disability in patients with primary progressive aphasia and their first-degree relatives. *Archives in Neurology, 65*(2), 244–248. https://doi.org/10.1001/archneurol.2007.34

Salinas, C. M., Cullum, C. M., Harder, L., & Bordes Edgar, V. (2020). Accelerating teleneuropsychology within diverse populations. *Archives in Clinical Neuropsychology, 35*(8), 1187–1188. https://doi.org/10.1093/arclin/acaa102

Sherwood, A. R., & MacDonald, B. (2020). A teleneuropsychology consultation service model for children with neurodevelopmental and acquired disorders residing in rural state regions. *Archives of Clinical Neuropsychology, 35*(8), 1196–1203. https://doi.org/10.1093/arclin/acaa099

Stern, Y., Albert, M., Barnes, C. A., Cabeza, R., Pascual-Leone, A., & Rapp, P. R. (2023). A framework for concepts of reserve and resilience in aging. *Neurobiological Aging, 124*, 100–103. https://doi.org/10.1016/j.neurobiolaging.2022.10.015

Stifel, S. W. F., Feinberg, D. K., Zhang, Y., Chan, M.-K., & Wagle, R. (2020). Assessment during the COVID-19 pandemic: Ethical, legal, and safety considerations moving forward. *School Psychology Review, 49*(4), 438–452. https://doi.org/10.1080/2372966X.2020.1844549

Strauss, E., Sherman, E. M. S., & Spreen, O. (2006). *A compendium of neuropsychological tests: Administration, norms, and commentary* (3rd ed.). Oxford: Oxford University Press.

Temple, V., Drummond, C., Valiquette, S., & Jozsvai, E. (2010). A comparison of intellectual assessments over video conferencing and in-person for individuals with ID: Preliminary data. *Journal of Intellectual Disability Research, 54*(6), 573–577. https://doi.org/https://doi.org/10.1111/j.1365-2788.2010.01282.x

Thomas, A., & Tranel, D. (2023). Mask wearing during neuropsychological assessment negatively impacts performance on verbal tests in older patients. *Psychological Assessment, 35*(11), 938–948. https://doi.org/10.1037/pas0001261

Tombaugh, T. N., & McIntyre, N. J. (1992). The mini-mental state examination: A comprehensive review. *Journal of the American Geriatric Society, 40*(9), 922–935. https://doi.org/10.1111/j.1532-5415.1992.tb01992.x

U.S. Department of Education. (2019). IDEA: Sec. 300.309: Determining the existence of a specific learning disability. https://sites.ed.gov/idea/regs/b/d/300.309

Walker, E. J., Kirkham, F. J., Stotesbury, H., Dimitriou, D., & Hood, A. M. (2023). Teleneuropsychological assessment of children and young people: A systematic review. *Journal of Pediatric Neuropsychology, 9*, 113–126. https://doi.org/10.1007/s40817-023-00144-6

Wechsler, D. (2014). *Wechsler Intelligence Scale for Children–Fifth Edition (WISC-V)*. San Antonio: Pearson Corporation.

Welsh, J. A., Nix, R. L., Blair, C., Bierman, K. L., & Nelson, K. E. (2010). The development of cognitive skills and gains in academic school readiness for children from low-income families. *Journal of Educational Psychology, 102*(1), 43–53. https://doi.org/10.1037/a0016738

10
Lessons for the Future

Available evidence suggests that, moving forward, many children of the COVID-19 pandemic will develop along different developmental trajectories compared to previous cohorts. There may be large-scale needs for this population, with at-risk and marginalized groups encountering far more disruption of expected development compared to other groups. Given that 4 years after the onset of the pandemic, there is still no cohesive national plan for recovery for students affected by prolonged educational disruption, there is an understandable concern about long-term impacts, as yet unknown. However, where there are challenges, there are opportunities for innovation and advancement.

Potential Strategies for Mitigation of Impacts

Interventions of a generational scale should be on the table, potentially including reparations for pandemic-related educational disruption. The response to the events that characterized the Massive Resistance, described in Chapter 1, set an example. Ultimately, a scholarship was established for Black adults who, as students, were locked out of Prince Edward County, Virginia, public schools in response to the *Brown v. Board of Education* decision (Pauly, 2023). Recently this scholarship program was extended to their descendants. In 1971, the state of Virginia passed a constitutional amendment to restructure financial and policymaking relationships between the Commonwealth and schools, adding Bill of Rights language (Clark, 2021). This symbolic verbal rejection of the Massive Resistance school closures was welcome at the time. Further, Pauly (2023) notes that adults who experienced the Massive Resistance closures are aging—longitudinal data are needed on their cognitive, physical, vocational, psychological, and medical outcomes.

Jordan (2023) published strategies for reducing chronic absenteeism in the post-pandemic era. This detailed report merits consideration by those interested in a vigorous and empirically based approach to mitigation

Neurodevelopment in the Post-Pandemic World. Molly Colvin, Jennifer Linton Reesman, and Tannahill Glen, Oxford University Press. © Oxford University Press 2024. DOI: 10.1093/9780197762660.003.0010

of learning losses during the pandemic. Jordan describes the three-tier system of strategies. Tier I encompasses schoolwide support and prevention, includes strategies like after-school interventions, transportation, and restorative discipline. Tier II targets support with home visits, mentors, and programs for special populations (e.g., students with disabilities). Tier III focuses on intensive support, involving case management, truancy interventions, and considerations for housing insecurity. Fahle et al. (2023) suggested empirically supported interventions, including summer programs and adding "double-dose" coursework, which refers to adding a second class in the desired subject.

The Center on Reinventing Public Education (CRPE; 2023) published clear recommendations for policymakers that merit discussion here. CRPE emphasized the urgent need for transparency regarding learning progress, listing Connecticut, Indiana, Louisiana, Mississippi, North Carolina, and Virginia as innovators in this area. Transparency also will help educate parents as to the extent of individual children's progress. Fahle et al. (2023) noted evidence that only 10% of parents believed their children were still behind and reported concerns about remediation. This number is shocking given the enormous breadth and magnitude of losses revealed by state and national testing, and it highlights both a serious caution and a major opportunity: schools may have social and economic disincentives to minimize the extent of learning loss; however, there is clear potential for a national initiative designed to educate parents about localized patterns of losses and available resources.

It was also recommended that policymakers scale up already proven interventions, such as high-dosage tutoring. Community colleges have suffered dramatic reductions in enrollment, so CRPE suggested innovative subsidized programs building on those resources. Most importantly, the organization highlighted the need for research to track progress and challenges of "the Covid generation."

Looking ahead to potential interventions and educational remediation for declines in math achievement, Ribner at al. (2018) note that cognitive abilities like processing speed and vocabulary have been modified with interventions, and there is some evidence to suggest cognitive remediation may have an impact on academic problems relating to learning disability (Malhotra et al., 2010).

Thus, perhaps remediation interventions targeting executive functions and other math-relevant cognitive skills may affect math academic skills.

Ardila and Rosselli (2019) reviewed the literature on cognitive rehabilitation in acquired math impairment, but existing literature is fairly limited and focused on groups such as adults with acquired brain injury. Wu et al. (2020) applied an 8-week cognitive intervention to randomly assigned primary school students with math learning disorder and found significant changes on several measures (e.g., backward number memory) in the intervention group. However, it is unclear if improvements were transient and/or related to practice effects or general effect of an intervention. Whatever the plan for recovery, Strunk et al. (2023) and Asadullah et al. (2023) warn against a return to "business as usual."

Future Mental Health Care Accessibility

Beyond the potential long-term outcomes for children growing up during the pandemic, there are also impacts on professional development and competency within the mental health field, at a time of overwhelming demand and low availability of providers. Within the field of psychology, pass rates for the licensure examination (the Examination for Professional Practice in Psychology [EPPP]) fell from 80.33% in 2017–2019 to 76.29% in 2020–2022 for students from accredited doctoral programs, and there were fewer test takers sitting for the licensure examination (Association of State and Provincial Psychology Boards [ASPPB], 2023). This presents a major concern for future mental health service access as the current cohort of psychologists ages and moves toward retirement. Further, new models of child and adolescent mental health care delivery may be timely and critically needed. Citing Dr. Jennifer Reesman, Borden King (2023) stated, "With a dearth of mental health staff as well as funding limits, [Dr. Reesman] says we will need to explore additional options beyond the 'one-therapist-one-child' model."

Research

Future research involving the cohort of pandemic-era children will need to take into account the factors described in this book, as they will likely contribute to later-life differences in vocational, educational, medical, neurological, and psychiatric outcomes. For example, researchers with the Nuffield

Foundation in the United Kingdom are engaged in a multiyear project, through 2025, to assess language and socioemotional development in children post-pandemic, and educational outcomes for children sustaining repeated disruptions to learning (Bowyer-Crane et al., n.d.). Similarly, in the United Kingdom, Bernardi et al. (2023) have published the first survey results from the Children of the 2020s (COT20s) birth cohort study, assessing physical and mental health, language development, financial well-being, service utilization, and early childhood education. Initial findings did not reveal significant differences between the 2020s cohort (age 9 ½ months) and pre-pandemic samples, but further data will be gathered annually until age 5 years.

In terms of future research, there are numerous avenues that are vital for development of our understanding of pandemic-era changes for youth. Research is needed to:

- Determine the role of early environment in later life cognitive functioning
- Understand how early adversity impacts adult functioning
- Prepare for future educational disruptions and defend against resultant harms
- Develop neuropsychological measures designed for remote administration to reach more individuals
- Develop risk-based assessment and consultation models allowing for screening and rapid classification of neurodevelopmental disorders and fiscal sustainability
- Elucidate and minimize known dementia risk increases with poorer quality education
- Compare timing of interventions (cochlear implantation, early intervention, speech therapy, occupational therapy) across groups and cohorts and developmental windows
- Determine how to increase access to protective factors like sports and school connectedness that impact later functioning
- Examine cohort effects on various topics of relevance, for example, development of later life psychological dysfunction (or protection against the same), lifetime earnings, and so on

Stern et al. (2023) suggested, for instance, longitudinal study to examine the relationship between brain changes (such as volume or white matter alterations) and cognition over time, as well as the potential impact of education. We would extend that idea to suggest the study of whether pandemic-era educational disruption is related to those factors.

Are We More Likely to Close Again in the Future?

A troubling question that has arisen during the writing of this book is whether individual public school systems are more likely to turn to school closure as an intervention when other threats arise. Examples include closures for student misbehavior, weather-related events, lack of infrastructure necessary for typical operations (e.g., lack of air conditioning in schools in Baltimore, Maryland; Quaranta, 2023), or isolated outbreaks of illness. There are some examples to suggest that policymakers are, indeed, turning to closures within the United States for heat, illness, and student behavior. Organizations that tracked school closures clocked 858 districts and 9,692 schools in November 2021 that were impacted by rolling school closures due to these issues. Speaking to National Public Radio on the topic of these sudden school closures in the fall and winter of 2021, Robin Lake of the Center on Reinventing Public Education pointed out the concerning trend: "I think we've gotten into this mode of, every time things get hard, our answer is closed school. That's really problematic" (Lake in Kamenetz, 2021).

Another concerning trend has been the rise of the 4-day school week (Hollingsworth, 2023). Some schools have turned to a shorter learning week to manage costs and attract teachers during a national shortage of instructors. In Missouri, for example, the number of districts planning 3-day weekends has doubled to 30%. Of note, limited reporting on this trend has already identified the logistical challenge of managing child care when parents are working (which may result in more unsupervised screen time). One school system is planning to offer one day per week for students to come in for additional academic help, presumably for challenges that were, ironically, exacerbated during pandemic school closures.

Moving forward, an important lesson gleaned from this work is that even relatively brief educational disruption comes with a steep cost to children and potentially to their development and longer term outcomes. To date, there have been well-researched mitigation strategies that can help blunt the impact of this disruption, but few of these techniques and resources have been delivered at a scale sufficient to make a difference in the larger trajectory of population-level child development. Policymakers, education leaders, and communities should consider the strong negative impact of closures and/or widespread use of remote instruction in response to tumultuous events—closing them removes not just instructional time but a multitude of other conferred benefits, as well as structure and support. Policymakers should remain mindful of the clear and consistent evidence of disparate and potentially long-term negative impacts from prolonged educational disruption.

Conclusion

In 2020, after extensive school closures in the early days of the COVID-19 pandemic, we began curating emerging data on the school closures cohort, with an eye toward predicting negative impacts on vulnerable students, in line with evidence from prior educational disruption related to disaster, war, and pandemics. As the year came to a close, with about half of schools still operating in virtual mode, and access to the usual supportive and mental health care services reduced, we understood there would be enormous negative impacts on learning and devastating psychosocial fallout, and that at-risk youth would bear the greatest burden.

For the next 2 years, it seemed the trickle of studies became a torrent, confirming what the Secretary-General of the United Nations, Antonio Guterres, referred to as "an education catastrophe" (UNESCO, 2020): attenuated learning gains and widening achievement gaps for students of color, emerging English speakers, students with economic disadvantage, and students with disabilities (National Assessment of Educational Progress (NAEP, 2022). Longer duration of school closures, which tended to occur in schools with greater numbers of vulnerable students (Goldhaber et al., 2022), led to greater loss of expected learning gains (Oxner, 2021). Chronic absenteeism exploded, students were lost to the system, and age at entry to the school system declined (Vazquez Toness & Lurye, 2023). The educational system as we know it is now facing fiscal cliffs, staffing shortages, and a burgeoning virtual education and evaluation industry poised to fill the gap.

These outcomes are consistent with our initial hypotheses: first, that pre-pandemic normative data, stratified by education, would no longer be a reliable estimate for comparison of neuropsychological scores; second, that diagnosis, and thus services for, learning disabilities has been complicated by existing exclusionary criteria; and third, that educational and societal shifts were so great that neurodevelopmental trajectories would be altered for some youth.

It is our hope that clinicians, educators, policymakers, and scientists are driven by these outcomes to take the opportunity to analyze, innovate, and inspire. The COVID-19 pandemic disruption to youth cannot go the way of the Massive Resistance, as Buesing Clark (2021) wrote, "from Massive Resistance to Quiet Evasion."

References

Ardila, A., & Rosselli, M. (2019). Cognitive rehabilitation of acquired calculation disturbances. *Behavioral Neurology, 2019*, 3151092. https://doi.org/10.1155/2019/3151092

Asadullah, M. N., Bouhlila, D. S., Chan, S. J., Draxler, A., Ha, W., Heyneman, S. P., ... Yemini, M. (2023). A year of missed opportunity: Post-Covid learning loss—A renewed call to action. *International Journal of Educational Development, 99*, 102770. https://doi.org/10.1016/j.ijedudev.2023.102770

Association of State and Provincial Psychology Boards (ASPPB). (2023). Psychology licensing exam scores by doctoral program. https://cdn.ymaws.com/www.asppb.net/resource/resmgr/eppp_/2023_dr_rpt_012024.pdf

Bernardi, M., Fish, L., van de Grint-Stoop, J., Knibbs, S., Goodman, A., Calderwood, L., ... Borges, T. (2023). Children of the 2020s: First survey of families at age 9 months. https://assets.publishing.service.gov.uk/media/65b11dbb160765000d18f7fb/Cot20s_age_9_months_research_report.pdf

Bowyer-Crane, C., Bonetti, S., Fricke, S., & Manzoni, C. The impact of COVID-19 on educational, language and socioemotional outcomes in KS1. *Nuffield Foundation*. https://www.nuffieldfoundation.org/project/impact-covid-19-educational-language-socioemotional-outcomes

Center on Reinventing Public Education. (2023). The state of the American student: Fall 2023. CRPE. https://crpe.org/the-state-of-the-american-student-2023/

Clark, J. B. (2021). From massive resistance to quiet evasion: The struggle for educational equity and integration in Virginia. *Virginia Law Review, 107*, 1115–1164.

Fahle, E. M., Kane, N. T. J., Patterson, T., Reardon, S. F., Staiger, D. O., & Stuart, E. A. (2023). School district and community factors associated with learning loss during the COVID-19 pandemic. Center for Education Policy, Harvard University, Cambridge MA. https://cepr.harvard.edu/sites/hwpi.harvard.edu/files/cepr/files/explaining_covid_losses_5.23.pdf

Goldhaber, D., Kane, T. J., McEachin, A., Morton, E., Patterson, T., & Staiger, D. O. (2022). The consequences of remote and hybrid instruction during the pandemic. Center for Education Policy, Harvard University, Cambridge MA.

Hollingsworth, H. (2023). More schools are adopting 4-day weeks. For parents, the challenge is day 5. *Associated Press*.

Jordan, P. (2023). Attendance playbook: Smart strategies for reducing student absenteeism post-pandemic. *FutureEd*. https://www.future-ed.org/wp-content/uploads/2023/05/Attendance-Playbook.5.23.pdf

Kamenetz, A. (2021). Parents are scrambling after schools suddenly cancel class over staffing and burnout. *NPR*. https://www.npr.org/2021/11/23/1057979170/school-closures-mental-health-days-families-childcare-thanksgiving-break

King, A. (2023). Middle-school minds in teenage bodies: The post-pandemic crisis in our high schools. *Healthy Debate*. https://healthydebate.ca/2023/11/topic/middle-school-minds-in-teenage-bodies-the-post-pandemic-crisis-in-our-high-schools/

Malhotra, S., Rajender, G., Bhatia, M., Kanwal, K., & Singh, T. (2010). Comparative efficacy of cognitive retraining techniques and remedial training in children with learning disability. *Delhi Psychiatry Journal, 13.*

National Assessment of Educational Progress (NAEP). (2022). Reading and mathematics scores decline during COVID-19 pandemic. *National Center for Education Statistics, Institute of Education Sciences, US Department of Education.* https://www.nationsreportcard.gov/highlights/ltt/2022/

Oxner, R. (2021, June 28). Texas students' standardized test scores dropped dramatically during the pandemic, especially in math. *The Texas Tribune.* https://www.texastribune.org/2021/06/28/texas-staar-test-results/

Pauly, M. (2023, January 23). Scholarships could be extended to descendants of Massive Resistance. *VPM.* https://www.vpm.org/news/2023-01-23/virginia-brown-v-board-scholarship-bill-massive-resistance-hb-1419

Quaranta, C. (2023, June 2). Many Baltimore city public schools dismiss early due to heat. *Baltimore Banner.* https://www.thebaltimorebanner.com/education/k-12-schools/baltimore-city-schools-air-conditioning-IQJVVYZTRVGUPLVKY5F7IGUBLA/

Ribner, A., Moeller, K., Willougby, M., & Blair, C. (2018). Cognitive abilities and mathematical competencies at school entry. *Mind Brain Education, 12*(4), 175–185. https://doi.org/10.1111/mbe.12160

Stern, Y., Albert, M., Barnes, C. A., Cabeza, R., Pascual-Leone, A., & Rapp, P. R. (2023). A framework for concepts of reserve and resilience in aging. *Neurobiological Aging, 124*, 100–103. https://doi.org/10.1016/j.neurobiolaging.2022.10.015

Strunk, K. O., Hopkins, B. G., Kilbride, T., Imberman, S. A., & Yu, D. (2023). The path of student learning delay during the COVID-19 pandemic: Evidence from Michigan. Education Policy Innovation Collaborative, College of Education, Michigan State University. https://epicedpolicy.org/wp-content/uploads/2023/05/Benchmark_WP2_StudentOutcomes_May2023.pdf

UNESCO. (2020). UN Secretary-General warns of education catastrophe, pointing to UNESCO estimate of 24 million learners at risk of dropping out. https://www.unesco.org/en/articles/un-secretary-general-warns-education-catastrophe-pointing-unesco-estimate-24-million-learners-risk-0

Vazquez Toness, B., & Lurye, S. (2023). Thousands of kids are missing from school. Where did they go? *T. A. Press.* https://projects.apnews.com/features/2023/missing-children/index.html

Wu, T., Shen, H., Sheng, Y., Zhao, F., Guo, N., Liao, L., . . . Dong, X. (2020). Use of cognitive correction training improves learning for children with mathematics learning disability. *Applied Neuropsychology: Child, 9*(2), 172–178. https://doi.org/10.1080/21622965.2018.1552866

Index

For the benefit of digital users, indexed terms that span two pages (e.g., 52–53) may, on occasion, appear on only one of those pages.

Tables and figures are indicated by an italic *t* and *f* following the page number.